Corinne
Clark

Corinne
Clark

CAMPING for
SPECIAL CHILDREN

CAMPING for SPECIAL CHILDREN

THOMAS M. SHEA

Professor, Department of Special Education,
and Coordinator, Camp R & R;
Southern Illinois University,
Edwardsville, Illinois

with 62 illustrations

THE C. V. MOSBY COMPANY

Saint Louis   1977

Library of Congress Cataloging in Publication Data

Shea, Thomas M   1934-
    Camping for special children.

    Bibliography: p.
    Includes index.
    1. Camps for the handicapped.   I.   Title.
GV197.H3S53   793′.019′6   76-17092
ISBN 0-8016-4566-2

GW/CB/B 9 8 7 6 5 4 3 2 1

To
Kevin and **Keith**
my sons, friends, and counselors

PREFACE

For the last 10 years I have attempted, with the help and encouragement of many people, to contribute to the well-being of handicapped children through a variety of camping programs. This volume is the outcome of my experiences. For me, these years have been exciting and fruitful. Having learned a great deal, I still have much to learn about camping for handicapped populations.

The children who have participated in the camps described in this volume number nearly a thousand at this time. As a group, they are children with hidden handicaps; that is, they are socially maladjusted, culturally different, emotionally disturbed, learning disabled, and educable mentally handicapped. They are boys and girls ranging in age from 4 to 16 years. These children have spent many happy and beneficial days with several hundred college students and community volunteers who have devoted their time and energy to the camps as counselors and instructors. I am indebted to these children and adults; I give them my sincere thanks.

Camping for Special Children is designed for students and professionals in the various disciplines concerned with the recreation, rehabilitation, and education of exceptional children.

The basic methodological approach applied in the text is prescriptive, clinical, or diagnostic teaching. The primary objective of prescriptive teaching (thus, the objective of the camp programs described here) is the development and implementation of activities in direct response to the strengths and weaknesses of the individual camper.

Section One introduces the topics: camping for special populations and prescriptive teaching. Chapter 1 is a description of the populations served in the special camp and a discussion of the benefits an exceptional child derives from attending camp. Chapters 2 and 3 are concerned with several prescriptive teaching models and procedures for application in the camp setting. Several models developed by researchers and practitioners in the disciplines of rehabilitation and special education are reviewed in Chapter 2. Chapter 3 presents a detailed description of a teaching model that I developed over a 10-year span and applied in the model camps. This chapter includes three case studies. Chapter 4 contains a taxonomy of 58 specific learning behaviors frequently confronting the staff of a camp for the handicapped. Behaviors from the affective, psychomotor, and cognitive learning domains are discussed. Special emphasis is focused on social-emotional problems. Each behavior is presented in descriptive terms and is exemplified in a brief case study. Several sources for further study are listed after each of the learning problems.

In Section Two the model camps are introduced and discussed in detail. The six camps are the day camp (Chapter 5), the evening camp and the preschool day camp (Chapter 6), the residential camp for special populations and the special purpose residential camp (Chapter 7), and the wilderness camp (Chapter 8). Each model is presented in a common format that includes (1) purposes and objectives; (2) administration and staffing; (3) physical facilities, equipment, and materials; (4) personnel training; (5) program description including hourly, daily, and weekly schedules, and example forms, schedules, and calendars; and (6) the advantages and disadvantages of the model.

The final section of the text, Section Three, discusses behavior management techniques for application in the camp setting (Chapter 9), and the programming, supervision, and administration of the special camps (Chapter 10). These two chapters include a variety of practical recommendations and suggestions derived from my actual experiences as a camp coordinator.

Appendixes include sample forms for use in the special camp (Appendixes A and D), additional readings (Appendix B), and a listing of resources for those seeking information about camping and recreation for the handicapped (Appendix C).

I have made every effort to write a practical text and usable handbook for those interested in camps and camping programs for handicapped children. My own experiences are applied with those of others derived from the literature of the field. The volume is replete with actual examples from the camp setting.

No single individual can develop and operate all the programs described in this volume without the assistance of many dedicated staff persons. I have been fortunate to have had many superior staff members over the years. I am deeply indebted to Dr. J. Crowner, Rev. and Mrs. T. L. Phillips, and M. Schaffer, who collaborated with me on the first residential camp in 1967 at Southern Illinois University at Carbondale. Thanks is given to A. Campbell, J. Halloway, W. Price, and L. Frietag, who collaborated on the residential camps at Carbondale in 1968 and 1969.

While I have resided at the Southern Illinois University at Edwardsville, I have received guidance and support from Dr. W. Whiteside, R. W. Egan, Dr. A. Foxworth, Dr. R. Long, M. Ott, and Dr. L. Olion. Assistant coordinators are largely responsible for the day-to-day operations of any camp. Consequently, I am especially grateful to G. Alstat, C. Alstat, C. Gunter, M. Fogle, C. Fogle, R. W. Egan, and R. Schusky, who served as assistant coordinators of the day camps between 1970 and 1976. R. W. Egan also helped prepare the case studies presented in Chapter 3.

The wilderness camp would not have been possible without the assistance of M. Beasley, J. Koehler, D. Lindsey, J. Stultz, and Dr. W. Whiteside.

Three persons are deserving of special thanks and recognition for their contributions to the camps: my sons, Kevin and Keith, to whom this volume is dedicated, and P. J. Sims. These three friends have guided me with patience and consistency for many years.

The photographs in this volume have been taken by several photographers: J. Koehler, P. J. Sims, Rev. T. L. Phillips, and D. J. Shea. A special thanks is given to Charles Cox of the University Photographic Service for providing several of the photographs.

Finally, thanks is given to Dolores, my wife, for her encouragement to write this book and to J. Holst for her clerical assistance during the preparation of the manuscript.

Thomas M. Shea

CONTENTS

INTRODUCTION

Section One of this text (Chapters 1 through 4) focuses on the rationale and unique benefits of camps for special children and on the application of prescriptive teaching methods in the camp setting.

In Chapter 1 a description is given of special children who have attended the model camps presented in Section Two. The specific benefits of camping for the handicapped are presented in this chapter.

In Chapter 2 prescriptive teaching is defined and several teaching models from the literature are presented. Chapter 3 is a detailed presentation of a prescriptive teaching model that I designed and implemented in the camp setting. Three actual case studies are presented in detail.

Staff members must work with the observable behaviors that a child manifests in the camp environment. To assist camp personnel in their efforts to define, clarify, and modify behaviors frequently manifested in the camp, a 58-item taxonomy of frequently observed behaviors is included in Chapter 4. Each behavior is defined, described, and exemplified. Specific suggestions for changing each behavior are presented. These recommendations are supplemented by several references for further study at the conclusion of the discussion of each item.

CHAPTER 1

An introduction to camping for special children

■ Mark and John struggle up the last pine-covered slope and come to the edge of a clearing in the dense forest. They stop for a moment to absorb the beauty of the lush green grass blowing gently in the warm summer breeze, the sparkling blue water of the stream that skirts this opening in the woods, and the multicolored wild flowers lining its banks. Under the weight of their heavy backpacks, the two boys move cautiously into the clearing with the hope of seeing a beaver, squirrel, or wild turkey before it scurries into the thick underbrush.

John and Mark will sleep here tonight with their classmates and teachers; they will set up their canvas homes and prepare their evening meal. They somehow feel freer in the forest, living among their friends and nature's beauty, away from the daily troubles and conflicts of the inner city.

■ Rosemary and Pat sit on the front steps of the old dilapidated gray house, working feverishly at their chosen task. They are making chocolate ice cream and must work quickly before the ice melts. The girls look across the lane to the field where their classmates and teachers are finishing a kickball game that was scheduled before the ice cream social. The two girls realize their responsibility to their friends.

What a chance this camping program is! Two emotionally handicapped girls have an opportunity to assume responsibility for their actions.

■ The big day is here! What activity! What excitement! The campground is cluttered with children and adults working alone, in pairs, and in small groups. Each one is busy with a special task that must be completed before the annual camp carnival can begin.

Yes, it is carnival day at camp. There are many inviting activities for the children, instructors, counselors, and parents. Ready for the first customers are the sponge throw, the pitch game, the makeup booth, the arts-and-crafts display, the puppet show, and the obstacle course. Joe, the old horse, is saddled so that everyone may take a ride around the playing field. Chimega, a cougar and the camp mascot, sits quietly in her cage, cleaning her paws with her long pink tongue, waiting to be visited and admired by the children. Even Officer Parker, dressed in his best uniform, awaits his guests with the radio of his police cruiser crackling and the big red lights slowly revolving in the early morning sun.

This is the last day of camp for this summer. It has been an exciting, productive 6 weeks of meeting new friends, engaging in new experiences, and learning new skills.

■ John and Tom work diligently on their vocabulary cards under a large oak tree on a bluff overlooking Grassy Lake. Occasionally,

3

they stop and glance in anticipation toward Ms. Patrick, their instructor. The boys know they must complete their academic tasks before going down to the lake for a midmorning dip. They will finish soon, race down the hill into the cool water, and enjoy their freedom.

■ Jim and George run quickly up and down the basketball court with eight of their classmates. They are on the same team tonight and six points ahead of the opposition. Jim, George, and the others must coordinate their efforts if they wish to win the game. The two boys have particular thoughts and feelings about each other as they race over the court.

"George is a good player," says Jim to himself. "I wonder why I was so mean to him in class this morning. Maybe we can still be friends."

"Guess Jim doesn't like me very much," George is thinking, "but maybe he'll change his mind and be my friend because I've scored so many points tonight. He sure was nasty this morning."

On and on the stories go. At camp, many successes are possible for the "unsuccessful": successes, little and big, for special children in camps designed to help them overcome or compensate for their disabilities.

This is the story of special children who are free to live and learn about life in the world of nature. It is the story of children involved in exciting, interesting, and meaningful camp activities designed to enhance their individual productivity and acceptability in a nonhandicapped world.

Their experiences, both of success and of failure, demand that we, as parents, administrators, recreation specialists, and teachers, continue to utilize the American man-made and natural resources for their benefit. The therapeutic and educational benefits derived from both simple and complex camping and recreational activities far exceed the time, effort, and funds needed to provide these opportunities.

Wading in a creek after a 6-mile hike.

THE CAMPING MOVEMENT

In recent years, teachers and recreation specialists have begun to explore in earnest, programming potentials of the innumerable playgrounds, community centers and parks, federal and state recreational areas, and wilderness areas for the millions of special children enrolled in school.

Although demonstration projects and experimental camps have been few in number during the last decade, they are rapidly increasing. The results of these beginning efforts have been publicized sufficiently in the professional and popular literature to stimulate the interest of many mental health, recreation, and educational professionals.

Many articles describing private camps and recreation projects have appeared in the popular literature, but the cost and complexities of these projects have discouraged professionals from organizing such camps in their communities. It is impractical for the teacher or instructor to contemplate replicating a complex, multithousand-dollar project without the availability of considerable outside financial resources.

Viable camping and recreational programs for the handicapped can be developed at minimal cost, however, with available local resources. Such programs are the focus of this volume.

The most significant trend affecting the development of special camps has been the dramatic increase in interest in camping and recreation among the general public. The American public has taken to the camping trail in recreational vehicles, handmade campers, and the family car. Throughout the year, we leave the cities and suburbs to weekend in the hundreds of camping areas developed throughout the United States and Canada during the 1960s.

The government has responded to this interest on federal, state, and local levels by investing millions of dollars in recreational and camping facilities. American industrial and business interests are frantically attempting to meet consumer demands for well-constructed, safe, compact, and economical equipment.

The taboos connected with the wilderness, so prevalent among adults of the last generation, have been dislodged and nearly forgotten. Parents no longer refuse to allow their children to go camping and hiking. A variety of formal and informal training programs have been developed for the average citizen relative to safety, comfort, and conservation in the out-of-doors.

BREAK FROM EDUCATIONAL TRADITION

A few professional educators have begun the break from educational traditions of the past. These teachers have rejected the personal security provided by the four walls of the classroom and have ventured with their students into the world of undomesticated animals, deep forests, arid plains, high mountains, and icy streams. In the camp setting they have attempted to apply lessons previously confined to the classroom.

The modern educator knows that a movie on forest fire prevention, no matter how well produced, cannot supplant the understanding a child derives from walking through a single mile of burnt-out forest. He recognizes that few works of art are as arresting and inspiring for a child as the view from a mountain top, the rim of a canyon, or a cliff above the seemingly endless ocean.

No unit of study on personal health and grooming can replace the experience a child derives from caring for himself during a single week in the wilderness or a residential camp. Slide presentations and lectures on running, jumping, skipping, throwing, and catching cannot replace the learning that takes place on the playing field.

Nature's classroom provides opportunities to add true meaning and understanding to the thinking, reading, and computing skills presented in the classroom. Nature provides opportunities to apply the principles of science, mathematics, physics, ecology, and conservation in the real world.

The opportunities to learn in nature and from nature are only limited by the imagination and will of the adults and children involved in the camp.

THE SPECIAL CAMPER

Handicapped children defy precise classification into presently accepted diagnostic categories, such as emotional disturbance, learning disabilities, mental retardation, and social maladjustment. It is infrequent that a child arriving at camp can be diagnosed as *only* emotionally disturbed or *only* learning disabled. Generally, the new arrival presents a variety of handicapping conditions. Although one of these conditions may appear to be the primary cause of the child's problem, the others can, and do, contribute significantly to his overall educational and social functioning in the school, community, and camp.

Consequently, the average special camper manifests a combination of disabilities, for example, experiential deprivation with learning and behavior problems. Although one of these disabilities may be offered as the primary reason for the child's referral to camp, this problem need not necessarily be the major focus of his remedial program.

The camping programs described in this volume are designed for children with "invisible" handicaps. Attention is focused on children who appear "normal" to the casual observer. These children are handicapped in situations demanding specific behaviors, such as paying attention in the classroom and being physically coordinated on the playground. This focus, of necessity, eliminates children with "visible" handicaps: the blind, the deaf, the severely retarded, the physically handicapped, and the chronically ill.

The children with "invisible" handicaps are the emotionally disturbed, the learning disabled, the mildly retarded, the disadvantaged, and the hyperresilient.

The following definitions should enable the reader to conceptualize the various groups of children who attend the special camps discussed in Section Two. It is evident that considerable overlap exists among the groups. In Chapter 4 the specific behaviors of these children are described in detail.

The emotionally disturbed child

The emotionally disturbed child is one "who cannot or will not adjust to the socially acceptable norms of behavior and consequently disrupts his own academic progress, the learning efforts of his classmates, and interpersonal relations" (Woody, 1969, p. 7).

As indicated by Woody's definition, the emotionally disturbed child presents the instructor with a wide variety of behavior problems that must be controlled if the child is to be a successful person.

These children, either because of intrapsychic conflict or social learning handicaps, have difficulty:

1. Accepting themselves as individuals worthy of respect
2. Interacting with peers in a consistently acceptable and personally productive manner
3. Interacting with authority figures, such as counselors, teachers, instructors, and parents, in a consistently acceptable and personally productive manner
4. Engaging in "normal" affective, psychomotor, and cognitive learning activities without inordinate frustration and conflict.

The problems they bring to camp include, among others, the following behaviors:

Emotional instability
Attention seeking
Verbal aggression
Physical aggression
Disruptive group behavior
Overcompetitiveness
Inattentiveness
Poor self-concept
Impulsiveness
Hyperactivity
Withdrawal
Passive-suggestible reactions
Age-inappropriate behavior
Sexual deviations
Psychosomatic complaints
Chronic disobedience
Negativism

Each of these behaviors are defined, discussed, and exemplified in Chapter 4.

The learning-disabled child

Children with special (specific) learning disabilities exhibit a disorder in one or more of the basic psychological processes involved in understanding or in using spoken or written language. These disorders may be manifested in problems with listening, thinking, talking, reading, writing, spelling, or arithmetic. They include conditions that have been referred to as perceptual handicaps, brain injury, minimal brain dysfunction, dyslexia, developmental aphasia, and so on. They *do not* include learning problems that are due primarily to visual, hearing, or motor handicaps, to mental retardation, to emotional disturbance, or to environmental disadvantage (National Advisory Committee on Handicapped Children, 1968, p. 34).

The learning-disabled child manifests a variety of motor, sensory, and cognitive handicaps. Among his motor problems are difficulties in gross motor activities, such as running, jumping, skipping, hopping, throwing, and catching. Poorly developed fine motor skills cause him difficulties in cutting, pasting, coloring within lines, and manipulating small objects. In addition, the learning-disabled child may have visual and auditory perceptual handicaps.

Most of these children present the teacher with academic problems in reading, arithmetic, spelling, writing, and so on.

The mentally retarded child

The mentally retarded child is one who manifests "subaverage general intellectual functioning which originates during the developmental period and is associated with impairment in adaptive behavior" (Heber, 1961, p. 3).

This definition of mental retardation necessitates the child's response to three criteria: subaverage general intellectual functioning, onset during the developmental period, and impairment in adaptive behavior. Consideration is given not only to the child's level of intellectual functioning but to his capacity to adapt to the environment. Consequently, some children with subaverage general intellectual functioning, as determined by an intelligence test, may not be classified as mentally retarded, because they can and do function successfully in the environment.

For educational purposes, the mentally retarded can be divided into four subgroups: slow learners, educable mentally retarded, trainable mentally retarded, and profoundly mentally retarded. However, it is generally acknowledged and accepted among practitioners working with the mentally retarded that there is considerable overlap among these subgroups and that precise classification of all retardates into the appropriate classification for educational purposes is impossible.

In this volume we are primarily concerned with those children classified in the first two subgroups: the slow learner and the educable mentally retarded. Their intelligence quotients range from 50 to 85, and their adaptability to the environment ranges from moderate to excellent. Those on the upper end of the intelligence-adaptability continuum function well in school, often graduate, and become contributing citizens. Those at the lower end of the continuum have difficulty in the regular classroom but adjust well in the more supportive environment provided by the special classroom.

Some mentally retarded individuals complete high school and enter the labor market as unskilled or semi-skilled workers. Others require sheltered workshop services throughout life. The majority, however, adapt well to community life and its responsibilities.

The socially, economically, and/or experientially disadvantaged child

The socially, economically, and/or experientially disadvantaged child is one who, because of the inadequacy, starkness, and/or harshness of his environment (in comparison with an environment generally assumed to be favorable), is unable to learn the skills anticipated among children of similar age and developmental stage.

Children within this classification are deprived of experiences that facilitate the development of their skills. This deprivation is a result of:

Lack of adequate family financial resources

Family disorganization

A significant difference between past and present environment (The child raised in a rural setting moves to an urban setting, and vice versa.)

An ethnic, cultural, racial, religious, and/or language background differing significantly from that of the majority of the children in the environment in which the child is attempting to function

To be more specific, these children are members of minority groups who because of the inadequacy of their education in comparison with others, the inflexibility of social institutions, prejudice, financial deprivation, and other factors, are deprived of an equal educational opportunity.

The healthy hyperresilient child

Redl (1971) defined another group of children long neglected by the helping professions: healthy hyperresilient children. These are children who are being encouraged toward deviance by their environment and by significant persons within their environment.

They are youngsters who are perfectly healthy—as normal, clinically speaking, as anyone might wish a youngster to be. In fact, being normal and healthy, they have a sharp nose for situations which are putrid, for life experiences which are sickening, for teacher or parent behavior which is downright impossible on any count. In short, these children smell situations which are bound to make them either nasty or sick. Their behavior is a means of preventing their becoming either. They defend themselves against damage and against threats to their inner balance. (Redl, 1971, p. vi)

Many hyperresilient campers present a variety of "problem behaviors" in their homes, schools, and communities in a determined, frantic effort to avoid accepting the "sick" role being forced on them by their parents, teachers, and peers. These children are observed by the camp staff as normal and frequently capable of positive leadership roles.

THE SPECIAL CAMP

If a camp is to be therapeutically beneficial to an exceptional child, it must be designed to meet the individual needs of that child. Consequently, no single camp model can be developed to respond to the diversity of needs of all potential campers. If this individualized approach to camping is accepted, then it is necessary to provide a variety of models that will respond to the presumed group needs of the children. In addition, each model must be designed to respond to the individual needs of each child.

In Section Two of this volume, six camp models are presented. Each camp is designed to respond to the group and individual needs of the campers. These models are the day camp, the evening camp, the preschool day camp, the residential camp for special populations, the special purpose residential camp, and the wilderness camp.

The commonality among these models lies in the application of prescriptive teaching procedures in the planning and implementation of educational and recreational programs for each child enrolled in the camp. Prescriptive teaching is discussed in detail in Chapter 2.

BENEFITS OF THE SPECIAL CAMP

Handicapped children, like nonhandicapped children, are curious, adventuresome human beings. They naturally seek learning, change, attention, enjoyment, and rest. They wish to accept themselves and to be accepted by others. They desire to be "someone" to themselves and to the others within their life-space.

Camping is the vehicle used to help the exceptional child meet his universal human needs and his individual special needs. In camp, whether residential or day, evening or weekend, the child is provided with the opportunity to learn, grow, succeed, and find pleasure in a planned, controlled setting. The benefits of camping are derived primarily by the child; however, his parents, brothers and sisters, teachers, and others can profit greatly by his attendance.

The benefits of the camps vary with the particular model being utilized. However, each child who attends accrues some personal, social, emotional, cognitive, and psychomotor benefits.

Diagnostic benefits

It is difficult to implement and carry out a comprehensive multidisciplinary diagnostic

Free to be yourself.

evaluation in a community setting without an inordinate expenditure of time, effort, and funds by the family and agencies involved. A community-based diagnostic process, even if staff, time, and funds are available, causes considerable inconvenience to the child, his parents, his teachers, and the mental health professionals.

The preciseness, intensity, and duration of the diagnostic process can be enhanced in the camp setting. For example, in the day, evening, or residential camp, the child needing a diagnostic evaluation can be made available to the diagnostician for the required length of time with little difficulty. Both camp and cooperating community agency personnel can arrange ample time for intensive evaluation of the child's strengths and weaknesses. A key element in the diagnostic process is direct observation of the child in a variety of structured and unstructured learning situations. Trained camp personnel can provide observational data to other members of the diagnostic team.

Placement benefits

Camps can be of benefit to the child in two ways when placement out-of-the-home is desirable. First, the camp can be used as a short-term placement center; second, the camp can be used for trial placement.

When family and community problems

make short-term (2 to 8 weeks) residential placement necessary, the camp is an ideal setting. Camp is almost universally accepted as a desirable placement for a child. The image of camp, in the eyes of the average citizen, connotes pleasure, fun, excitement, normalcy, and health. It avoids the stigma commonly attached to foster homes, special schools, children's centers, and detention centers.

Camp is an excellent placement when the family is trying to determine the child's reaction to living away from home. Trial placement in a camp can answer such parental concerns as:

Can my child tolerate residential placement?

Can my child benefit from residential placement?

Can our family tolerate placing our handicapped child in a residential setting?

Camp may benefit the handicapped child as a placement before or after special class placement. Before special class placement, the child's specific needs can be determined in the camp setting and an individualized program prescribed. When the child is being discharged from the special class, the camp setting is an ideal transition one in which to prepare him to return to the regular classroom.

Remedial benefits

A camp with a well-designed remedial program assists the child by providing him with opportunities:

To acquire knowledge and skills needed for school success

To reinforce newly acquired but not habituated behavior

To revitalize and apply previously learned and neglected knowledge and skills

To apply knowledge and skills in the environment

Camp remediation programs ensure that the child remains an active learner during vacation periods. In this way, the child avoids the commonly observed academic and social-emotional regression that is characteristic of many children and adolescents during long vacation periods.

Personal benefits

Camping is instrumental in helping the child improve self-care skills, build self-confidence, and improve self-awareness of unrealized potential. At camp, the child can be trained in personal hygiene as well as in the care and use of personal and community property. Older children can learn self-care and survival skills, such as first aid, cooking, shelter building, fire building, safety, and the conservation of human and natural resources.

Special campers are given a variety of opportunities to learn how to utilize their leisure time in an enjoyable, productive way by playing field and table games, by engaging in arts and crafts, and by reading and listening for pleasure. At camp, particularly in residential and wilderness camps and on field trips, the children are involved in exciting new adventures. They are afforded acceptable opportunities to test their personal, social, and emotional strengths in unknown but supportive situations.

Camping with acceptable and accepting adults has a positive effect on the exceptional child's perception of himself as a human being, a child, a learner, and a friend. Camp activities also modify the camper's perceptions of others, especially adult authority figures, such as counselors, instructors, and parents.

Social benefits

In the camp setting the handicapped child has an opportunity to learn and experiment with newly acquired social skills in a controlled environment. He learns how to get along with others in a communal setting. He quickly discovers that community living requires much give and take and that his personal wishes must frequently be subordinated to the wishes of the group. He learns that he must engage in personally undesirable tasks if he is to participate in some group activities. He recognizes that his behavior affects other members of his group and that the behavior of his peers and counselors will frequently affect his behavior. He learns to accept responsibility for others and to re-

A race with a new friend.

spond positively when others in his group act responsible toward him.

Cooperative work skills are difficult to learn for many emotionally handicapped children. At the special camp children learn that they must work cooperatively with others, peers and adults, if projects are to be completed. For example, if a puppet show is to be produced, lunch is to be served, games are to be played, or a tent is to be erected, all members of the group must cooperate. Learning to work together is initially frustrating; however, as the camp program continues, the arguing, bickering, and fighting decrease.

For older children camping of any kind can be an experience in self-government. The boys and girls are encouraged to plan, implement, and evaluate their own programs and activities.

Emotional benefits

Emotional release is permitted and occasionally encouraged in the camp environment. In this environment children have many opportunities to express their real and imagined fears and hostility without concern for punishment or embarrassment. In camp, the handicapped child can be honestly afraid of the unknown and become angry at the world of real obstacles under the guidance of counselors who help him understand his fear and channel his energies into meaningful activity.

Children learn self-control through discussion of their unacceptable behaviors with peers and counselors. They are encouraged to experiment with alternative behaviors that are more acceptable to their peers, thus less personally harmful.

They learn that group living requires limits

that must be followed for the benefit of others. Most important, they learn that discipline can be impersonal, consistent, and nonviolent. They learn that even though their behavior is occasionally unacceptable, they are accepted and acceptable.

Physical benefits

Campers can improve their physical stamina and increase their motor skills through participation in remedial and recreational activities in a well-planned cycle of work, play, and rest. In camp, the child has an opportunity to increase his physical strength as well as to develop the physical-social skills he needs to participate in games with his friends. Through sequential individualized activities, each child learns to achieve increasingly more complex physical feats. In this way, the child learns to take satisfaction in physical achievements.

Benefits to family, teachers, counselors, volunteers, and trainees

Each adult involved in a camping program for the handicapped grows in awareness of himself as a human being and of his effect on the behavior of others. The adult learns that achievement for the handicapped child is not simply a matter of desire but of hard work over an extended period of time. The child's efforts require extraordinary self-control, concentration, and persistence.

For instructors and counselors, camp is an opportunity to observe themselves and the children in a unique environment. So obvious in the school or clinic, handicaps are frequently less evident at camp.

Teachers discover that the parent of the handicapped child has many problems of which they, as professionals, are unprepared to manage.

For the parent, the child's attendance at camp may be a brief respite from years of constant concern and anxiety. Those persons without a handicapped child in their home have little idea of the intense involvement demanded of parents who must live 24 hours a day, 365 days a year, with a severely or moderately handicapped child.

SUMMARY

In this chapter it has been emphasized that the special camp is *not just another camp or just another school.* It is a unique educational, recreational, and therapeutic vehicle that, to be effective, must be responsive to the individual needs of each child in attendance.

Although the camp is conducted in a nontraditional setting, its impact can be as profound as the traditional mental health and educational institutions. It is not a panacea for all of the difficulties of all handicapped children, but it can be an important facet of the child's overall rehabilitation and remediation program.

Perhaps most important, the special camp is one setting in which a child not only can learn many needed skills, he can have fun in the process.

REFERENCES

Avedon, E. M. *Therapeutic recreation service: an applied behavioral science approach.* Englewood Cliffs, N.J.: Prentice-Hall, Inc., 1974.

Bavley, F. New horizons for disadvantaged youth. *Camping Magazine,* 1970, **42**(2), 16-34.

Bavley, F. Two year experiment proves camp can change camper attitudes. *Camping Magazine,* 1972, **44**(7), 18.

Heber, R. A manual on terminology and classification in mental retardation. *Monograph supplement to American Journal of Mental Deficiency* 1959 (2nd ed., 1961), p. 64.

Heber, R. Modifications in the manual on terminology and classification in mental retardation. *American Journal of Mental Deficiency,* 1961, **65**, 499-500.

Hewett, F. M., and Forness, S. R. *Education of exceptional learners.* Boston: Allyn & Bacon, Inc., 1974.

Kronick, D. Regular camp, special camp, or no camp. *Academic Therapy Quarterly,* 1969, **4**, 207-211.

Lowry, T. P. (Ed.). *Camping therapy: its uses in psychiatry and rehabilitation.* Springfield, Ill.: Charles C Thomas, Publisher, 1974.

Magner, G. W. Mental health and camping. *Camping Magazine,* 1967, **39**(8), 22-29.

McCreary-Juhasz, A., and Jensen, S. E. Benefits of a school camp experience to emotionally disturbed children in regular classrooms. *Exceptional Children,* 1968, **34**, 353-354.

National Advisory Committee on Handicapped Children. *Special education for handicapped children, first annual report.* Washington, D.C.: U.S. Department of Health, Education, and Welfare, Office of Education, 1968.

Redl, F. Foreword. In N. J. Long, W. C. Morse, and R. G. Newman (Eds.), *Conflict in the classroom: the education of emotionally disturbed children*. Belmont, Calif.: Wadsworth Publishing Co. Inc., 1971.

Scheidlinger, S., and Scheidlinger, L. From a camp of a child guidance clinic: the treatment potentialities of the summer camp for children with personality disturbances. *Nervous Child*, 1947, **6**, 232-242.

Stein, J. U. The mentally retarded need recreation. *Parks and Recreation*, 1966, **1**(7), 574-578.

Woody, R. H. *Behavioral problem children in the schools*. New York: Appleton-Century-Crofts, 1969.

Individual instruction with a personal teacher and counselor.

CHAPTER 2

Prescriptive teaching

MAKING NAME TAGS

It is 10 o'clock in the morning on a bright sunny July day at Camp Kibo in the foothills of the Green Mountains of Vermont. Camp Kibo is a camp for children with behavior and learning problems.

Daily during this time, the children gather in their cabin groups for arts and crafts. The project selected for this particular session is making name tags. This activity involves the application of a variety of motor skills. Each child must be able to saw a piece of wood from a 2-inch sapling, shave the bark from the wood, sand the surface, carve his name, paint the carved name with one or more bright colors, wait for the paint to dry, coat the surface with plastic coating, bore a small hole in the tag, thread a necklace through the hole, and tie the ends of the lace. Of course, the child must have some awareness of the concepts "his name" and "name tag." This complex activity also involves many less obvious skills, such as patience, persistence, and motivation.

Mr. Bob, the arts and crafts instructor, has prepared the necessary materials and equipment. He has a sapling, saws, drills, paints, cutting tools, plastic coating, and several bright spools of "boondoggle" on the workbenches. He has instructed the counselors-in-training (CITs) in the procedures of name tag production.

At 10:05 AM Ms. Peggy arrives with her cabin group, the Chicksaws. The tribe includes six boys ranging in age from 8 to 10 years. They are a fine-looking group of campers and are very excited about this project, which Mr. Bob announced the previous day.

The boys enter the work area and, after a bit of nudging and bickering, are seated at the benches. Mr. Bob gives them verbal instructions.

Ms. Peggy remains with the group and makes the following observations during the half-hour activity.

GROUP: Most members of the tribe are interested, well behaved, and involved in the activity during the first 15 minutes of the session. In the latter part of the session, a number of fights, negative comments, and some bickering are observed among the group members. Only two of the six boys, Jim and Bill, complete the task as prescribed.

JIM AND BILL: Jim and Bill have little difficulty understanding the directions and completing the task. They make beautiful tags and are obviously proud of their accomplishment. They show their tags to everyone in the work area and to others who pass through. It is noteworthy that the two boys help each other throughout the session.

GEORGE: Initially, George is very enthusiastic about making his name tag. He has no difficulty sawing the piece of wood from the sapling, drilling a hole, or shaving the bark from the tag. However, when he begins to carve his name into the wooden surface, he becomes physically restless. He is unable to carve the letters in recognizable form. At 10:15 George throws the cutting tool to the ground and refuses to participate for the remainder of the session, although he is encouraged to do so by the CITs.

PAUL: Paul proceeds in much the same way as George but becomes frustrated and aggressive when he is unable to position his name on the tag properly. He attempts time and time again to sketch the letters of his name on the wooden surface with a carpenter's pencil. Each time, however, he fails to leave space for the "l" in "Paul." About 20 minutes into the session, he starts a fight with George and is removed from the work area.

ELMER: Elmer does an excellent job cutting, drilling, sanding, and carving. However, he refuses to use the paint and plastic coating. He repeatedly begs one of the CITs to paint the letters for him but is refused. Elmer finishes his tag without painting it. He appears satisfied with his "final" product.

KEITH: Keith does not attempt the project. He seems unaware of the purpose of being in the arts-and-crafts area. However, he is quiet throughout the session. Keith sits on the ground and plays with two pieces of wood. Mr. Bob and the CITs try repeatedly to engage him in the activity.

What can be done to improve this activity? Why is the project less than successful for four of the six boys in the tribe? Why do the various boys abandon the project at a particular time or during a specific operation?

LEARNING ARITHMETIC

Ms. Stillman is the mathematics instructor at Camp Hope. She has each cabin group daily for a 30-minute session. The Arapho Tribe, 1 boy and 3 girls, 6 and 7 years of age, attend the 9 o'clock session. Today, Ms. Stillman is going to focus their lesson on the addition of simple numbers. She has instructed her aide in the lesson's content and teaching procedures. The necessary materials and equipment—pencils, paper, counting frames, counting sticks, and a felt board with various animal forms—are available.

Promptly at 9 o'clock, Mr. Beasley arrives

with the Arapho Tribe. With a little confusion, the children gather around the worktable. They appear eager to learn their addition facts. Mr. Beasley sits quietly in the corner of the area, making the following observations.

GROUP: All the children are alert and active this morning. There was no resistance to coming to the mathematic's center, other than that by Charlie, who repeatedly said, "No, I won't" but came to the work area without physical resistance.

PATTIE: Pattie does well on this lesson. She attends to the directions of the teacher and manipulates the felt board animals with skill. She writes her name on the work sheet and completes all of the problems correctly. She is very pleased with the gold star Ms. Stillman puts on her paper.

CHARLIE: Charlie completes his assignment correctly and is rewarded with a gold star. Most of his verbal negativisms are ignored by the teacher and aide. At 9:15, however, Ms. Stillman responds to Charlie's "No, I won't" with "Oh, yes, you will, young man." This incident results in Charlie's disengagement from the activity for approximately 5 minutes. During this time, with his arms folded over his chest and a scowl on his face, he sits in his seat and glares at the teacher, who ignores him.

DEBBIE: Debbie attends to the lesson for approximately 3 minutes. She then begins to fidget in her chair and aimlessly looks about the work area. Ms. Stillman gives her individual attention and assistance with the task. She completes approximately half of the work sheet. She is distracted throughout the session except when the teacher or aide is at her side.

JUNE: June tries very hard and successfully gives correct verbal responses to the teacher's questions. She completes the felt board and counting frame activities with little difficulty. However, she does not complete her work sheet. June has difficulty writing her name and numbers. Although she receives a gold star, her paper is torn and smudged as a result of repeated erasures and write-overs. She does not respond positively to receiving the star. She tears her paper and throws it on the floor as the group prepares to leave the area.

What can be done to improve this lesson? How can the instructor become aware of and prepare for similar problems to be confronted in future lessons with these children? Could the lesson be planned to increase the probability that each child will succeed at his or her assigned tasks? Why do the individual children respond as they do to the lesson?

Prescriptive teaching is designed to enable an instructor to respond to children's learning problems such as those evident in the above vignettes. Prescriptive teaching, properly applied, increases the probability of success for each child attending camp.

DEFINITION

During the past several years, prescriptive teaching has become encumbered with many questionable characteristics. It has developed a mystique and has been burdened by a great quantity of unneeded educational jargon. Unfortunately, these characteristics have effectively hidden a very simple, straight-forward methodological concept. Prescriptive teaching is a set of procedures for conceptualizing, implementing, and evaluating individualized instructional programs for children (in this case handicapped children).

At various times and by various authors, prescriptive teaching has been called educational therapy, diagnostic teaching, clinical teaching, individualized programming, and prescriptive programming.

The primary focus of the prescriptive teaching method is the child as a "learner." Consideration is given to the utilization of the child's known strengths and weaknesses in an effort to enhance the probability of his success. In this case "learner" is defined in a broad sense to include the affective and psychomotor learning skills, as well as the more recognized cognitive learning skills.

The following definition was adapted from one proposed by Peter (1965, p. 1): Prescriptive teaching is a method utilizing assessment data for the development and/or modification of an instructional program for a child with one or more handicaps. This is accomplished by determining the relevance of the child's assessed strengths and weaknesses in relation to the skills and knowledge he is to learn. Prescriptive teaching includes

devising teaching methods that yield to the individual learner's characteristics in an effort to enhance the probability that learning will occur. In addition, prescriptive teaching includes a continuous evaluation process that enables the instructor to modify, as necessary, the prescription and thus continue to increase the probability of learner success.

Prescriptive teaching assumes the existence of a child with "a problem," or in this case, a handicapped camper. Too often, it is accepted by the professional that "the problem" is *within* the child. This conclusion may be true in certain cases, but all children function in environments that include many persons, places, and objects that determine their behavior in part. Rhodes (1967, 1970) recommends that educators analyze the reciprocal or transactional relationships existing between the child and his environment. It is plausible that the child's problem may be a symptom of a problem belonging to his teacher, counselor, parents, peers, or significant others within the environment; or his problem may be the result of a noxious environment.

The instructional procedures recommended in this volume assume the availability of assessment data from instructors, counselors, parents, and allied professionals, and, most important, from the handicapped child. If acceptable assessment data are not readily available for application, they must be collected before a prescription can be designed and implemented.

The instructional procedures suggested here assume the capability of modifying the child's present program for his benefit. Among the factors that must be accessible for modification are (1) the curriculum, (2) the conditions of learning, and (3) the consequences of learning (Hewett, 1974). The specific variables to be considered within these broad categories are (1) the type and level of subject matter, (2) the method of presentation, (3) the interpersonal interaction patterns, (4) the general and specific instructional objectives, (5) group placement, (6) the materials and equipment available, and (7) the rewards for learning.

SELECTIVE REVIEW

Before the specific prescriptive teaching strategy applied in the special camp is described, several models of prescriptive teaching reported in the literature during the past 2 decades are briefly reviewed: the interdisciplinary-psychodynamic approach, the perceptual-motor approach, the psycholinguistic approach, and the psychoeducational approach. In addition, consideration is given to other strategies that are variations of these.

Interdisciplinary-psychodynamic approach

Peter. Peter (1965) was among the first professionals in the field of special education to present a prescriptive teaching method in

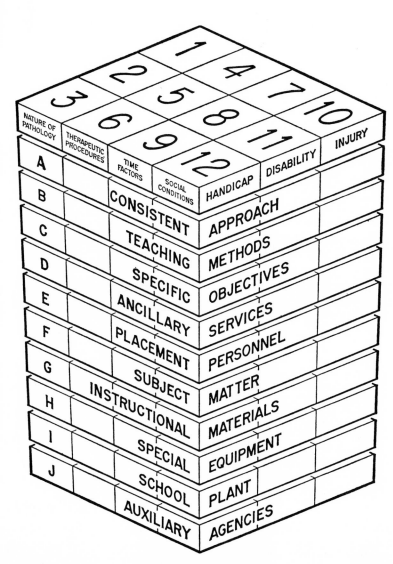

Fig. 1. Model for translating diagnostic findings into a prescription for teaching. (From *Prescriptive teaching* by L. J. Peter. Copyright 1965, McGraw-Hill Book Co. Used with permission of McGraw-Hill Book Co.)

a systematic format. Before publication of *Prescriptive Teaching*, the various components of prescriptive teaching existed in the literature independently of each other.

Peter's theoretical orientation (1965) appears to be of the traditional psychoanalytic-psychodynamic school of thought. He perceives prescriptive teaching as an interdisciplinary-clinical team effort. The clinical team is composed of a child psychiatrist, school psychologist, physician, nurse, guidance counselor, social worker, administrator, and teacher. Considerable emphasis is placed on the role of the guidance counselor as coordinator of the team activities.

In this strategy, programming efforts are initiated during the diagnostic-assessment phase. The teaching prescription is based on data derived from a comprehensive diagnostic case study. The diagnostic study includes all available social, psychological, educational, biographical, and medical evidence about the child. Data are obtained from all relevant professionals and nonprofessionals in the child's life-space.

After the diagnostic-assessment data are obtained, they are entered into the appropriate cells of the prescriptive teaching model (Fig. 1).

The model has three dimensions: problem variables, situation variables, and school variables.

The variables within each of the dimensions are arranged on a continuum from the most modifiable to the least modifiable. The variables within the *problem* and *situation* dimensions are the foundation of the prescription for teaching. The prescription itself is developed utilizing the *school* variables as guidelines.

The problem variables are (1) injury, (2) disability, and (3) handicap. Handicap is the most modifiable; injury, the least modifiable.

Peter's definitions of the individual problem variables are unique in the literature; thus, they are presented here. *Injury* is defined as physical harm or damage. *Disability* refers to the incapacity to function. Disability involves the nonorganic capacities of sensa-

tion, motion, communication, perception, cognition, integration, and the like.

"*Handicap* refers to that which impedes, hinders, or hampers some kind of action" (Peter, 1965, p. 65). Handicap is action or activity bound. The specific handicap that a child has may be incapacitating only under certain environmental conditions. For example, a child who has lost the use of his lower extremities is not normally incapacitated in academic pursuits, such as reading and writing. However, this same child is severely handicapped during physical education activities that require skill in jumping, running, and the like.

The situation variables are (1) the nature of the disorder, (2) the therapeutic procedures, (3) time factors, and (4) social conditions. In this dimension social conditions are the most modifiable, whereas the nature of the disorder is the least modifiable.

The *nature of the disorder* refers to the classification and description of the handicap, disability, or injury. It is the target of the prescription. *Therapeutic procedures* refer to those nonteaching activities designed to assist the child, such as hospitalization, institutionalization, medication, psychotherapy, physical therapy, social service, and so on. *Time factors* consist of a number of elements that have a direct bearing on the remediability of the handicap. Time factors include the study of the child's development and the history and probable duration of the handicap, disability, or injury. The timing of both therapeutic and teaching interventions must be considered in planning. *Social conditions* refer to various cultural and social variables affecting the child's overall functioning.

The interactions between these two dimensions, problem and situation variables, are represented by 3 × 4 matrix on the horizontal surface of the model (Fig. 2). Case study data are organized into the various cells of this problem-situation matrix. The interactions of these two dimensions are represented by the individual cells of the matrix. They are evaluated relative to their effect on the teaching of the child by means of the school variables.

As previously noted, the teaching prescription itself is designed by the clinical team utilizing the school variables as guidelines. This third and final dimension includes consideration of:

Consistency of teaching: The consistency of the interpersonal transactions between the teacher and the child

Teaching method: The appropriateness of the modes of communication utilized for enhancing the child's learning

Specific instructional objective(s): Instructional objectives in any of the learning domains—cognitive, affective, or psychomotor

Ancillary services: The availability of instruction-related services provided by school personnel

Child's placement and the personnel assigned to his program: The appropriateness of the child's teacher, grade, and class

Subject matter or instructional content: The topics to which the child is responsive

Instructional materials: The availability of traditional and special materials required for instruction

Special equipment: The availability of record players, visual aids, and the like

School plant: The availability of the physical facilities needed to permit and encourage learning

Auxiliary agencies: The availability of nonschool clinical and social services

Peter recommends continuous monitoring and evaluation of remediation in order to facilitate the modifications needed to improve the child's prescription.

In 1972 Peter published three works designed to augment the implementation of his model: *Individual Instruction, Individual Instruction Workbook*, and *Individual Instruction Record*. These works constitute a program for training personnel in the application of prescriptive teaching. Included in this training program are directions, simulation exercises, activities, and sample forms. Peter discusses and exemplifies the concepts of referral, diagnosis, observations, general and specific objectives, elicitors, reinforcers, and evaluation.

Although complex, Peter's model for prescriptive teaching is an excellent one. However, his strategy lacks precision in two areas: specific diagnostic-assessment procedures for application by the teacher, and specific recommendations and guidelines for remedial interventions applicable by the teacher.

The model is too general and organizationally impractical for implementation in camp settings.

Perceptual-motor approaches

Several prescriptive teaching strategies have been developed by proponents of the perceptual-motor theory. Among the strategies of the best known theorists and practitioners in this group are those of Kephart (1971); Roach and Kephart (1966); Frostig, LeFever, and Whittlesey (1961); and Frostig and Horne (1964).

The perceptual-motor development advocates have one central hypothesis in common, that higher-level mental processes, for the most part, develop out of and after adequate development of the perceptual-motor system (Gearheart, 1973). There has been considerable discussion of the theme that perceptual-motor development is significantly related to the development of academic skills and higher thought processes. The hypothesis has neither been proved nor disproved by the experimental research thus far reported in the literature.

It is my position that a logical, if not mathematically demonstrable, relationship does exist between perceptual-motor development and success in academic pursuits, such as, reading, writing, and computing. It is difficult to conceive how a child could be a successful learner in school without adequate perceptual and motor skills. The child, for example, must have considerable visual-perceptual, as well as motor, skill if he is to learn to read and write. He must be able to form letters and numbers, color within the lines, and so on, if he is to succeed in the traditional school curriculum.

The child must also develop adequate perceptual and motor skills if he is to socialize appropriately with his peers. He must develop ability in running, jumping, skipping, hopping, throwing, catching, and the like. These are universally required play skills.

In this section two perceptual-motor strategies of prescriptive teaching, the Kephart and Frostig models, are reviewed. These two strategies are measurement based; that is, they utilize test or survey results as the basis for a remedial program.

Kephart. Kephart's prescriptive teaching strategy is presented in two basic references: The Purdue Perceptual-Motor Survey (Roach and Kephart, 1966) and *The Slow Learner in the Classroom* (Kephart, 1971).

The Purdue Perceptual-Motor Survey, a diagnostic instrument for administration by a teacher or counselor, is designed to evaluate the child's skills in five perceptual-motor areas. The manual provides very specific directions for administering and rating each item. The five areas are balance and posture, body image and differentiation, perceptual-motor match, ocular control, and form perception. Each of these areas is rated by means of several specific items, as indicated on the following outline:

I. Balance and postural flexibility
  A. Walking board
    1. Forward
    2. Backward
    3. Sideways
  B. Jumping
    1. Both feet
    2. One foot
    3. Skipping
    4. Hopping
II. Body image and differentiation
  A. Identification of body parts
  B. Imitation of movement
  C. Obstacle course
    1. Going over
    2. Going under
    3. Going between
  D. Kraus-Weber test (evaluates physical strength and muscular fitness)
  E. Angels-in-the-snow test (evaluates neuromuscular differentiation and sidedness)
III. Perceptual-motor match
  A. Chalkboard
    1. Circle
    2. Double circles
    3. Lateral lines
    4. Vertical lines
  B. Rhythmic writing
    1. Rhythm
    2. Reproduction
    3. Orientation
IV. Ocular control
  A. Ocular pursuits
    1. Both eyes
    2. Right eye
    3. Left eye
    4. Convergence
V. Form perception
  A. Visual achievement forms
    1. Form
    2. Organization

The results of the child's performance on the Survey can be directly translated into individualized remedial programs such as the ones presented in *The Slow Learner in the Classroom*. Chapters 8 and 13 of *The Slow Learner* provide detailed instructions and suggestions for remediation of the assessed ability. In this text the author also presents an extensive discussion of the theoretical formulations underlying the Survey and training programs. Effective implementation of the Kephart program is not feasible without an understanding of his theory.

The remedial activities proposed by Kephart include walking board and balance beam exercises, trampoline activities, stunts, games, rhythm activities, gross motor tasks, games utilizing partial and total body control, hand-eye and eye-hand activities, and training in ocular control and pursuit. Also included are chalkboard drawing and copying, training in form perception via form recognition, object matching, form board activities, puzzles, form construction, pegboard tasks, building block construction, and cutting-and-pasting activities.

The majority of the activities suggested by Kephart are fun. Children are highly motivated to participate in this program.

The Kephart approach to prescriptive teaching is well organized and can be effectively applied in the special camp setting. The translation of diagnostic data into a practical remedial program is easily accomplished by the teacher or counselor. Both the rating and remediation phases of the program can be conducted with little training. In addition, specialized equipment and materials required for implementation of this approach are minimal.

Frostig. As a result of clinical experiences at The Marianne Frostig Center of Educational Therapy in Los Angeles, Frostig and her colleagues developed a perceptual-motor approach to prescriptive teaching, which, although comprehensive in nature, places emphasis on visual-perceptual development. The Frostig approach includes The Developmental Test of Visual Perception (DTVP) (Frostig and others, 1961), The Frostig Program for the Development of Visual Perception (Frostig and Horne, 1964), and the Move-Grow-Learn (MGL) program (Frostig and Maslow, 1969a, 1969b, 1970).

The importance Frostig and her collaborators place on perception is indicated by the following:

Perception is one of the prime psychological functions. It is the bridge between the human being and his environment, and without perception all but the simplest body functions, such as breathing and elimination, would stop and survival would be impossible.

. . . Perception is defined as the ability to recognize stimuli. This ability includes not only the reception of sensory impressions from the outside world and from one's own body, but the capacity to interpret and identify the sensory impressions by correlating them with previous experiences. This recognition and integration of stimuli is a process that occurs in the brain, not in the receiving organ, such as the ear or the eye. (Frostig and Horne, 1964, p. 7)

The DTVP is designed to measure five operationally defined visual-perceptual skills: eye-motor coordination, figure-ground discrimination, constancy of shape, position in space, and spatial relationships (Table 1). The test may be used as a screening or clinical assessment instrument. As a screening instrument, it is applicable to preschool, kindergarten, and first-grade children. For clinical purposes, the DTVP may be applied with older learning-disabled children. It can be administered by a trained teacher or counselor. It can be administered in either a group or individual setting. Frostig suggests that the learning disabled and severely disturbed be individually tested.

The child's performances on the DTVP guides the teacher in the selection of an ap-

propriate remedial program. Although Frostig emphasizes test performance as the most important variable in the selection of a remedial program, she cautions that test results are not infallible. The teacher or counselor must consider his personal observations of the child's behavior, as well as the child's performance on other formal and informal evaluation instruments during the selection process.

The MGL program, the first of the two remedial programs developed in correlation with the DTVP, has been largely ignored in discussions of the efficiency of this approach to remediation. The MGL program provides the teacher or counselor with 160 activities to facilitate the teaching of movement skills and the development of creative movement. "The program is designed to enhance the total development of young children—their physical and their psychological abilities, their ability to learn, their ability to get along with one another, their feelings about themselves, and their relationships to the environment" (Frostig and Maslow, 1969a, p. 5). This program includes suggestions for developing movement skills, body awareness, language development, and so on. The facilities and equipment needed to implement the program are listed, as well as suggestions for working with handicapped children.

The other remedial program, the Frostig Program for the Development of Visual Perception, emphasizes two-dimensional pencil-and-paper remedial activities. This program includes approximately 350 work sheets divided into the five visual-perceptual skill areas. Within each of the areas, the work sheets progress from the simple to the complex. Although frequently overlooked, a variety of games and exercises are suggested to precede or parallel the pencil-and-paper activities.

Although Frostig and her collaborators have placed considerable emphasis on visual-perceptual skill development, their approach, when viewed in its entirety, has considerable to offer the teacher and counselor in the camp setting. This is a highly organized and easily applied prescriptive teaching system.

Table 1. Overview of Frostig DTVP

Subtest	Definition of skill	Examples of correlated disability	Example item
Eye-motor coordination	Ability to coordinate vision with movements of the body or with a part or parts of the body	Clumsiness in dressing self and in motor activities; difficulty in sports and games; difficulty in cutting, pasting, drawing	
Figure-ground discrimination	Ability to select from the mass of incoming stimuli a limited number of stimuli which become the center of attention	Inattentiveness; distractibility; disorganization; reversals in letters, words, numbers; difficulty locating objects	
Constancy of shape	Ability to perceive an object as possessing invariant properties, such as shape and size	Difficulty in determining size, shape, color, brightness; difficulty in determining letters, numbers, symbols	
Position in space	Ability to perceive the relationship of an object to self	Visual distortion; directionality; reversals	
Spatial relationships	Ability to perceive the position of two or more objects in relation to self and each other	Sequencing of symbols, letters, numbers, words, patterns; academic problems in reading, writing, spelling, computing	

Other perceptual-motor approaches. Other works by educators associated with perceptual-motor and visual-perceptual approaches to remediation include those by Strauss and Lehtinen (1947); Barsch (1967); Cratty (1967, 1971); Fitzhugh and Fitzhugh (1966); and Getman, Kane, Halgren, and Mckee (1968). Space does not permit a detailed discussion of these important theorists and practitioners; however the reader is encouraged to review the basic premises expounded by each through the references provided at the conclusion of this chapter.

Psycholinguistic approaches

Since the publication of the Illinois Test of Psycholinguistic Abilities (ITPA) (Kirk, McCarthy, and Kirk, 1961; rev. ed., 1968), there has been an explosion in the application of prescriptive teaching strategies based on the language model, including those by Orton (1937), Kirk (1966, 1968), Kirk and Kirk (1971), and Johnson and Myklebust (1967). A review of all of the strategies proposed by all of the contributors is not feasible; the ITPA, which has been utilized by many professionals as a foundation upon which teaching prescriptions are designed for remediation, is reviewed and consideration is given to the remedial recommendations proposed by Bateman (1965) and Wiseman (1965).

The following is an expression of the commonality among the proponents of the psycholinguistic model:

Since language defects or lags are often characteristic of children with learning disabilities, it could be expected that certain remedial procedures that put the primary stress on ameliorating language problems (i.e., listening, speaking, reading, writing) would be evolved. It is not the rather widespread prevalence of language problems among children with learning disabilities that justifies this approach, however, since almost all handicapped children have language defects. It is rather, the positive relationship of language ability to measured intelligence and to school achievement that makes such approaches important for children with learning disabilities. For presumably, improvements in language function can lead to improvements in intellectual function and/or academic achievement, and these latter are precisely the areas in which children with learning disabilities need improvement. (McCarthy and McCarthy, 1969, p. 54)

Illinois Test of Psycholinguistic Abilities. The importance of the ITPA lies in its nearly universal acceptance and application in the field of special education as a diagnostic instrument. Since its original publication in 1961, it has been used as a basis for teaching prescriptions for thousands of handicapped children. Seldom used alone but given as part of a battery of diagnostic tests, it is usually one of the most useful tests for programming purposes because several remedial programs are available that correlate with its results.

The ITPA is primarily a test of communications abilities based on a modification of a theoretical model designed by Osgood (1957).

The 1968 revision of the ITPA is composed of 12 subtests that evaluate the two major channels of communications: visual-motor and auditory-vocal. Within these two channels of communication, three psycholinguistic processes are evaluated: receptive, organizing, and expressive. Two levels of organization are evaluated: representational and automatic. The relationships between these various components of the ITPA are presented in Fig. 2.

Representational level functions. Three general types of functions are tested at the representational, or symbolic, level: the receptive process, the organizing process, and the expressive process.

The *receptive process* may be defined as the process whereby children are able to comprehend symbols. Receptive process tests include the auditory reception test and the visual reception test.

The *auditory reception test* assesses the child's ability to derive meaning from the spoken word. Fifty short, direct questions requiring only yes or no answers are included.

The *visual reception test* assesses the child's ability to derive meaning from visual symbols. The child is shown a stimulus picture for 3 seconds and is told, "See this." A page of pictures, one of which is conceptually similar to the stimulus, is then shown, and the child is asked to choose the one most like

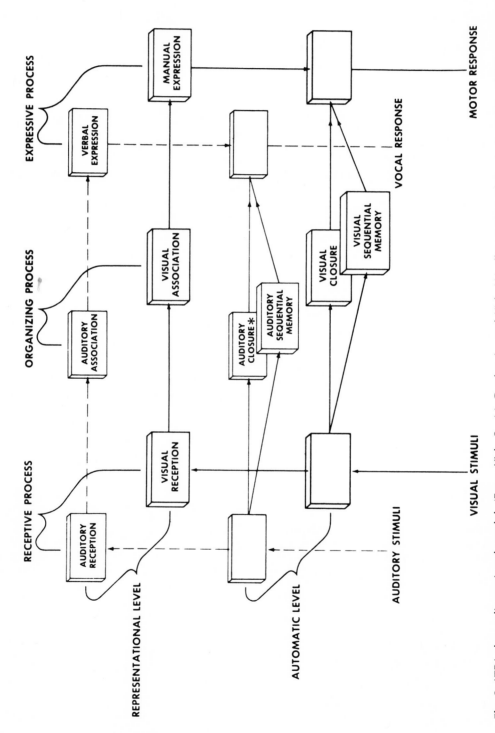

Fig. 2. ITPA three-dimensional model. (From Kirk, S., McCarthy, J., and Kirk, W. *Illinois Test of Psycholinguistic Abilities: examiner's manual*, Rev. ed. Urbana, Ill.: University of Illinois Press, 1968.)

the stimulus picture. Other choices may have structural instead of functional similarity to the stimulus, or they may be associated in some nonfunctional way with either the stimulus picture or the correct-choice picture.

The *organizing process* may be defined as the ability to organize or relate symbols in a meaningful way. Organizing process tests include the auditory-vocal association test and the visual-motor association test.

The *auditory-vocal association test* assesses the child's ability to relate concepts presented orally. Sentence completion, including such statements as "I pound with a _____," is the technique used.

The *visual-motor association test* uses a picture association technique. A single stimulus picture is surrounded by four optional pictures. The child is asked which of the optional pictures goes with the central stimulus picture.

The *expressive process* may be defined as the ability to transmit an idea through symbols. Expressive process tests include the verbal expression test and the manual expression test.

The *verbal expression test* involves asking the child to tell about a number of different pictures. The score indicates the relevance and factualness of the concepts expressed.

The *manual expression test* assesses the child's ability to use manual expression in response to "show me what we do with" questions. The child is to pantomine the response he wishes to give.

Automatic level functions. Two general types of functions are tested at the automatic, nonsymbolic level: closure and short-term sequential memory.

Closure may be defined as the ability to fill in the missing parts in an incomplete picture or expression, that is, to sense the whole. Closure tests include the grammatic closure test, the visual closure test, the auditory closure test, and the sound-blending test.

The *grammatic closure test* assesses the child's ability to fill in the missing parts of expressions. Items are presented orally,

along with pictures portraying the content of the expressions.

The *visual closure test* assesses the child's ability to identify common objects from an incomplete picture.

The *auditory closure test* (supplementary test 1) is a test of the child's ability to fill in the missing parts of words, such as might be heard in a faulty telephone connection.

The *sound-blending test* (supplementary test 2) involves pronouncing the sounds of a word with intervals of silence between. This, like the auditory closure test, is a means of assessing the organizing process at the automatic level in the auditory-vocal channel.

Sequential memory may be defined as the ability to reproduce a sequence of stimuli. Sequential memory tests include the auditory sequential memory test and the visual sequential memory test.

The *auditory sequential memory test* assesses the child's ability to reproduce sequences of digits that have been presented auditorially.

The *visual sequential memory test* assesses the child's ability to reproduce sequences of figures from memory. Nonmeaningful figures are used; the child is given "chips" of these figures to place in the same sequence as those he has seen.

The ITPA is recommended for use with children between the ages of 2½ and 10 years. It yields a raw score for each of the 12 subtests, as well as a psycholinguistic age (PLA), which is based on the scaled scores of the 10 basic subtests. Each raw score may be converted into a scaled score and plotted on the "profile of abilities." This graphic presentation, or profile, is very useful to the professional prescribing a remedial program for a child.

The basic focus of the ITPA is on comparing *intratest* differences rather than *intertest* differences among children. The results of the ITPA must be interpreted by a professional trained in the administration, scoring, and interpretation of the instrument.

Bateman. Bateman (1965) presented a five-stage diagnostic-remedial model to be used to obtain and translate diagnostic information into a teaching prescription. This model responds to "what to do with the child" and "how to better teach the child." It depends heavily, but not exclusively, on the results of the ITPA. Bateman suggests using the ITPA as one of a battery of diagnostic instruments.

The stages of Bateman's diagnostic-remedial strategy (Bateman, 1965) are:

Stage one: "Determining whether a learning problem exists." During this stage the diagnostician attempts to differentiate between the learning-disabled child and those children functioning unacceptably because of mental retardation, developmental lags, experiential deprivation, poor instruction, and so on.

Stage two: "Obtaining a behavioral analysis and description of the disability." Here, attention is focused on *how* the child functions in a descriptive sense rather than on *where* or at *what level* he functions.

Stage three: "Examining correlates of a disability." This is the "heart" of the diagnosis. At this point in the diagnostic-remedial process, Bateman identifies two classes of correlates: paraconstitutional and educational. Paraconstitutional correlates include familial factors, sex distribution, "soft" signs of neurological dysfunction, and motor awkwardness. Educational correlates include subject matter performance, auditory discrimination, visual discrimination, and sound blending.

Stage four: Formulating "a clear, concise, and accurate diagnostic hypothesis." At this time, the diagnostician sums up the diagnostic process and proposes a remedial program. The program must include recommendations for remediation.

Stage five: "Making educational recommendations based on the diagnostic hypothesis." In this final section, Bateman discusses the need for remedial programs that correlate with the findings of diagnostic procedures.

Remedial programs. Since the publication of Bateman's diagnostic-remedial model in 1965, several remedial programs based on the ITPA have been presented in the literature. The most useful of these programs have been offered by Kirk, McCarthy, and Kirk (1968), Bush and Giles (1969), Kirk and Kirk (1971), and Wiseman (1965). It is not feasible to review each of these programs here; rather, the Wiseman program and the Kirk and Kirk program are discussed briefly.

Wiseman's remedial program is based on the 1961 edition of the ITPA; thus, he uses the words "decoding," "association," and "encoding" rather than "receptive," "organizing," and "expressive," which are used in the 1968 revision. Wiseman offers exercises for remediation in the various ability areas: decoding (auditory and visual); association (auditory and visual); memory (auditory, visual, general, sequential, relative to environmental cues, immediate, intermediate, and long term); automatic closure (auditory and visual); and encoding (vocal and motor). Each of his language ability programs are correlated with the results of the ITPA subtests.

In general, Wiseman recommends teaching directly to the disability.

The Kirk and Kirk program is an excellent source of ITPA remedial techniques. The authors give both general and specific guidelines for the remediation of learning abilities. They stress that their guidelines are neither a curriculum nor a step-by-step sequence of activities for remediation, but are merely a guide. They provide specific suggestions for the remediation of disabilities evaluated by each of the subtests.

The ITPA strategy is excellent for the remediation of psychomotor and cognitive learning disabilities. However, it does not provide assistance for social and emotional handicaps. In addition, the highly trained personnel required to administer and interpret the ITPA are frequently not available in a camp.

Psychoeducational survey approaches

In recent years, several psychoeducational survey approaches to the remediation of the learning and behavior problems of children have been published. Most notable among the efforts to systematize assessment and remediation processes are the works of Valett (1967, 1968a, 1968b, 1969a, 1969b), Farrald and Schamber (1973), Mann and Suiter (1974), and Cawley (1973).

Each strategy is an effort to organize and translate formal and informal psychoeducational test, inventory, and/or survey assessment results into appropriate remedial programs. The systems vary greatly in the specific assessment and remedial techniques used to attain this objective. Some of the models focus exclusively on formal, standardized assessment techniques, whereas others focus on informal, teacher-made techniques. However, each strategy offers a variety of recommendations and guidelines for the assessment and remediation of learning and behavior problems.

Valett. Valett has published several books for teachers and psychologists concerning the assessment and remediation of learning and behavior problems. Among his major publications are *Programming Learning Disabilities* (1969), *The Remediation of Learning Disabilities: A Handbook of Psychoeducational Resource Programs* (1967), *Developmental Task Analysis* (1969), and *A Psychoeducational Inventory of Basic Learning Abilities* (1968).

Programming Learning Disabilities and *Developmental Task Analysis* are ability and skill evaluation surveys for children from preschool to junior high school. Valett correlates these instruments with a variety of remedial programs, which he presents in the *Handbook*.

Valett classifies learning handicaps into six areas: gross motor development, sensory-motor integration, perceptual-motor skills, language development, conceptual skills, and social skills. He further divides each of these areas into component skills. In the *Handbook*, Valett defines, exemplifies, and presents specific remedial programs for the following learning skills:

A. Gross motor development
   1. Rolling
   2. Sitting
   3. Crawling
   4. Walking
   5. Running
   6. Throwing
   7. Jumping
   8. Skipping
   9. Dancing
   10. Self-identification
   11. Body localization
   12. Body abstraction
   13. Muscular strength
   14. General physical health
B. Sensory-motor integration
   1. Balance and rhythm
   2. Body-spatial organization
   3. Reaction-speed dexterity
   4. Tactile discrimination
   5. Directionality
   6. Laterality
   7. Time orientation
C. Perceptual-motor skills
   1. Auditory acuity
   2. Auditory decoding
   3. Auditory-vocal association
   4. Auditory memory
   5. Auditory sequencing
   6. Visual acuity
   7. Visual coordination and pursuit
   8. Visual form discrimination
   9. Visual figure-ground differentiation
   10. Visual memory
   11. Visual-motor memory
   12. Visual-motor fine muscle coordination
   13. Visual-motor spatial-form manipulation
   14. Visual-motor speed of learning
   15. Visual-motor integration
D. Language development
   1. Vocabulary
   2. Fluency and encoding
   3. Articulation
   4. Word-attack skills
   5. Reading comprehension
   6. Writing
   7. Spelling
E. Conceptual skills
   1. Number concepts
   2. Arithmetic processes
   3. Arithmetic reasoning
   4. General information
   5. Classification
   6. Comprehension
F. Social skills
   1. Social acceptance
   2. Anticipatory response
   3. Value judgements
   4. Social maturity

ADAPT (Farrald and Schamber). ADAPT (**A** **D**iagnostic **A**nd **P**rescriptive **T**echnique) (Farrald and Schamber, 1973) is a multidisciplinary teaching process that developed logically from the educational needs of children. This strategy is designed for teachers of regular classes but can be of great assistance to special education teachers attempting to reintegrate handicapped children into the educational mainstream. Farrald and Schamber's definition of "learning disability" is generic; thus, it includes children with social-emotional problems. These authors discuss several social-emotional handicaps, such as disorganization, distractibility, weak automatization ability, hyperactivity, impulsivity, inflexibility, perseveration, affective figure-ground confusion, emotional vulnerability, and interpersonal skills. Farrald and Schamber correlate these psychosocial characteristics with the problems of auditory reception, visual reception, and verbal expression. Throughout their work, they provide a variety of formal and informal suggestions for assessment and remediation of these various disabilities.

Mann and Suiter. Mann and Suiter's *Handbook in Diagnostic Teaching: A Learning Disabilities Approach* (1974) is designed to help teachers bridge the gap between *what they know* as a result of training and *what they must do* to help children with learning handicaps. Applying a task analysis approach to learning, the teacher is encouraged to determine the child's:

Rate of input: How fast does he learn?
Amount of input: How much does he learn?
Sequence of input: In what order and via what modes of communication does he learn?

Primarily, Mann and Suiter's work is concerned with what a child needs to accomplish in order to succeed in school. By delineating the critical skills necessary for academic success in reading, writing, spelling, and arithmetic, the teacher can identify deficits in a child's language skills. The authors include chapters on spelling, reading, and arithmetic. In each chapter they suggest standardized and teacher-made assessment techniques.

In the chapter on developmental screening, focus is primarily on the readiness skills. Mann and Suiter provide a model for a defi-cit-level, process-oriented curriculum and specific suggestions for remediation.

Cawley. In 1973 Cawley and his collaborators published the *Behavior Resource Guide*, which is designed to assist in the systematic assessment, analysis, and remediation of learning problems. In the *Guide* attention is focused on three groups of handicapped children: learning-disabled children, emotionally disturbed children, and slow learners. Guidance in prescriptive instruction is provided in the areas of auditory skills, visual skills, and social-emotional development.

A listing of 266 desired learner outcomes (DLOs) is included in the *Guide*. Each of the DLOs, presented in specific behavioral terminology, are correlated with several hundred specific test items from over 40 widely used psychoeducational tests and with over 1,000 commercially available instructional items.

In addition, a listing of the publishers of the tests and instructional materials and an extensive glossary of terms are provided. The *Guide* is a well-organized and highly usable volume.

The most obvious weakness (perhaps a necessary one) of the *Guide* is a nearly total reliance on commercially published assessment instruments and instructional materials. This inhibits implementation of this particular system in many camp settings because of financial restrictions.

APPLICATION IN THE CAMP SETTING

Each of the prescriptive teaching strategies discussed in this chapter offers assistance to camp personnel. The authors have offered models or frameworks that, when applied in a camp setting, give direction to the choice and implementation of the activities to be provided for the campers.

Sometimes, perhaps frequently, the proponents of a particular model overemphasize their particular approach as being "the way" to remediation. This is perhaps understandable, since it is generally a life's work that is being offered. However, an overemphasis on one approach to the exclusion of all others can be detrimental.

What is needed is an approach that recognizes the importance of each of the learning domains—affective, psychomotor, and cognitive—in relation to the child's overall functioning. Such an approach must recognize and emphasize the relationships existing between these learning domains. The strategies classified under psychoeducational appear to approximate the desired model.

Gearheart has presented nine variables to be considered in the selection of an education strategy. Although his concern is with the selection of a strategy for use in the public school setting, his suggestions are germaine.

The final answer can be determined only after consideration of a host of variables such as (1) age of children to be served, (2) type of learning disability, (3) degree, or severity, of learning disabilities, (4) facilities available for educational programming, (5) diagnostic/assessment personnel available, (6) funds available for personnel, materials, and equipment, (7) state regulations that limit or delimit educational approaches, (8) teacher competence, and (9) school district philosophy. (Gearheart, 1973, p. 155)

Although the camp is not, in the traditional sense of the word, a *school*, these two social institutions have considerable in common. Among the variables to be considered in the camp setting are:

1. Purpose of the camp
2. Specific objectives of the camp
3. Ages of the children to be served
4. Type of handicapped children to be served
5. Degree, or severity, of the handicaps
6. Length of the camp session
7. Educational facilities available
8. Recreational facilities available
9. Living facilities available
10. Precamp referral and diagnostic-assessment data
11. In-camp diagnostic-assessment personnel and the data generated by them
12. Supportive community services
13. Materials and equipment available
14. Regulatory and ethical limits on programming
15. Number of personnel available
16. Staff competency
17. Camp philosophy

The overall purpose for conducting a camping program in large part determines the choice of the prescriptive teaching approach. The purposes for conducting special camps vary greatly. The following are some examples:

To keep the children busy during vacation periods

To keep the inner-city child off the streets and out of trouble

To enrich the child's school program

To facilitate the child's general social-emotional development

To facilitate the child's general and/or specific recreational skills

To help the child develop a proper attitude toward the use of leisure time

To assess and diagnose the child's handicap and to prescribe treatment and remediation to be implemented in another setting

To provide instruction in specific physical education, camping, and survival skills

To provide an opportunity for the child to study topics that are correlated with his academic school program, such as conservation, ecology, forestry, history, and nature

To serve as a temporary placement center before and/or after placement in an institution, foster home, or special class placement center

These are but a few of the reasons for operating a special camp. Each camp has, or should have, its individual purposes for being.

The specific individual and group objectives of the camp are another variable determining what strategies will be applied in the program. Whether the camp is concerned with the total group of campers, the individual campers, or with both makes a great difference in the selection of strategies. The total group approach tends to assume that campers are more alike than they are different and may overlook the individual camper's needs and desires. In addition, those using the group approach frequently assume that all children in a program have the needed prerequisite skills to perform prescribed activities (until the child demonstrates otherwise). The group approach may be acceptable for some nonhandicapped children, but the heterogeneity of the handicapped population prohibits this approach.

A camp serving preschool children will certainly differ from a camp serving pre-adolescent boys. Consideration must be given not only to the chronological age of the children but also to the developmental age; these factors affect individual and group needs, desires, interests, experiences, and rewards.

The type of handicap (physical, emotional, social, cognitive, and so on) will determine the camping program. What campers do, what they are expected to do, where they go, and so on, vary greatly with handicapping conditions. You cannot provide the same program for a group of autistic children that is provided for a group of slow learners from the inner city.

The degree of handicap within a specific population has many implications for the numbers, types, and competencies of the personnel to be employed, as well as the physical facilities, materials, and equipment required for the program.

Far more can be accomplished in behalf of the handicapped child during a 6- or 8-week session than can be done in a 1- or 2-week session. If an organized educational program is to be offered to the children, facilities must be available. Out-of-door classrooms work very well with the majority of handicapped children, but they must be quiet and of a size that encourages attention and study. It is nearly impossible to efficiently conduct a recreational program without adequate space, materials, and equipment.

If the purpose of the camp is assessment, diagnosis, and remediation, or any one of these, then adequately trained personnel must be available. These individuals may be either camp personnel or cooperating community agency personnel. If assessment and diagnostic data are to be obtained before the child attends camp, then a mechanism for obtaining and routing such data must be devised.

The staff is the key to a successful camping program. We are long past the day when anyone can serve as a camp director, counselor, instructor, or aide. The personnel must have, or be willing to learn, skills that are congruent with the purpose and objectives of the program.

Materials and equipment must be available to support the objectives of the program. It is possible, but difficult and inefficient, to attempt to provide an arts-and-crafts program without adequate materials.

Fortunately, we have state health, safety, and programming regulations and professional ethics that are designed to protect the rights of the child. These restrictions require that camps provide proper supervision, adequate programs, and safe facilities. They also prohibit physical and psychological punishments. They discourage overpermissiveness by defining our responsibility for protecting and assisting the child.

Finally, each camp has a written or unwritten philosophy, which sets the tone of the camp as permissive or structured, demanding or challenging, caring or unconcerned. The camp's philosophy has a great bearing on what, when, how, where, and with whom a child participates in the activities comprising the program.

REFERENCES

Barsch, R. *Achieving perceptual-motor efficiency.* Seattle: Special Child Publications, 1967.

Bateman, B. D. An educator's view of a diagnostic approach to learning disorders. In J. Hellmuth (Ed.), *Learning Disorders* (Vol. 1). Seattle: Special Child Publications, 1965.

Bush, W., and Giles, M. *Aids to psycholinguistic teaching.* Columbus, Ohio: Charles E. Merrill Publishing Co., 1969.

Cawley, J. F. *Behavior resource guide.* Wallingford, Conn.: Educational Sciences, Inc., 1973.

Cratty, B. J. *Developmental sequences of perceptual-motor tasks.* Baldwin, N.Y.: Educational Activities, Inc., 1967.

Cratty, B. J. *Activity learning: games to enhance academic abilities.* Englewood Cliffs, N.J.: Prentice-Hall, Inc., 1971.

Farrald, R. R., and Schamber, R. G. *A diagnostic and prescriptive technique: handbook I: a mainstream approach to identification, assessment and amelioration of learning disabilities.* Sioux Falls, S.D.: ADAPT Press, 1973.

Fitzhugh, K. B., and Fitzhugh, L. *The Fitzhugh Plus Program.* Galien, Mich.: Allied Education Council, 1966.

Frostig, M., and Horne, D. *The Frostig Program for the Development of Visual Perception: teacher's guide.* Chicago: Follett Corp., 1964.

Frostig, M., LeFever, W., and Whittlesey, J. R. B. *Administration and scoring manual for the Marianne Frostig Developmental Test of Visual Perception.* Palo Alto, Calif.: Consulting Psychologists Press, 1966.

Frostig, M., LeFever, W., and Whittlesey, J. R. B. *Developmental Test of Visual Perception.* Palo Alto, Calif.: Consulting Psychologists Press, 1961.

Frostig, M., and Maslow, P. *Frostig MGL: Move-Grow-Learn: movement education activities.* Chicago: Follett Corp., 1969 (a).

Frostig, M., and Maslow P. *Frostig MGL: Move-Grow-Learn: teacher's guide.* Chicago: Follett Corp., 1969 (b).

Frostig, M., and Maslow, P. *Movement education: theory and practice.* Chicago: Follett Corp., 1970.

Gearheart, B. R., *Learning disabilities: educational strategies.* St. Louis: The C. V. Mosby Co., 1973.

Getman, G., Kane, E., Halgren, M., and McKee, G. *Developing learning readiness: teacher's manual.* St. Louis: McGraw-Hill Book Co., 1968.

Hewett, F. M., and Forness, S. R. *Education of exceptional learners.* Boston: Allyn & Bacon, Inc., 1974.

Johnson, D. J., and Myklebust, H. R. *Learning disabilities: educational principles and practices.* New York: Grune & Stratton, Inc., 1967.

Kephart, N. C. *The slow learner in the classroom* (2nd ed.). Columbus, Ohio: Charles E. Merrill Publishing Co., 1971.

Kirk, S. *Diagnosis and remediation of psycholinguistic abilities.* Urbana, Ill.: University of Illinois Press, 1966.

Kirk, S. The Illinois Test of Psycholinguistic Abilities: its origin and implications. In J. Hellmuth (Ed.), *Learning disorders* (Vol. 3). Seattle: Special Child Publications, 1968.

Kirk, S. A., and Kirk, W. D. *Psycholinguistic learning disabilities: diagnosis and remediation.* Urbana, Ill.: University of Illinois Press, 1971.

Kirk, S., McCarthy, J., and Kirk, W. *Illinois Test of Psycholinguistic Abilities: examiner's manual.* Urbana Ill.: University of Illinois Press., 1961; Rev. ed., 1968.

Lerner, J. W. *Children with learning disabilities: theories, diagnosis, and teaching strategies.* Boston: Houghton Mifflin Co., 1971.

Mann, P. H., and Suiter, P. *Handbook in diagnostic teaching: a learning disabilities approach.* Boston: Allyn & Bacon, Inc., 1974.

McCarthy, J. J. The importance of linguistic ability in the mentally retarded. *Mental Retardation*, April 1964, **2**, 90.

McCarthy, J. J., and McCarthy, J. F. *Learning disabilities.* Boston: Allyn & Bacon, Inc., 1969.

Myers, P. I., and Hammill, D. D. *Methods for learning disorders.* New York: John Wiley & Sons, Inc., 1969.

Orton, S. T. *Reading, writing and speech problems in children.* New York: W. W. Norton & Co., Inc., 1937.

Osgood, W. A behavioristic analysis. In J. S. Bruner and others, *Contemporary approach to cognition,* Symposium, University of Colorado. Cambridge, Mass.: Harvard University Press, 1957.

Peter, L. J. *Individual instruction.* New York: McGraw-Hill Book Co., 1972.

Peter, L. J. *Prescriptive teaching.* New York: McGraw-Hill Book Co., 1965.

Radler, D. H., and Kephart, N. C. *Success through play.* New York: Harper & Row, Publishers, 1960.

Rhodes, W. C. The disturbing child: a problem of ecological management. *Exceptional Children*, 1967, **33**, 449-455.

Rhodes, W. C. A community participation analysis of emotional disturbances. *Exceptional Children*, 1970, **36**, 309-314.

Roach, E. G., and Kephart, N. C. *The Purdue Perceptual-Motor Survey manual.* Columbus, Ohio: Charles E. Merrill Publishing Co., 1966.

Strauss, A. A., and Lehtinen, L. *Psychopathology and education of the brain-injured child.* New York: Grune & Stratton, Inc., 1947.

Valett, R. E. *The remediation of learning disabilities: a handbook of psychoeducational resource programs.* Palo Alto, Calif.: Fearon Publishers, 1967.

Valett, R. E. *A psychoeducational inventory of basic learning abilities.* Palo Alto, Calif.: Fearon Publishers, 1968 (a).

Valett, R. E. *Workbook to accompany a psychoeducational inventory of basic learning abilities.* Palo Alto, Calif.: Fearon Publishers, 1968 (b).

Valett, R. E. *Developmental task analysis.* Belmont, Calif.: Fearon Publishers, 1969 (a).

Valett, R. E. *Programming learning disabilities.* Palo Alto, Calif.: Fearon Publishers, 1969 (b).

Wiseman, D. A classroom procedure for identifying and remediating language problems. *Mental Retardation*, April 1965, **3**, 20.

Learning to "do it yourself" with the help of a friend.

CHAPTER 3

A model for prescriptive teaching in the special camp

The prescriptive teaching model presented in this chapter is but one of several that would be appropriate for application in the camp setting. However, when consideration is given to the diversity existing among camps as a result of the variability of campers, disabilities, purposes, personnel, and facilities, this plan seems to be the most adaptable for general implementation.

This particular model, as are all prescriptive teaching models, is designed as a guide to the ordering of assessment data, instructional objectives, remedial interventions, and evaluation procedures.

Although the model provides the necessary structure for efficient and effective remediation, it does not place unnecessary restriction on the selection of the intervention to be imposed on the child. Interventions can be on a continuum from the interdisciplinary-psychodynamic approach to the psychoeducational approach. Consequently, instructors and counselors are not confined to a "best" method or methods of intervention. However, the model does require the instructor to organize the prescription for

learning in a manner that makes both success and failure equally evident.

If the intervention is successful, the instructor may continue the remediation process with confidence. However, if the instructor has adhered to the prescription for learning and has failed to bring about the sought after changes in the child's behavior, he is secure in the knowledge that this particular intervention is not successful. The intervention may be discarded and an alternative intervention implemented, or it may be modified.

The prescriptive teaching model presented is a synthesis of the components of several of the approaches discussed in Chapter 2. These components have been drawn together into a workable system for application in the camp setting.

Three case studies are presented to exemplify implementation of the model. These cases demonstrate the application of this model in each learning domain: affective, psychomotor, and cognitive.

A summary of the model is presented in Table 2.

Table 2. Prescriptive teaching model

Phase number	Phase title	Components
1	Collecting and synthesizing assessment data	Preadmission assessment; formal assessment; informal assessment
2	Describing present and terminal behaviors	
3	Selecting and writing instructional objectives	General objectives; specific objectives
4	Designing and implementing specific interventions	Determining or guiding variables
5	Evaluating the intervention	Implementation; effectiveness

PHASE 1: COLLECTING AND SYNTHESIZING ASSESSMENT DATA

All activities that contribute information or data to the teacher's knowledge of the child and his problem constitute the total evaluation process. It is this information that is synthesized and used to formulate an appropriate instructional intervention for a particular child. (Hammill, 1971, p. 341)

Although Hammill uses the words "evaluation" in lieu of "assessment" and "teacher" in lieu of "instructor," he clarifies with considerable precision the purpose of phase 1 of the prescriptive teaching process. Four sources are utilized to obtain assessment data on each child attending camp: preadmission data, formal assessment data, informal survey or inventory assessment data, and data obtained by direct observation of the child in the camp setting.

Preadmission data

Preadmission data may be obtained from a variety of sources, such as the application form, referral reports, referring agency personnel, parents, teachers, and physicians. These initial data provide camp personnel with an overall description of the child and his problem.

It is desirable to establish an application procedure that facilitates obtaining as much objective information about the child seeking admission to camp as possible.

One method, productive of considerable data about a child, is an application procedure authorizing camp personnel to seek information from noncamp personnel who have dealt with the child and from records concerning the child. If this procedure is to be followed, the application for admission should request the following information and permissions:

Child's name, sex, age, and birthdate

Parents' names, home address and telephone number, business address and telephone number, and emergency telephone number

Child's school, preschool, or day-care center; school address and telephone number; school district; teacher's name; and permission to contact the school or teacher

Extraordinary services provided child, such as special education, welfare, social, mental health, medical, remedial, and recreational services; names, addresses, and telephone numbers of persons and/or agencies providing these services; and permission to contact them

Statement of reason for seeking admission to camp

Brief description of child's behavior problem

Brief description of child's learning disability

Brief description of child's physical handicap

Basic information on referring person, if not the parent: name, address, position, title, relationship, and telephone number

Name, address, and telephone number of child's physician; date of last physical examination; a written report concerning the examination; and permission to contact the physician.

An application form requesting this information and permission to contact other professionals will allow camp personnel to efficiently accumulate relevant information about the child. A sample application form is presented in Appendix A; this form should be modified to respond to the needs of the specific camp.

If the parent or guardian gives permission to seek additional information about the child from other professionals, this information may be obtained either through face-to-face consultation or through written communications. Three sample forms to be completed by the teacher, the physician, and the social service professional are included in Appendix A. As with the application form, these forms should be modified to meet the needs of the specific camp.

The first form, the *educational assessment form*, should, at a minimum, include the information presented below. This form is to be completed by the teacher with the help of other instructional specialists in the school having significant contact with the child, such as the physical education teacher, the art teacher, the music teacher.

Identifying data: Child's name, age, sex, and birthdate; parents' name, address, and telephone number; name and position of person or persons completing form

Statement of problem: Severity, frequency, and duration; when first observed; changes since onset; consistency of the problem over time; child's awareness of the problem; child's response to the problem

School adjustment: Name of school, grade, test data, attendance, age at school entrance, average grades during last 4 years, aptitudes, interests, attitude toward school and school personnel

Work habits: Attention span, ability to complete task and follow directions, neatness, handling of material and equipment

Readiness skills: Using pencil and crayon; coloring; cutting and pasting; identifying colors, shapes, sizes, letters, and numbers; reproducing shapes; tracing; copying; recognizing similarities and differences

Motor skills: Walking, running, jumping, skipping, climbing, going up and down stairs, catching, throwing, bouncing, batting, aiming, hitting a target

Motor control: Balance; rhythm; coordination; ability to chew, swallow, grasp, roll, sit, crawl, and run with and without a change in pace, and locate body parts

Language: Clarity of expression; verbal expression of wants and needs; conversational skills, use of eye contact when conversing; use of words, phrases, and sentences; ability to listen to and follow directions

Reading: Recognizing and writing child's name and the letters of the alphabet, writing on lines, comprehending and telling stories, recognizing differences and similarities of words, having basic sight vocabulary, reading with assistance, reading alone, working in workbooks, reading in a group, using context clues and punctuation, and analyzing words

Spelling: Level, skill

Mathematics: Rote counting, recognizing numbers, writing numbers, adding, subtracting, multiplying, dividing, solving problems, counting money, telling time, measuring

Sensory-motor integration: Spatial orientation and movement in the environment, reaction speed, dexterity, tactile discrimination, laterality, awareness of time

Perceptual-motor skills: Auditory—comprehension of spoken words, meaningfulness of response to auditory clues, retention and recall of auditory data, recall of sequenced auditory data; *visual*—eye movement coordination, visual tracking, figure-ground discrimination, recall of visual experiences, motoric reproduction of visual experiences, fine muscle coordination, head turning, squinting, eye inflammation and watering

Speech: Quality and quantity of verbalizations, articulation, speech difficulties

Behavioral adjustment: Responsiveness to peers, adults, objects, and changes in environment; self-image; self-confidence (Is child nervous, shy, rude, disobedient, selfish, destructive, hostile, aggressive, or overactive? Does child show off, have tantrums, whine, cry, fight, soil, or wet?)

Social development: Ability to function in a group; group role; relationships with peers and older children; friendships; hobbies and recreations; interest in books, magazines, and movies; courtesy; interest in helping others; respect for others' property

These behaviors and characteristics are only suggestive of the areas that may be explored with the aid of school personnel. The sample educational assessment form in Appendix A was designed and used in a special day camp serving 5- to 11-year-old exceptional children. The form must be modified to respond to the needs of other programs.

The second form for collecting data about the child seeking admission to camp, the *physician's assessment form,* is completed by the child's parents and physician. At a minimum, forms of this type must request the following information:

Prenatal: Accidents and unusual conditions during pregnancy, type of delivery, birth injuries

Postnatal: Convulsions, injuries, feeding problems, illnesses, diseases

Early development: Age when first tooth erupted, child held head erect, stood, crawled, walked, talked, had control of bowel and bladder, fed and dressed self

Medical history: Age of occurrence and severity of mumps, measles, whooping cough, chicken pox, pneumonia, hay fever, asthma, allergies, rashes, hives, fevers; permanent effects of diseases, illnesses or surgery; description of physical injuries, handicaps, disabilities, stamina, strength, and handedness; restrictions on physical activities

Medication: Present medication, schedule for administering medication, and authorization to administer medication during camp session

The final preadmission form, the *family information form,* is designed to assist camp personnel in obtaining minimal information about the child's family, home, and community. This form can be completed by a social worker, case worker, school nurse, or other professional associated with the child and his family. The basic information to be requested on a form of this type includes:

Names, ages, residence, vocation, education, outstanding personality traits, and physical and emotional health of those adults and children living in the home

Family's attitude toward the child

Child's attitude toward his family

Child's role in the family

Methods of child training and discipline

Child's response to discipline

Economic, social, and cultural conditions of the family

Languages spoken in the home

Child's duties and responsibilities in the home

It is important to have an application procedure that facilitates the accumulation of objective data about children seeking admission to camp. The data derived from the completed forms is the *only* information available to personnel deciding whether to admit a child to camp. Although there is frequently a discrepancy between the information reported about the child and the real situation, such data are useful in answering such questions as:

Is the child within the age, sex, and disability ranges of the children to be admitted to camp?

Can the camp make provisions to remediate this child's learning and/or behavior problems?

Can the camp make provisions for this child's physical disabilities?

Is the staff competent, individually and as a group, to help this child?

In addition, preadmission data assist the administrator or camp program coordinators in making decisions concerning space, dates, personnel, transportation, materials, equipment, special events, and so on.

Finally, preadmission data are used to verify the results of the formal and informal assessment to be conducted at camp.

Formal assessment

There are hundreds, perhaps thousands, of standardized assessment instruments available in the market place. These instruments vary in purpose, validity, reliability, and usability. It has been frequently debated whether some of these tests evaluate the factors they presume to evaluate. It is difficult to select instruments that will be reliable, valid, and useful in all camp settings.

There are several methods of overcoming or reducing the weaknesses inherent in a camp's formal assessment program:

Employ personnel trained to administer, score, and interpret the tests to be used at camp.

Organize an assessment program that ensures that each characteristic to be assessed is evaluated by at least two instruments.

Correlate the formal, preadmission, and informal assessment programs to verify and serve as checks on each other.

Select assessment instruments that can be conveniently translated into prescriptive teaching interventions; the results of the child's performance on the instruments should be directly translatable into a remedial program.

Do not become overly concerned with overall scores and performance indicators: intelligence quotients, language quotients, and so on. These quotients are abstract constructs that may have little or no meaningful application in camp.

Focus assessment at the skill level; can the child perform the specific tasks he assumably should be able to perform?

The formal assessment program is conducted during the initial days of each camping session. The program is designed to respond to the objectives of the specific camp and the needs of the children attending that camp. Each camp will have a unique formal assessment program designed to fit its needs.

There are, however, certain general areas of the children's functioning that should be assessed. These areas are (1) sensory-motor development, (2) perceptual and perceptual-motor skills, (3) language skills, (4) higher thought processes, (5) emotional develop-

ment, (6) social development, and (7) general and specific achievement.

The standardized assessment instruments listed below have been successfully applied in camps for handicapped children between the ages of 3 and 11 years. Many of these are correlated with remedial programs available on the commercial market.*

Sensory-motor development
   Harris Tests of Lateral Dominance: Tests right and left preferences of hand, eye, and foot. The Psychological Corp.
   Lincoln-Oseretsky Motor Development Scale: Tests a variety of motor skills. Western Psychological Services.
   Purdue Perceptual Motor Survey: Tests motor development and skill. Charles E. Merrill Publishing Co.
Perceptual and perceptual-motor skills
   Auditory Discrimination Test (Wepman): Assesses auditory discrimination of phonemes. Language Research Associates.
   Developmental Test of Visual-Motor Integration: Assesses child's ability to copy designs; focuses on visual perception and motor coordination. Follet Corp.
   Frostig Developmental Test of Visual Perception: Assesses five facets of visual perception. Consulting Psychologists Press.
Language skills
   Illinois Test of Psycholinguistic Abilities, Revised: Assesses a variety of language-related skills in 12 subtests. University of Illinois Press.
   Peabody Picture Vocabulary Test: Assesses receptive language. American Guidance Service.
Higher thought processes
   Slosson Intelligence Test for Children and Adults: Brief screening test of intelligence. Slosson Educational Publications.
   Stanford-Binet Intelligence Scale, Revised (3rd ed.): Individual test of intelligence composed of a variety of subtests; useful for prescriptive purposes. Houghton Mifflin Co.
   Wechsler Intelligence Scale for Children: Individual intelligence test composed of a variety of subtests; useful for prescriptive purposes. The Psychological Corp.

---

*The assessment instruments suggested here must be administered and interpreted by appropriately trained personnel.

Wechsler Preschool and Primary Scale of Intelligence: Individual intelligence test composed of a variety of subtests; useful for prescriptive purposes. The Psychological Corp.

Emotional development

Children's Insight Test: Projective personality test (Engel, 1958).

Minnesota Personality Profile II: Assesses general adjustment and nine component characteristics. University of Minnesota Institute of Child Development and Welfare.

Behavior Checklist: Assesses disorientation and maladaptation to environment, antisocial behavior, unassertiveness, overconforming behavior, neglect, infantile behavior, immaturity, and irresponsibility (Rubin, Simpson, and Betwee, 1966).

Devereux Child Behavior Rating Scale (DCB), Devereux Adolescent Behavior Rating Scale (DAB), and *Devereux Elementary School Behavior Rating Scale:* Behavior rating scales designed to describe the behavior of the emotionally handicapped child regardless of his or her pathological classification; provide a profile of the child's problem. The Devereux Foundation Press.

Social development

Vineland Social Maturity Scale: Interview technique for assessing social maturity and independence. American Guidance Service.

Achievement, general

California Achievement Tests: Comprehensive battery. California Test Bureau.

Iowa Every-Pupil Tests of Basic Skills: Comprehensive battery. Houghton Mifflin Co.

Metropolitan Achievement Tests: Brief test of word recognition, spelling, and arithmetic; excellent for screening purposes. Guidance Associates.

Achievement, specific

Durrell Analysis of Reading Difficulty. Harcourt Brace Jovanovich, Inc.

Gray Oral Reading Tests: Assesses rate, accuracy, and comprehension. The Bobbs-Merrill Co., Inc.

Stanford Diagnostic Reading Test. Harcourt Brace Jovanovich, Inc.

Diagnostic Test and Self-Help in Arithmetic. California Test Bureau.

Stanford Diagnostic Arithmetic Test. Harcourt Brace Jovanovich, Inc.

Picture Story Language Test: Assesses written language. Grune & Stratton, Inc.

Others (Broader in scope, these assessment instruments frequently include items to assess a variety of learning and developmental skills.)

Denver Developmental Screening Test: Identifies serious developmental delays in infants and preschoolers. University of Colorado Medical Center, Denver.

Handbook in Diagnostic Teaching (Mann and Suitor, 1974).

Valett Developmental Survey of Basic Learning Abilities. Fearon Publishers.

The reader is reminded that this list of formal assessment instruments is only suggestive of those that may be appropriate for a specific camping program.

Informal assessment

The informal evaluation is that part of the total diagnostic process characterized (1) by the use of informal procedures, (2) administered by the educational diagnostician (usually a teacher), (3) in a continuing educational setting and (4) is frequently called "diagnostic teaching." The goals of this part of the total evaluation are to expand, probe, verify, and, if need be, discard the conclusions and recommendations of formal assessment. (Hammill, 1971, p. 348)

The instructor and counselor are primarily responsible for the informal assessment process. They must systematically and continuously assess the child's performance in various camping activities. Attention is focused on the verification of data derived from the preadmission and formal assessment processes. The instructor and counselor seek to expand their understanding of the child's *functional* strengths and weaknesses.

This informal assessment of the child begins the moment he arrives at camp and continues until the teaching prescription is completed and the child departs.

The instructor and counselor have two primary aids in conducting this part of the total assessment process: informal surveys or inventories and direct observation of ongoing activities. Although both of these techniques are useful and provide a focus for informal assessment, the instructor and counselor are heavily dependent on their own ingenuity, knowledge of children, and knowledge of the activities conducted as part of the camping program.

The educational assessment form (see Ap-

Child's name _____ Instructor's name _____

		3	4
		Evaluation of results	
1 Test	**2** Subtest	Adequate	Inadequate
Purdue Perceptual- Motor Survey	Walking board Jumping Identification of body parts Movement imitation Obstacle course Kraus-Weber Angels in the snow Chalkboard Rhythmic writing Ocular pursuits Visual achievement		
Frostig Developmental Test of Visual Perception	Eye-hand coordination Figure-ground discrimination Form constancy Position in space Spatial relationships		
Wepman Test	Auditory discrimination		
Illinois Test of Psycholinguistic Abilities, Revised	Auditory reception Visual reception Auditory association Visual association Verbal expression Manual expression Grammatic closure Auditory closure Sound blending Visual closure Auditory sequential memory Visual sequential memory		
Wechsler Intelligence Scale for Children	Information Comprehension Arithmetic Similarities Vocabulary Digit span Picture completion Picture arrangement Block design Coding Object assembly		
Wide Range Achieve- ment Test	Arithmetic Reading Spelling		
Vineland Scale	Social maturity		

Fig. 3. Assessment synthesizer.

Date _____

5	6	7	8
Verification		Training prescribed	Training implemented
Yes	No		

pendix A) may be used as an informal assessment inventory or survey. Using this form, the instructor systematically verifies the information provided by the child's teacher by assigning the child a series of tasks. In addition, the instructor and counselor may verify the information by observing the child during daily activities.

Several of the models discussed in Chapter 2 include surveys and inventories that can be used to systematize and facilitate the informal assessment process. Of particular value for this purpose are the inventories provided by Valett (1968), Mann and Suiter (1974), Cratty (1967), and Myers and Hammill (1969).

Perhaps the most useful technique instructors and counselors have available to them is direct observation of the child during activities. However, these observations cannot be haphazard. The observer must focus attention on a specific skill or group of skills. Observations should include structured and nonstructured situations as well as academic and nonacademic ones. The observer should define in specific descriptive terms the behavior he is observing.

The observation report should be objective. Subjective opinions, evaluations, and criticisms have no place in the observation report. In essence, the observer reports *what took place, not what he thinks, feels, or hopes took place.*

Both the formal and informal assessment procedures are continuous processes. The instructor need not wait until the formal assessment procedures are completed before beginning to explore and expand his knowledge of the child via informal assessment.

The total assessment process is like the atoms in a molecule—constantly moving, probing, changing, and colliding in an effort to fulfill their purpose, total knowledge of the child's functioning.

Synthesis of assessment data

Some method of organizing and synthesizing the large quantity of data collected must be available. Assessment data are of *little or no value* for prescriptive teaching purposes unless they are rendered into a form that facilitates instruction.

The *assessment synthesizer* (Fig. 3) is used for this purpose. The synthesizer presented here was designed for a day camp serving learning-disabled children of elementary school age. A synthesizer must be designed for each specific camp program.

The formal assessment instruments are utilized as a base for the synthesizing process. Preadmission and informal assessment data are used to verify the formal data.

Properly utilized in the following manner, the assessment synthesizer can be an invaluable aid to the instructor and counselor:

1. The assessment instrument is administered, scored, and interpreted by the appropriate diagnostician.
2. The child's performance is judged to be adequate or inadequate, and the appropriate column (3 or 4) is checked.
3. Data obtained from preadmission information and informal assessment either verify or do not verify the results of the formal assessment. Column 5 or 6 is checked. If the formal assessment results are not verified, a second effort at verification is made by obtaining additional formal or informal assessment data.
4. A remedial program is prescribed, and column 7 is checked.
5. The prescribed program is implemented, and column 8 is checked.

Assessment must be a cooperative effort of camp and noncamp personnel. The effectiveness of the total assessment process depends on the efficiency and care with which all relevant data are collected, analyzed, and synthesized. Data analysis is generally conducted at an assessment meeting attended by all pertinent personnel. The goal of this meeting is to describe the child's performance and design a prescription for learning.

PHASE 2: DESCRIBING PRESENT AND TERMINAL BEHAVIORS

Phase 2 of the prescriptive teaching model includes two subphases: describing present behaviors and describing terminal behaviors. The descriptions prepared during this phase

are used to facilitate the tasks to be accomplished during the remaining phases of the model: selecting and writing instructional objectives, designing and implementing specific interventions, and evaluating the interventions.

When preparing behavior descriptions, the instructor or counselor brings together all data derived from the assessment. These behavioral descriptions must respond to the following queries:

How *does* the child behave under specified environmental conditions?

How *does* the child behave with specified individuals and groups?

How *should* the child behave under specified environmental conditions?

How *should* the child behave with specified individuals and groups?

Behavior descriptions are written in precise behavioral terms. They are devoid of all evaluative words and phrases.

EXAMPLE: John is a 12-year-old, *middle-class* boy who *appears to become aggressive* when he is in a *bad mood*. This behavior is a result of *poor home training*. In addition, John *can't read* and *won't play* field games with his group.

This entire description of John's behavior is unacceptable for prescriptive teaching purposes. It is an overgeneralization, replete with subjective evaluations and judgments. The objectionable words and phrases are in italics.

EXAMPLE: John is a 12-year-old boy. Observations have demonstrated that he refuses (says "No" and physically resists) when commanded to perform activities if not given an alternative. In her report, John's mother states: "I never insist that John perform activities he resists initially, such as eating certain foods, brushing his teeth, making his bed, and so on." According to the WRAT, John reads at the 3.5 grade level. He demonstrated gross motor coordination handicaps on the Purdue Perceptual-Motor Survey. These handicaps make participation in field games difficult.

This second example describes John's behavior with precision; that is, it alerts the instructor and counselor to the child's probable responses under specific environmental conditions. The description enables the staff to plan responses to John's behaviors when they occur. It also enables the staff to intervene to prevent certain behaviors from occurring.

The following categories should be used for writing a precise description of a child's present and terminal behaviors:

1. *General description of behavior:* Overall description of the child's behavior in the camp setting. Attention is centered on general behavioral characteristics, both positive and negative, in the three learning domains: psychomotor, affective, and cognitive. Special consideration is given to those handicaps that, in the opinion of the staff, are the child's central problem areas, such as physical disabilities, motor coordination handicaps, academic learning problems, emotional difficulties, speech defects, and social handicaps.

2. *Relations with instructor:* Description of how the child relates to the instructor in various specified settings: academic, nonacademic, structured, nonstructured, person-to-person, and group.

3. *Relations with counselor:* Description of how the child relates to the counselor in the various specified settings listed in category 2. (The use of categories 2 and 3 demonstrates awareness of the differences in the traditional roles of the instructor as teacher and the counselor as guide, companion, and confidante.)

4. *Relations with peers:* Description of how the child relates to his peers in the various settings listed in category 2.

5. *Relations in camp settings other than the instructional setting:* Description of the child's behavior and changes in his behavior as he interacts in various settings: cabin, playing field, lake, dining hall, arts-and-crafts area, and so on.

6. *Relations in the instructional setting:* Description of the child's relations in the instructional setting, that is, in the classroom or other areas used for instructional purposes. Attention is focused on how he relates with personnel, materials, equipment, and the instructional methods applied.

7. *Affective behavior:* Description of the child's general emotional tone or responsiveness to his environment. Is the child positive or negative, curious or fearful, aggressive or submissive, dominant or compliant?

8. *Adaptive functioning:* Description of how the child adapts to the camp environment and the planned and unplanned changes within the environment.

PHASE 3: SELECTING AND WRITING INSTRUCTIONAL OBJECTIVES

An instructional objective is an intent communicated by a statement describing a proposed change in a learner —a statement of what the learner is to be like when he has successfully completed a learning experience. (Mager, 1962, p. 3)

During phase 3 of the prescriptive teaching process, instructional objectives are selected and written for each individual child. These objectives are generated from the assessment data and the description of the child's present behaviors. Instructional objectives are of two kinds: general instructional objectives, and specific instructional objectives.

General objectives are broad objectives focusing on the tasks to be accomplished during a 6- or 8-week camping session. The specific instructional objectives focus on the sequence of tasks making up the general objectives. Specific objectives are daily or weekly objectives.

Instructional objectives are stated in specific behavioral terms and translated into remedial interventions during phase 4 of the prescriptive teaching process.

Properly stated, instructional objectives (1) clarify the instructional intent in terms of the learner, (2) describe the behavior the learner will engage in, and (3) state the criteria and conditions for acceptable performance.

Gronlund (1970) cautions that the writing of objectives can be like using a two-edged sword. The one edge is *too dull*, resulting in *overgeneralization;* the other is *too sharp,* resulting in *overspecification*. In the model under discussion, stating both general and specific instructional objectives in precise terminology enables one to avoid these two errors.

The following instructional objectives are stated in acceptable form:

Maintain the number of times Jim volunteers to answer questions during group discussions.

Increase the number of problems Sally completes correctly during math period.

Decrease the number of critical remarks George makes about other players during field games.

Increase Benji's skill in recognizing and naming the types of trees in the camp.

An instructional objective in its written form should respond to the following guidelines (Walker and Shea, 1976):

1. What is the camper or group of campers whose behavior is being changed expected to do or not to do?
    a. Use action verbs to denote the behavior change process.
    b. List the specific resources and materials to be used by the camper during the behavior change process.
    c. Indicate specifically the desired interaction between the camper and his environment, including both persons and objects.
2. What is the rate or level of performance (in terms of accuracy, duration, and skill or knowledge) expected of the camper?
3. What percentage of time or what percentage of the occurrences of the desired behavior is the child expected to perform at the criterion level?
4. How will the anticipated changes in behavior be measured for evaluative purposes? What instrumentation is needed for evaluation?
5. How long will the proposed intervention program be in force before its effectiveness is evaluated?

There are several sources available in the literature to assist in the selection and writing of instructional objectives. Those by Mager (1962) and Gronlund (1970) are especially useful to readers interested in developing skill in the writing of instructional objectives. McAshan's text (1974) serves

as a guide to selecting and writing objectives in the cognitive and affective learning domains.

Three taxonomies of value for the selection of objectives in the three learning domains are those by Krathwohl (1956) (affective learning domain), Bloom (1956) (cognitive learning domain), and Harrow (1972) (psychomotor learning domain).

Cawley (1973) lists 266 desired learner outcomes (DLOs) that can be utilized as instructional objectives. These DLOs are correlated with the results of formal assessment instruments and remedial programs.

In addition, many of the publications discussed in Chapter 2 are helpful to instructors and counselors selecting and writing objectives.

PHASE 4: DESIGNING AND IMPLEMENTING SPECIFIC INTERVENTIONS

The design of the remedial intervention is a staff function. All pertinent staff members (instructors, counselors, diagnosticians, and administrators) meet together to decide which of the child's disabilities are to be modified and how this modification is to be implemented.

The intervention may be simple or complex; it may be based on psychodynamic, ecologic, or behavior modification theory. Many of the sources of remedial interventions discussed in Chapter 2 can serve as a guide for the selection of an appropriate intervention. In Chapter 4 a variety of interventions for psychomotor, cognitive, and affective handicaps are discussed.

An intervention should not be applied without staff consideration of the following problem variables.

First, the impact of the child's handicap on his overall present and future functioning must be determined. The child may be, and in all probability will be, multiply handicapped. Some handicaps have considerable impact on the child's overall functioning. They are extremely important and should be remediated if possible. Other handicaps are relatively unimportant when viewed from the perspective of the child's overall functioning. They are given a low priority for remediation.

Second, a method for establishing positive interpersonal relations between the child and others must be selected. For example, the most effective method of interacting with the child may be one that is positive, neutral, aggressive, distant or impersonal, and so on. On the basis of the available information and actual experiences with the child, the staff determines which method for developing productive interpersonal relations may be most successful. All staff members must agree to apply the method selected.

Third, a teaching method must be selected that responds to the query "What communications channels are available to this child for learning?" Some children (and adults) are visual learners; others are auditory learners, motor learners, or kinesthetic learners. Selecting the appropriate method will facilitate the child's learning.

Fourth, camp personnel must be realistic concerning the services they can provide for a child. Services can only be provided when they are available. The type and variety of service depends on facilities, materials, equipment, and personnel. In addition, a low-priority service cannot be provided child A if this deprives child B of a high-priority service.

Fifth, camp personnel must judge whether the knowledge and skills the child is to learn are appropriately presented in the camp setting. Many normal children have common growth and learning problems. These may be due to the extremely high and unrealistic standards established for them by their parents or school. Such problems, although important, are not the concern of the special camp; the concern of the special camp is to serve moderately and severely handicapped children.

Sixth, camp personnel must determine the potential impact of the proposed intervention of the child's camping group. Will the intervention conflict with the intervention needed by another child in the same group? Can this conflict, if it exists, be eliminated?

Finally, consideration must be given to the availability of facilities, materials, and equipment. For example, it is of *no* value to prescribe time-out, or isolation, as an intervention if facilities are not available.

When prescribing an intervention, the staff must be realistic. They must respond to the query "Can we implement and conduct this intervention in this camp with the available or obtainable staff, materials, and equipment?"

PHASE 5: EVALUATING INTERVENTIONS

The evaluation of the intervention includes two subphases. The first of these is to determine if the intervention is being implemented by the instructor and counselor as prescribed. For example, if the intervention is "to ignore John's negative behavior," the evaluator must determine if, in fact, John's negative behavior is being ignored by the instructor and counselor.

The second subphase of the evaluation process is to determine if the intervention is having the desired effect on the behavior to be changed.

Evaluation of the implementation of the intervention is usually determined by direct observation of instructor-child interactions.

Evaluation of the effectiveness of the intervention is determined by comparing a current description of the child's behavior with the "present" and "terminal" descriptions written during phase 2. *How far* has this child *progressed* along the continuum from his *initial present behavior* to his *desired terminal behavior?*

In prescriptive teaching, evaluation results are only meaningful if they are communicated to the instructor and counselor working with the child. Direct feedback permits the instructor and counselor to adjust either their implementation of the intervention or the intervention itself on the basis of an objective evaluation.

CASE STUDIES

Three case studies are presented. The children represent a range of learning problems (affective, cognitive, and psychomotor) and ages (preschool or kindergarten, primary, and intermediate grade levels). The cases were selected as examples, not only because they represent a variety of handicapping conditions and age groups, but because they clearly exemplify the prescriptive teaching procedures recommended in this volume.

Comprehensive case studies would require several dozen pages; these cases are presented in an abbreviated form with the following format:

1. *Background information:* Information from the application, educational assessment, family information, and physician's assessment forms
2. *Assessment data:* Relevant information from formal and informal assessment
3. *Descriptions of behavior:* Brief descrip-

Child's name ____Marie____   Instructor's name ____Ms. Sims____

1	*2*	*3*	*4*
		Evaluation of results	
Test	**Subtest**	**Adequate**	**Inadequate**
Stanford-Binet	Comprehension	X	
Form L-M	Visual-motor skills	X	
	Mental arithmetic	X	
	Retention of verbal skills		X
	Retention of visual skills	X	
	Vocabulary		X
	Verbal abstract ability		X
	Reasoning	X	
Denver Developmental	Personal-social skills		X
Screening Test	Fine motor adaptive skills	X	
	Language		X
	Gross motor skills	X	
Frostig Developmental	Eye-hand coordination	X	
Test of Visual	Figure-ground discrimination	X	
Perception	Form constancy	X	
	Position in space	X	
	Spatial relationships	X	
Wepman Test	Auditory discrimination	(Responses unintelligible)	
Illinois Test of	Auditory reception	X	
Psycholinguistic	Visual reception	X	
Abilities, Revised	Auditory association		X
	Visual association	X	
	Verbal expression		X
	Manual expression		X
	Grammatic closure		X
	Auditory closure		X
	Sound blending	X	
	Visual closure	X	
	Auditory sequential memory		X
	Visual sequential memory	X	
Vineland Social			X
Maturity Scale			

Fig. 4. Assessment synthesizer (Marie).

tions of relevant present and terminal behaviors

4. *Instructional objectives:* Selected examples of general and specific instructional objectives
5. *Interventions:* Prescribed interventions for the selected instructional objectives
6. *Evaluation:* Techniques of evaluation of the selected interventions

te _____5/30/75_____

	5	6	7	8
	Verification		Training prescribed	Training implemented
	Yes	No		
		X		
		X		
		X		
	X			
		X		
	X			
	X			
		X		
	X			
		X		
	X			
		X		
	X			
	X			
	X			
	X			
	X			
		X		
		X		
		X		
	X			
		X		
	X			
	X			
	X			
	X			
		X		
		X		
	X			
		X		
	X			

While studying the cases, one should keep firmly in mind that the typical child enrolled in the camp is generally multiply handicapped. He may exhibit problems with symptoms less obvious than the ones in the examples given here.

CASE 1: MARIE
BACKGROUND INFORMATION

Marie is 5 years and 6 months of age. She will enter kindergarten in the fall. She has had no formal preschool experience.

Marie lives on a farm with her mother (Mary) and father (Clyde). She has one sibling, a brother (Kirk), who will complete high school in the spring. Kirk is an above-average academic student (*A* and *B* grades). He does not participate in extracurricular activities. He works with his father on the farm.

Referral. Marie was referred to the camp by her mother through the county prekindergarten screening project. Marie's mother and project personnel are concerned about Marie's development and readiness for school.

Problem. Marie is occasionally enuretic. Wetting occurs during the day when she is in unfamiliar settings, such as a store, a strange house, or a doctor's office.

Marie clings to her mother in the presence of unknown adults and children. On these occasions, her speech is inaudible and verbalizations are infrequent. She does not make eye contact with others when speaking or being spoken to. The staff at the screening project described Marie as "shy and withdrawn." However, in her report, Marie's mother states that Marie is a "noisy and outgoing little girl" around the home.

According to the mother's report, Marie has no age peers with whom to play on the farm. She has few contacts with children her age because "We prefer to keep to ourselves."

No exceptional growth and development patterns are noted on the physician's assessment form. No injuries or illnesses of an exceptional nature have occurred. There are no activity restrictions. No physical reason is reported for her enuresis.

The family information form was completed by screening project personnel. Both parents were high school graduates. The family is characterized as (1) "loners," (2) "intact," and (3) "hardworking, successful grain farmers."

Marie was an unplanned birth. She is accepted

and loved by all the members of her family. Marie is the center of the family unit; all activities focus on her needs and wishes. She is overprotected. The methods of discipline in her home are deprivations, reprimands, and infrequent spankings. Marie's mother is the disciplinarian. Marie responds to parental discipline.

ASSESSMENT DATA

Marie's formal assessment was conducted during the initial week of the camping session. On the Stanford-Binet Form L-M, Marie had a mental age of 5 years, 7 months and an intelligence quotient of 102. Strong performance areas were mental arithmetic, motor skills, and nonverbal tasks. Performance in language and verbal expression was below average.

In addition to the Stanford-Binet test, Marie was given the Denver Developmental Screening Test, the Frostig Developmental Test of Visual Perception, the Wepman Auditory Discrimination Test, and the Illinois Test of Psycholinguistic Abilities, Revised.

Marie's behavior was observed during the initial 2 weeks of the camping session by her instructor and counselors. During this time, she was informally assessed by means of the educational assessment form (see Appendix A).

The Vineland Social Maturity Scale was administered to Marie's mother before Marie's admission to camp. No general or specific achievement tests were administered because of Marie's age and lack of previous educational experience.

The results of the formal and informal assessment appear on the assessment synthesizer (Fig. 4).

Comments. The informal assessment and observation data collected by the instructors, counselors, and counselors-in-training during the initial weeks of the session verified the formal assessment data with one exception: enuresis. Pants wetting occurred only once during the first week of the session—the evening of the first day.

It was verified that Marie is less adequate than the members of her peer group in verbal expression, language, and social skills. She was shy and withdrawn around both children and adults during initial contact but formed some tentative interpersonal relationships with her counselor and a few children. She spoke only when spoken to and generally responded with one- or two-word answers.

Marie performed all activities adequately with the exception of activities requiring verbal-social

transactions. She did not manifest any overt behavior problems.

DESCRIPTIONS OF BEHAVIOR

Present. Marie is a 5½-year-old prekindergarten child. She is a member of an intact but socially isolated farming family. Marie's measured intelligence is average.

Her measured strengths are in the areas of visual-motor skills, nonverbal expression, reasoning, and comprehension.

Her verified deficits are in verbal expression, language development, and social skills. She is shy and uncomfortable during group activities, especially activities requiring verbal transactions with children and adults. Marie does not make eye contact with individuals with whom she is interacting. She is occasionally enuretic.

Terminal. Marie will express herself verbally when interacting with children and adults in both individual and group settings. She will make eye contact during interpersonal transactions. She will develop and utilize age-appropriate expressive language. She will respond to questions with complete sentences, be able to tell stories, and relate personal experiences. Marie will demonstrate appropriate social skills for a child of her age; that is, she will interact with children and adults in work and play situations. She will develop bladder control when she is in situations that are unfamiliar to her and when she is in the company of persons who are strangers.

INSTRUCTIONAL OBJECTIVES

General. Increase quantity of verbal expressions.

Specific. Increase spoken vocabulary.

Increase use of phrases, complete sentences, and multiple sentences in response to questions.

Increase initiation of verbalizations.

General. Increase social skills to an appropriate age level as measured by the Vineland Social Maturity Scale.

Specific. Increase social transactions with peers and adults.

Increase verbal-social interaction with a peer, an adult, and a peer-adult pair.

Increase verbal-social interaction in a small group of four or five members, first including an adult, and then of peers only.

Increase verbal-social interaction in large groups of 20 or 25 members (peers and adults).

Increase eye contact with peers and adults with whom she is interacting.

General. Eliminate enuresis.

Specific. Eliminate enuresis in situations or settings that are unfamiliar and when confronted with persons who are unfamiliar.

INTERVENTIONS

Verbal expression and language. A language development program will be conducted by an instructor in a one-to-one setting or in a small group setting. Vocabulary words should be acted out through dramatic play. The words to be learned should be related to objects, settings, and activities in the camp. Counselors should be familiar with Marie's "new words" and reinforce her use of them during the noninstructional day. The formal instructional period should be limited to 20 minutes daily. In teaching, emphasis should be placed on the use of her visual-motor and fine and gross motor skills to facilitate verbalization.

The language-learning environment should be positive, including immediate reinforcement for appropriate language behavior. Suggested references: Peabody Language Development Kits (American Guidance Service), Valett (1968), and Johnson and Myklebust (1967).

Social skills. Game-learning experiences requiring social interaction with peers and adults, (small-group games and problem-solving activities) will be provided. Interaction should proceed from a one-to-one situation with a counselor to a one-to-one situation with a peer (the peer to be selected by Marie), to a peer-adult pair, to a small group with both peers and a counselor, to a small group of peers only, and finally to a large group of peers and adults.

After Marie has established a positive interpersonal relationship with an instructor or counselor during which she can respond to questions consistently and verbally, an intervention to increase her eye contact should be implemented. The instructor will respond to Marie's verbalizations *only* when she makes eye contact. She may be reminded to look at the individual with whom she is interacting, with the statements "Look," "Look at me," or "Marie, you're not looking." These statements should be of a neutral tone, that is, nonpunitive.

Enuresis. Marie's enuresis will be ignored during the initial 2 weeks of the camping session with the following exceptions: she will be kept clean and dry, and a log recording the frequency, time, and situation of the occurrences of wetting will be maintained.

All preschool campers (including Marie) will be asked on an average of once per hour if they have to go to the bathroom.

If it is observed that Marie's pants are wet, the counselor or instructor will say *very quietly* to her, "I see you have had an accident. Perhaps you would like to change." No additional discussion is necessary. At that time, Marie will be escorted directly to her cabin for dry clothing and then to the wash house, where she will change. After she has changed and put her wet clothing in the appropriate place in her cabin, Marie will return to her activities.

EVALUATION OF INTERVENTIONS
Implementation

Counselors, instructors, and counselors-in-training working with Marie will observe each other for a minimum of 30 minutes per day to evaluate the implementation of the interventions.

Effectiveness

Verbal expression and language. The instructor will keep a frequency count of the new vocabulary words Marie knows and uses appropriately.

The instructor and counselor will keep a frequency count on Marie's self-initiated verbalizations.

Social skills. The instructor and counselor will keep a frequency count of Marie's self-initiated social transactions with peers and adults in one-to-one group settings.

The instructor will maintain a frequency count of Marie's eye contacts during verbalizations.

Enuresis. The log recording the frequency, time, and situation of the occurrences will be maintained by the counselor.

CASE 2: MARK
BACKGROUND INFORMATION

Mark is 7 years and 2 months of age. He is scheduled to repeat the first grade in the fall. Mark did not attend a preschool or kindergarten.

Mark resides in a surburban area with his mother, father, and two younger brothers.

Referral. Mark was referred by his teacher for academic difficulties and behavior problems. She has indicated that he probably will not successfully complete the first grade again next year unless he receives help of a remedial nature.

Problem. According to the teacher, Mark is "not motivated, is lazy, and will not learn to read." He disrupts the class frequently during reading lessons. However, he is "fairly cooperative" at

Child's name   Mark   Instructor's name   Mr. Dee

1	2	3	4
		Evaluation of results	
Test	**Subtest**	**Adequate**	**Inadequate**
Wechsler Intelligence	Information	X	
Scale for Children	Comprehension	X	
	Arithmetic		X
	Analogies/similarities	X	
	Vocabulary	X	
	Digit span	X	
	Picture completion		X
	Picture arrangement		X
	Block design		X
	Object assembly	X	
	Coding		X
Purdue Perceptual-	Walking board	X	
Motor Survey	Jumping	X	
	Identification of body parts		X
	Movement imitation	X	
	Obstacle course	X	
	Kraus-Weber	X	
	Angels in the snow	X	
	Chalkboard		X
	Rhythmic writing		X
	Ocular pursuits		X
	Visual achievement		X
Frostig Developmental	Eye-hand coordination		X
Test of Visual	Figure-ground discrimination		X
Perception	Form constancy		X
	Position in space		X
	Spatial relationships		X
Wepman Test	Auditory discrimination	X	
Illinois Test of Psycho-	Auditory reception	X	
linguistic Abilities,	Visual reception		X
Revised	Auditory association	X	
	Visual association		X
	Verbal expression	X	
	Manual expression	X	
	Grammatic closure	X	
	Auditory closure	X	
	Sound blending	X	
	Visual closure		X
	Auditory sequential memory	X	
	Visual sequential memory		X
Wide Range Achieve-	Arithmetic		X
ment Test	Reading		X
	Spelling		X
Devereux Child	Poor coordination		X
Behavior Rating Scale*	Social aggression		X

*Only inadequate factors reported.

Fig. 5. Assessment synthesizer (Mark).

te ___5/30/75___

	Verification		Training prescribed	Training implemented
5	**6**		**7**	**8**
Yes	**No**			
	X			
	X			
X				
	X			
	X			
	X			
X				
X				
X				
	X			
X				
	X			
	X			
X				
	X			
	X			
	X			
	X			
X				
X				
X				
X				
X				
X				
X				
X				
X				
	X			
	X			
X				
	X			
X				
	X			
	X			
	X			
	X			
	X			
X				
	X			
X				
X				
X				
X				
X				
X				

other times. Although he makes errors on arithmetic work sheets, he quickly corrects them when they are brought to his attention.

According to the educational assessment form, Mark has many friends in his classroom and in the school. He enjoys out-of-doors activities, although he is not highly skilled in field sports. Although Mark is disruptive, his temper outbursts are not severe. He generally reacts to frustration by saying, "Damn, damn, damn," or by pushing a book, pencil, or some other object off his desk onto the floor. This behavior stops if he is verbally reprimanded by the teacher.

No exceptional physical characteristics or problems are noted on the physician's assessment form. Mark has had measles, chicken pox, and other childhood illnesses—all without complications. He is not on medication. His physical activities are not restricted.

Mark's physician referred him to an opthalmologist, who reported that Mark needs visual-perceptual training and corrective lenses. He prescribed corrective lenses.

The family information form was completed by a mental health clinic social worker serving Mark's school as a consultant. Mark comes from an intact family. His parents have expressed little concern about his reading problem. Both his mother and father have stated that they had difficulty learning to read and do so now only when necessary. Mark's mother, a high school graduate, is employed in a local plastics factory. Mark's father, an eighth-grade graduate, is a custodial engineer for the city. Although the family has many friends, they prefer to stay home on weekends and evenings to "watch T.V. and putter around the house." Mark's siblings are reported by the mother as being "healthy and happy and no problem."

The family method of discipline is a slap by the mother and "if they're really bad," a strapping by the father.

ASSESSMENT

With the exception of an intelligence test that was administered by a school psychologist during the spring, Mark's formal assessment was conducted during the initial week of the camping session.

Mark was administered the Wechsler Intelligence Scale for Children. He received a full-scale intelligence quotient of 110, with a verbal quotient of 119 and a performance quotient of 99.

Mark's strengths were on the information, comprehension, similarities, vocabulary, and object assembly subtests. His weaknesses were in areas dependent on visual-perceptual skills: arithmetic, picture completion, picture arrangement, block design, and coding.

Mark was also administered the Frostig Developmental Test of Visual Perception, the Wepman Auditory Discrimination Test, the Illinois Test of Psycholinguistic Abilities, Revised, the Purdue Perceptual Motor Survey, the Devereux Child Behavior Rating Scale, and the Wide Range Achievement Test.

Mark was informally assessed by instructors and counselors during the initial weeks of the camping session.

The results of the formal and informal assessment phases appear on the assessment synthesizer (Fig. 5).

Comments. Mark's visual-perceptual handicaps were noted during formal assessment and by the opthalmologist. These findings were verified during the informal assessment phase.

It was noted that temper outbursts were confined exclusively to instructional settings. Mark learns well verbally. He has above-average social skills. He is selected frequently by his peers as group leader.

Counselors agree that Mark is "an average camper" and "a good kid."

DESCRIPTIONS OF BEHAVIOR

Present. Mark is 7 years and 2 months old. He failed the first grade and will repeat it.

Mark is the oldest son from an intact family. His parents do not appear concerned about his school problems.

Mark's measured intelligence is above average. There is a significant difference between his verbal and performance scales (the verbal scale is 20 points higher).

Although Mark has temper outbursts, they are not severe. His social skills are above average.

Mark has good verbal and auditory abilities. He learns rapidly through these modalities.

Deficiencies have been noted in the visual-motor and visual-perceptual areas. Mark becomes frustrated easily in tasks that require reading.

Terminal. Mark will develop self-control over his temper outbursts and will demonstrate an increased ability to tolerate frustration.

Mark will develop age-appropriate visual-motor and visual-perceptual skills. He will learn to read at the appropriate grade level.

INSTRUCTIONAL OBJECTIVES

General. Increase visual-motor and visual-perceptual skills to the appropriate age level.

Specific. Increase motor skills, such as throwing, catching, lacing, tying, and painting.

Increase visual-perceptual skills, such as copying, tracing, printing, and writing.

General. Increase reading skills to the appropriate grade level.

Specific. Increase reading skills in a one-to-one instructional program using a multisensory approach.

Increase reading skills to the appropriate grade level in a small group setting.

General. Increase self-control of aggressive behavior.

Specific. Demonstrate socially appropriate behavior when frustrated, such as asking for assistance.

INTERVENTIONS

Visual motor and visual-perceptual skills. Approaches suggested by Cratty (1967), Valett (1968), Frostig and Maslow (1969), and Kephart (1971) will be used.

Opportunities will be provided for Mark to engage in brief arts-and-crafts activity periods, progressing from activities requiring gross motor skills to activities requiring fine motor skills.

Mark will practice in brief sessions the component skills making up various field sports. After he has learned the component skills, he will practice them in the combinations comprising games.

Frustration will be avoided in all motor and perceptual activities. Positive reinforcement will be used.

Reading. The multisensory approach to reading as proposed by Fernald (1943) will be initiated.

When Mark has acquired the basic reading readiness and reading skills, the program will be accelerated to the appropriate grade level in a small-group setting.

Frustration will be avoided. Positive reinforcement will be used.

Behavior control. Temper outbursts will be ignored. Outbursts will be prevented through brief reading sessions and a change of activity when outbursts occur or can be predicted.

Mark's self-concept will be improved through positive reinforcement of approximations and successes.

EVALUATION OF INTERVENTIONS
Implementation

Counselors and instructors will observe each other 1 hour per week. Observation will focus on the positive and negative reinforcement frequencies in the positive interpersonal teaching method suggested for Mark.

Effectiveness

Visual-motor and visual-perceptual skills. Mark's visual-motor and visual-perception skills will be evaluated through direct observation of performance, and his performance on the Purdue Perceptual Motor Survey and the Frostig Developmental Test of Visual Perception will be reassessed.

Reading. Mark's reading skills will be evaluated through a diagnostic reading test, an informal reading inventory, and observation of his performance.

Behavior control. The counselor will maintain a log recording the following information:
1. Number of outbursts per day
2. Time of each outburst
3. Duration, in minutes, of each occurrence
4. Immediate result of each occurrence
5. Setting in which the outburst occurred
6. Activity during which the outburst occurred

CASE 3: RODNEY
BACKGROUND INFORMATION

Rodney is 9 years and 7 months of age. He will enter the fourth grade in the fall. In his third-grade teacher's opinion, Rodney should be placed in a class for children with behavior disorders. Services of this nature are not available in his community.

Rodney lives with his mother and two older sisters in the inner city. Rodney's mother is a domestic worker in the suburbs. Her place of employment is approximately 15 miles from the home. She has an eighth-grade education. Rodney's sisters attend the local high school.

Rodney is a *D* and *F* student.

Rodney's father is present in the home for a few weeks each year.

Referral. Rodney was referred, with his mother's cooperation, by Rodney's third-grade teacher.

Problem. The teacher has reported that Rodney is hyperactive and uncontrollable. According to her, Rodney could do much better work academically if he would try. He is frequently involved in fights: "He beats up on kids who bug him." The teacher feels that Rodney has both academic potential and leadership ability. He has many friends in "his gang," which meets on the playground during recess, lunch hour, and after school.

The physician's assessment form was completed by personnel at the city health clinic. No injuries, illnesses, or growth problems were noted by the physician. Rodney is not on medication, nor are his activities restricted.

Rodney was referred to Children's Hospital for a neurological examination. An appointment has not been made at this time.

The family information form was completed by welfare department personnel. They noted that the family receives welfare funds because the mother's salary is not adequate to meet the family's financial needs. The father does not contribute financially to the family. The mother is a hard worker, but because she is unskilled, she cannot find a better-paying job.

The family lives in a city housing project. The apartment, although sparsely furnished, is clean. The daughters assist the mother with housecleaning. They supervise Rodney during the mother's absence. Rodney has duties to perform in the home, such as making his bed and emptying trash. He always completes these jobs. Rodney has many friends in the project and plays outdoors during his free time. Although Rodney's gang is "noisy and loud," they are not destructive.

Discipline is the mother's responsibility. She generally "just yells at him." She does not approve of physical punishment. On the rare occasions when the father is home, he will slap and hit the mother and children.

ASSESSMENT

Rodney's formal assessment was conducted during the initial week of the camping session. His intelligence quotient on the Wechsler Intelligence Scale for Children was 116 (verbal scale, 110; performance scale, 120). With the exception of the information and vocabulary subtests, all areas were above average.

Rodney was also given the Frostig Developmental Test of Visual Perception, the Wepman Auditory Discrimination Test, the Illinois Test of Psycholinguistic Abilities, Revised, the Purdue Perceptual-Motor Survey, the Wide Range Achievement Test, and the Devereux Child Behavior Rating Scale.

Informal assessment was conducted by camp personnel during the initial 2 weeks of the session.

Child's name	Rodney	Instructor's name	Ms. Bailey	

1	2	3	4
		Evaluation of results	
Test	**Subtest**	**Adequate**	**Inadequate**
Purdue Perceptual Motor Survey	Walking board	X	
	Jumping	X	
	Identification of body parts	X	
	Movement imitation	X	
	Obstacle course	X	
	Kraus-Weber	X	
	Angels in the snow	X	
	Chalkboard	X	
	Rhythmic writing	X	
	Ocular pursuits	X	
	Visual achievement	X	
Frostig Developmental Test of Visual Perception	Eye-hand coordination	X	
	Figure-ground discrimination	X	
	Form constancy	X	
	Position in space	X	
	Spatial relationships	X	
Wepman Test	Auditory discrimination	X	
Illinois Test of Psycho-linguistic Abilities, Revised	Auditory reception	X	
	Visual reception	X	
	Auditory association	X	
	Visual association	X	
	Verbal expression	X	
	Manual expression	X	
	Grammatic closure		X
	Auditory closure	X	
	Sound blending	X	
	Visual closure	X	
	Auditory sequential memory	X	
	Visual sequential memory	X	
Wechsler Intelligence Scale for Children	Information		X
	Comprehension	X	
	Arithmetic	X	
	Similarities	X	
	Vocabulary		X
	Digit span	X	
	Picture completion	X	
	Picture arrangement	X	
	Block design	X	
	Coding	X	
	Object assembly	X	
Wide Range Achievement Test	Arithmetic	X	
	Reading	X	
	Spelling		X
Devereux Child Behavior Rating Scale	Distractability	X	
	Poor self-care	X	
	Pathological use of senses	X	
	Emotional detachment	X	
	Social isolation	X	
	Poor coordination and body tonus	X	
	Incontinence	X	
	Messiness, sloppiness	X	
	Inadequate need for independence	X	
	Unresponsiveness	X	
	Proneness to emotional upset		X
	Need for adult contact	X	
	Anxious fearful ideation	X	
	Impulse ideation	X	
	Inability to delay gratification		X
	Social aggression		X
	Unethical behavior	X	

Fig. 6. Assessment synthesizer (Rodney).

5	6	7	8
Verification		Training prescribed	Training implemented
Yes	No		
	X		
	X		
	X		
	X		
	X		
	X		
	X		
	X		
	X		
	X		
	X		
	X		
	X		
	X		
	X		
	X		
	X		
	X		
	X		
	X		
	X		
X			
	X		
	X		
	X		
	X		
	X		
X			
	X		
	X		
	X		
X			
	X		
	X		
	X		
	X		
	X		
	X		
	X		
	X		
X			
	X		
	X		
	X		
	X		
	X		
	X		
	X		
	X		
X			
	X		
	X		
	X		
X			
X			
	X		

Results of the assessment appear on the assessment synthesizer (Fig. 6).

Comments. Camp staff, by means of direct observation and an informal educational inventory, verified Rodney's strengths and weaknesses as assessed by the formal tests and scales noted on the assessment synthesizer.

With the exception of information, behavior control, spelling, and grammar, Rodney was found to have considerable strength in all areas. He manifests no particular preference for a modality of learning. Both auditory and visual learning channels are excellent.

After only 2 weeks at camp, Rodney has been elected his cabin leader. He is skilled at most out-of-doors physical activities, such as field games and swimming. He has some difficulty with table games, such as Monopoly and checkers. He has demonstrated his willingness to help counselors, instructors, and peers on several occasions.

He will challenge authority in situations where he is reprimanded publicly.

Although he has been in "fights," they have not been severe. Usually involving shouting and shoving another child who, according to Rodney, is "bugging him," the conflicts have lasted only a minute or two at the longest.

DESCRIPTIONS OF BEHAVIOR

Present. Rodney is 9 years and 7 months old. He is a member of an inner-city family that includes himself, his mother, two older sisters, and occasionally his father. The family lives in a city housing project.

Rodney's measured intelligence is above average. He has superior strengths in all areas of functioning except self-control, general information, spelling, and grammar.

He demonstrates leadership potential in the camp setting.

Terminal. Rodney will increase his self-control and develop alternative techniques to fighting for dealing with "kids who bug him."

Rodney will increase his store of general knowledge about persons, places, and things in the city and in the camp environment. Rodney's skill in spelling will be increased to the appropriate grade level.

INSTRUCTIONAL OBJECTIVES

General. Increase self-control and develop alternative behavior responses.

Specific. Decrease frequency of shouting and hitting.

Increase repertoire of alternate responses to being "bugged."

General. Increase general information reservoir.

Specific. Increase knowledge of persons, places, and things in the city and in the camp.

General. Increase spelling skill.

Specific. Increase spelling skill to the appropriate grade level.

INTERVENTIONS

Behavior. The frequency of Rodney's fights will be decreased through positive reinforcement for *not fighting*. He will be reinforced consistently every 15 minutes for *not fighting* during the first week of the intervention. The frequency of reinforcement will be decreased each week thereafter until it is phased out. Rodney will select his reward. The use of a tangible reinforcer, such as food or drink (Walker and Shea, 1976), will be avoided.

Rodney will be encouraged to identify, discuss, and implement socially acceptable alternatives to fighting when "being bugged" by other children. This will be accomplished through discussions with the counselor. The discussions will be conducted after a fight and after Rodney is calm.

Information. Rodney will participate in weekly field trips to the city and suburbs. He will visit the zoo, the post office, the government center, the sports arena, and other places of interest. He will be accompanied by a counselor, who will point out and explain persons, places, and things in the environment. The counselor will encourage Rodney to discuss these trips.

Field trips will be coordinated with pictures, slides, movies, and reading material presented during daily social studies lessons.

Rodney will be encouraged to explore, question, and discuss persons, places, and things in the camp environment.

Spelling.* Rodney will maintain a spelling "workbook" (a small 3 × 5 inch notebook). Rodney's instructor will reward him for finding new words to write in the book. His counselor will assist him in spelling the words. Rodney will be rewarded for spelling the new words correctly.

Fifteen-minute spelling lessons using Rodney's new words and a multisensory approach will be given daily.

---

*Rodney's spelling and grammer problems appear to be related to his particular dialect of the American language rather than to any innate disability; these problems are social rather than cognitive.

EVALUATION OF INTERVENTIONS
Implementation

The interventions recommended for Rodney are self-evaluating.

Effectiveness

Behavior. A frequency count of Rodney's fights will be maintained daily. A graph will be drawn weekly to determine whether the behavior is increasing or decreasing.

The counselor and instructor will observe and note Rodney's successful and unsuccessful efforts to substitute an alternative response.

Information. Alternate forms of previously administered tests and a general achievement test will be given.

Spelling. The number of new words in Rodney's "workbook" and the number of new words spelled correctly during spelling lessons will be counted.

A spelling test or informal inventory (Mann and Suiter, 1974) will be administered.

SHORT FORM

During initial implementation of the five-phase prescriptive teaching method, the five phases must be followed as described in this chapter. Adhering to these recommended procedures assures the staff that the individual camper's needs are responded to in both the general camp program and in the specific activities comprising that program. However, as the staff's prescriptive teaching competencies increase, modification of the model is possible.

For example, if some of the programmed materials discussed in Chapter 2 are available to the staff, the overall time devoted to collecting and synthesizing assessment data (phase 1), describing behaviors (phase 2), and selecting objectives (phase 3) can be greatly reduced. Much of the instructional material discussed in Chapter 2 incorporates the objectives of these three phases into the programming procedures.

In addition, if the procedures recommended for phase 3 (selecting and writing instructional objectives) are followed closely, it is possible to skip phase 2 (describing behaviors) entirely. In this way, the five-phase method is reduced to four phases: collecting and synthesizing assessment data, selecting and writing instructional objectives, designing and implementing specific interventions, and evaluating the interventions.

REFERENCES

Bloom, B., and others. *Taxonomy of educational objectives: handbook I: cognitive domain.* New York: David McKay Co., Inc., 1956.

Cawley, J. F. *Behavior resource guide.* Wallingford, Conn.: Educational Sciences, Inc., 1973.

Cratty, B. J. *Developmental sequences of perceptual-motor tasks.* Baldwin, N.Y.: Educational Abilities, Inc., 1967.

Engel, M. Children's Insight Test. *Journal of Projective Techniques,* 1958, **22,** 13-15.

Fernald, G. *Remedial techniques in basic school subjects.* New York: McGraw-Hill Book Co., 1943.

Frostig, M., and Maslow, P. *Frostig MGL: Move-Grow-Learn: movement education activities.* Chicago: Follett Corp., 1969.

Gronlund, N. E. *Stating behavioral objectives for classroom instruction.* New York: MacMillan, Inc., 1970.

Hammill, D. C. Evaluating children for instructional purposes. *Academic Therapy,* September 1971, **6,** 341-353.

Harrow, A. J. *A taxonomy of the psychomotor domain: a guide for developing behavior objectives.* New York: David McKay Co., Inc., 1972.

Johnson, D. J., and Myklebust, H. R. *Learning disabilities: educational principles and practices.* New York: Grune & Stratton, Inc., 1967.

Johnson, O. G., and Bommarito, J. W. *Tests and measurements in child development: a handbook.* San Francisco: Jossey-Bass, Inc., Publishers, 1971.

Kephart, N. C. *The slow learner in the classroom* (2nd ed.). Columbus, Ohio: Charles E. Merrill Publishing Co., 1971.

Krathwohl, D. R., and others. *Taxonomy of educational objectives: handbook II: affective domain.* New York: David McKay Co., Inc., 1956.

Lerner, J. W. *Children with learning disabilities: theories, diagnosis and teaching strategies.* Boston: Houghton Mifflin Co., 1971.

Mager, R. F. *Preparing instructional objectives.* Palo Alto, Calif.: Fearon Publishers, 1962.

Mann, P. H., and Suiter, P. *Handbook in diagnostic teaching: a learning disabilities approach.* Boston: Allyn & Bacon, Inc., 1974.

McAshan, H. H. *The goals approach to performance objectives.* Philadelphia: W. B. Saunders Co., 1974.

Myers, P. I., and Hammill, D. D. *Methods for learning disorders.* New York: John Wiley & Sons, Inc., 1969.

Rubin, E. Z., Simpson, C. B., and Betwee, M. L. Emotionally handicapped children and the elementary schools. Detroit, Mich.: Wayne State University Press, 1966.

Valett, R. E. *A psychoeducational inventory of basic learning abilities.* Palo Alto, Calif.: Fearon Publishers, 1968.

Walker, J. E., and Shea, T. M. *Behavior modification: a practical approach for educators,* St. Louis: The Mosby Co., 1976.

CHAPTER 4

Characteristics of handicaps and their remediation in the special camp

The classification of exceptional children into distinct categories (giving them labels), such as "mentally retarded," "learning disabled," "socially maladjusted," and "behavior disordered," places unwarranted emphasis on the common characteristics of the children within these groups. Emphasis should be focused on each individual child's unique functional characteristics.

Regardless of his group label, the exceptional camper experiences difficulties at a functional level in one or more of the learning domains: psychomotor, affective, and/or cognitive. The classification of children with handicapping conditions by means of the learning domains facilitates staff efforts to plan and implement remedial programs responsive to the individual's functional strengths and weaknesses rather than to his assumed group needs.

In this chapter the handicaps of exceptional campers are classified into the three learning domains. Considerable overlap exists within and among the problems presented under each of the domains. Several of these could have been classified under two, or even all three, of the domains.

This classification scheme is applied for the purposes of organization and clarity only. A precise and comprehensive explanation and discussion of the learning domains and their components is presented in Bloom and others (1956), Krathwohl and others (1956), and Harrow (1972).

It is not feasible in this volume to present all of the handicapping conditions of exceptional children who apply for admission to camp. The handicaps presented here were selected because they are frequently observed in the camp and because they are remediable through the camping programs described in Section Two.

In addition, it is assumed in this volume that certain handicapping conditions *are not* represented in the camp population. The application and assessment procedures described in Chapter 2 were designed, in part, to screen from the population:

Trainable mentally handicapped children
Profoundly mentally handicapped children
Children who are blind or who have a severe visual impairment
Children who are deaf or who have a severe hearing impairment

Crippled children

Children with chronic health problems restricting physical activity

These exclusions should not be construed to imply that children with these handicaps cannot benefit from a camp program. However, the staff, programs, and facilities described in this volume are neither sufficient nor appropriate to meet their needs.

BASIC LEARNING HANDICAPS

There are four basic learning skills that every child must learn if he is to profit from his environment: awareness, attentiveness, responsiveness, and organization of responses. If he is to learn, a child must be aware of his environment, attend to specific stimuli within the environment, respond to environmental stimulation, and organize his responses in a meaningful way.

Awareness

Some severely handicapped children admitted to camp are not responsive to their environment (camp or other). These autistic-like children must be made aware of their environment if they are to learn even the simplest of tasks.

In the camp setting such children require constant supervision and precise programming. The task of helping these children establish meaningful contact with the environment is exhausting from the perspective of time, effort, and personnel involved in remediation. Progress is slow, and the normally anticipated interpersonal rewards desired by counselors and instructors are few in number and difficult to observe.

EXAMPLE: Five-year-old Peter was diagnosed as "a severely retarded and withdrawn child with autistic-like behaviors."

A reward for a task well done.

On the first day of summer camp, Peter arrived by bus and was escorted by a counselor through the day's activities. He neither resisted nor participated in any activities. He did not speak, although he was repeatedly encouraged to do so by the counselor. He showed no awareness of where he was, whom he was with, or what others were doing. If an object (ball, pencil) was placed in his hand, he either held it passively or let it fall to the ground. When approached by a child or an adult, Peter remained unresponsive or slowly turned his head away from the other person. The only behavior he initiated that day was to lead the counselor to the restroom.

During lunch hour, Peter sat quietly. He made no effort to feed himself. However, when certain foods (Cheerios and hotdogs) were put in his mouth, he chewed and swallowed them.

Peter's affective behavior was described as "flat"; that is, he did not resist or initiate any activity, laugh or cry, indicate likes or dislikes, or express satisfaction or dissatisfaction.

During remediation of the autistic-like child, behavior modification interventions are applied in a continuous and consistent effort to alert the child to the environment. Interventions implemented must respond to the child's inordinate desire to remain in an unchanging environment.

It is not my intention in this volume to discourage services for autistic-like children in the camp setting. However, it should be emphasized that remedial programs for such children must be well planned and carefully implemented if these children are to make measurable progress.

For further study on awareness, see Hamblin and others (1971), Kugelmass (1970), Rhodes and Tracy (1972b), Wing, J. K. (1966), and Wing, L. (1972).

Attentiveness

As the child develops awareness of his environment, he must learn to attend to specific stimuli within that environment—on demand (his or another's) and for a sufficient time to learn and complete a task.

Some children enrolled in a camp attend to one or two stimuli in the environment and exclude all others. Other children attempt to attend to all stimuli in the environment. The former group of children must learn to attend to a greater variety of stimuli; the latter must be provided an environment that limits the stimuli to which they can attempt to attend.

During remediation, this first group of children are trained to attend to specific stimuli. As they develop their attending skills, the number and variety of stimuli to which they attend are expanded. During the learning process, directions must be clearly and precisely communicated. Both successful performances and approximations of successful performances are rewarded during the initial phases of the remedial process.

The second group of children, those attending to many stimuli, are trained in a structured environment to attend to a decreasing quantity of stimuli.

EXAMPLE: With training, Peter (see preceding example) became aware of his environment. His awareness was initially limited to a few objects, activities, and persons. Peter learned to play with Tinker Toys, building blocks, a soft rubber ball, and a deck of cards. Any time he was not being led through activities by his counselor, he returned to play with these toys to the exclusion of all others.

If guided by his counselor, Peter would participate in fine motor activities such as finger painting, cutting and pasting, and simple arts-and-crafts projects. He did not participate in gross motor activities.

As Peter's awareness developed, he began to interact with his counselor and a few other adults. However, he ignored his peers.

Peter's attending handicaps were remediated by a continuation of the interventions described previously.

EXAMPLE: Tommy, a 5-year-old handicapped summer camper, was diagnosed as "hyperactive, impulsive, and distractible."

According to his counselor, during the initial days of the session Tommy was "all over the place" and "into everything." Tommy tried to respond to every object, place, activity, and individual in the environment. His attention did not appear to be organized in any specific way or for any specific purpose.

Remediation for Tommy's handicap involved placing him in a structured activity program in an uncluttered environment. He was given clear, precise directions for all his activities, and he was required to complete one task before he could begin another. As the summer progressed, Tommy began to consistently attend to specific stimuli for sufficient periods of time to complete tasks.

For further study on attentiveness, see Hewett (1968), Kugelmass (1970), Rhodes and Tracy (1972b), Wing, J. K. (1966), and Wing, L. (1972).

Responsiveness

After a child learns to attend to specific stimuli in his environment for an adequate period of time, he must learn to respond to various stimuli consistently and appropriately. To develop this skill, the staff must design an intervention that increases the probability of the child responding consistently to the presentation of specific stimuli. Initially during the remedial process, any consistent response or approximation by the child is accepted and rewarded. However, as the child progresses, he is required to respond to specific stimuli not only consistently but appropriately.

EXAMPLE: Peter (see previous examples) learned to be aware of his environment and to attend to specific stimuli. It was observed at this phase of his remediation, however, that his responses were frequently inconsistent and inappropriate for the stimulus presented.

Peter would play a game or participate in a learning activity only when he wished to do so. One day he would participate in table games, arts and crafts, and verbal transactions with his counselor; the following day he would not engage in these behaviors. Not only were his responses inconsistent but they were frequently inappropriate; that is, he would run rather than walk, stand rather than sit, and scream rather than sing.

At this time, especially during the daily language development lessons, a concerted effort was made by the instructors to increase the consistency and appropriateness of Peter's responses to specific environmental stimuli.

For further study on responsiveness, see Hewett (1968), Kugelmass (1970), Wing, J. K. (1966), and Wing, L. (1972).

Organization of responses

Many children attending camps for special populations are unable to order (organize) their responses to the environment. This is especially true when required responses are complex. The child's complex responses are frequently either incomplete, out of sequence, or both.

In such cases the intervention must progress from requiring simple responses to requiring complex ones. Directions for completing a task must be clear and concise. Counselors must provide close supervision.

Through this process the child can learn to order complex motor responses, as well as his affective and cognitive responses.

EXAMPLE: Scott, a 10-year-old summer camper, was diagnosed as having minimal brain damage as the result of an automobile accident at the age of 7 years.

Scott was a willing participant in field sports. He always volunteered to join in the morning softball games.

Scott enjoyed playing first base. However, he had great difficulty during the game if he was required to make the complex response of (1) talking it up, (2) fielding the ball, (3) running to first base, and (4) tagging the base with his foot. On these occasions, Scott would frequently either not complete the response or complete it out of sequence. He might, for example, run to the base before fielding the ball, or catch the ball and stop to talk it up before tagging the base or the runner.

Over the course of a 6-week camp session with coaching from his counselor, Scott learned to successfully complete this and other complex response sequences.

For further study on organization of responses, see Hewett (1968), Kugelmass (1970), Rhodes and Tracy (1972b), Wing, J. K. (1966), and Wing, L. (1972).

PSYCHOMOTOR HANDICAPS

The majority of exceptional children attending camps for special populations have motor, sensory, or perceptual handicaps. These problems are not only handicapping in themselves, they appear to cause many affective and cognitive problems. It is a generally accepted fact among practitioners that children with psychomotor disabilities have difficulty learning academic subjects. A perfect correlation has not been established between lack of perceptual-motor skills and learning disabilities in such areas as reading and computing (Goodman and Hammill, 1973), but it is logical to assume that a child with a visual-perceptual disability will have difficulty learning to read. It is also logical to assume that the child with inadequate fine motor skills will have difficulty writing.

A child with poorly developed gross motor skills will have difficulty playing field sports, such as baseball and kickball. In addition, he may become anxious and frustrated because of his persistent failure in these games.

Academic failure causes the child to become frustrated; thus, his level of anxiety is increased. Anxiety is frequently made manifest in interpersonal behavior conflicts.

The interrelatedness of psychomotor, affective, and cognitive learning cannot be overemphasized. It is of major concern to those responsible for remedial programs for exceptional campers.

The pyschomotor handicaps discussed in this section are those most frequently observed among exceptional children in the camp setting.

Physical health and muscular strength

In this discussion of psychomotor handicaps, it is assumed that the camper is in excellent general physical health and has adequate muscular strength to perform camp activities.

The physician's assessment form (see Chapter 3) is designed in part to assure camp personnel that the child has good physical health. If the child is prohibited by his physician from participating in certain activities, an appropriate modification must be made in his camp schedule.

If muscular strength is inadequate, a program of physical activities ranging from the least strenuous to the more strenuous is implemented for the child. Throughout each camp session, the staff must be alert to ensure that each child has an adequate diet and sufficient rest.

For further study on physical health and muscular strength, see Arena (1966), Conover (1972), Geddes (1974), Harvat (1971), and Kephart (1971).

Body awareness and identification

Occasionally, young children enrolled in camp demonstrate a lack of awareness of their physical being. These children are unaware of their body, its functions, and the functioning of its parts. Training is implemented to increase the child's awareness of his body.

EXAMPLE: Four-year-old Mary was diagnosed by her psychiatrist as "childhood schizophrenic." An active child, Mary used her body to perform a wide variety of tasks: running, jumping, crawling, manipulating toys, and knocking objects and children to the ground. However, she did not appear to comprehend the cause-and-effect relationships between her actions and the effects of those actions in the environment. Mary was often surprised when she could not walk through solid objects or crawl through space smaller than her body and when she knocked her lunch or juice to the ground with a hand or an arm. She registered no observable recognition of herself when she stood before a mirror or was shown her photograph.

During remediation, Mary learned awareness of her body and its functions. She learned about her size and density and about the functions of her arms, legs, hands, fingers, feet, and so on. She learned to recognize herself in a mirror and in individual and group photographs.

For further study on body awareness and identification, see Barsch (1967), Cratty (1967), Frostig and Maslow (1969), Geddes (1974), Kephart (1971), and Valett (1967).

Identification and localization of body parts

A child's awareness of himself increases as he learns to identify the parts of his body and those of the bodies of others. Through the remedial process, a child with inadequate self-awareness learns to recognize that he is a separate and independent entity, by learning to locate and recognize the parts of the body:

head, neck, shoulders, chest, trunk, arms, legs, and so on. Next, the child's attention is shifted to naming the body parts. Finally, the child learns to name the body parts of others.

EXAMPLE: Mary (see preceding example) continued her training in body awareness by learning to locate and identify the parts of her body through movement. She accomplished this task by imitating her counselor and practicing before a mirror. During this phase of the remedial process, Mary was not required to name the body parts.

As the remedial process progressed, Mary learned to name her body parts as she pointed to and/or moved them. Finally, she learned to point to and name the body parts of her peers and counselor. She learned to identify and name the body parts of children and adults in photographs.

For further study on identification and localization of body parts, see Barsch (1967); Cratty (1967); Karnes (1968); Lerner (1971); Montessori (1965); Reger, Schroeder, and Uschold (1968); Valett (1967); and Wedemeyer and Cejka (1970).

Gross motor skills

Gross motor development includes many varied skills involving the use of the large muscles. Among the gross motor skills a child must learn to execute with competency are rolling, sitting, crawling, walking, running, throwing, jumping, skipping, and dancing. The child must be competent in performing these skills individually, in combination, and in sequence. In addition, he must learn variations of the basic skills, such as hopping, duck walking, taking giant and baby steps, and the like.

Frequently, normal children and adults take competency in large muscle activities for granted. We tell the exceptional child to "go play" without being consciously aware of the myriad of skills involved in "playing." Many children enrolled in camps for special populations are unable to run, walk, skip, hop, catch, or throw properly.

It is extremely difficult, if not impossible, for a child lacking competency in gross motor skills to participate effectively in activities such as foot races, kickball games, softball games, and swimming.

The social and emotional implications of these skills for peer acceptance should not be overlooked. The skills are necessary if the child is to be an accepted member of his peer group.

The exceptional child may acquire competency in gross motor skills by practicing the component skills required to perform certain activities and games. After the component skills are mastered, the child is trained to combine them into the complex responses required for the activities and games.

EXAMPLE: Russell, a 13-year-old junior high student, wanted to be an outfielder on his eighth-grade baseball team. Every time Russell threw the ball, however, it went in the wrong direction. He released the ball too soon during the forward motion of his arm. This obvious lack of skill had two immediate consequences: Russell was a discouraged and frustrated outfielder, and he was usually selected last when his classmates chose teams.

Russell's handicap was observed by his physical education instructor. A remedial intervention was implemented to improve Russell's throwing skill. For the next several weeks, Russell practiced throwing at various-size targets with various-size balls at increasingly greater distances. With practice, coaching, and encouragement from his instructor and peers, Russell learned to throw accurately.

EXAMPLE: Ten-year-old Harold arrived at camp very enthusiastic about the sports program. He believed that he was a "superior" athlete. On the first day of camp, however, the boys in his age group ran the obstacle course and, of the six boys in the race, Harold was the last to finish. He was very disappointed.

During his observation of the race, Harold's counselor noted that Harold had difficulty running (his legs appeared stiff, and he kicked his ankles). He anticipated actions so far in advance of actually needing to perform them that he would begin crawling or prepare to jump several feet before it was necessary.

During the camp session, Harold was trained in the individual skills needed to complete the obstacle course. During morning physical education lessons, Harold practiced running, jumping, crawling, and so on. As the summer progressed, he learned to perform simple and then complex combinations of these skills.

For further study on gross motor skills, see Barsch (1967), Cratty (1967), Frostig and Maslow (1969), Geddes (1974), Harvat (1971), Kephart (1971), Valett (1967), and Van Witsen (1967).

Fine motor skills

Equal in importance to the child's gross motor competency is his ability in fine motor skills. The exceptional camper must be provided a variety of opportunities to improve his fine motor skills. If the child is to be a successful camper, he must learn to cut and paste, trace, color within the lines, lace and tie strings, draw and paint, and manipulate small objects with skill.

EXAMPLE: Six-year-old Mark was referred to camp by the social welfare department. He was described by the social worker as "experi-entially deprived." This label is interpreted to mean that he did not have the childhood experiences common to most 6-year-old boys. Assessment indicated that Mark's gross motor skills were well developed. However, his fine motor skills were below average for a child his age.

Mark was unable to cut a sheet of paper with a scissors, color with crayons within the lines of simple drawings, or manipulate small objects, such as pencils, Tinker Toys, and blocks, with ease. He could not button his shirt, zip his pants, or lace his shoes.

Evidently, Mark had not been provided the opportunities to develop these skills at home. During his 6 weeks at camp, Mark had daily arts-and-crafts lessons and informal sessions with his counselor during which he practiced fine motor skills.

For further study on fine motor skills, see Barsch (1967), Cratty (1967), Edgington (1968), Frostig and Maslow (1969), Kephart (1971), Montessori (1965), Valett (1967), Van Witsen (1967), and Wedemeyer and Cejka (1970).

Learning by modeling.

Motor integration

If a child is to successfully perform the many tasks demanded of him at camp, his gross and fine motor skills must be integrated into complex response sequences. This integration process must be systematically learned by many exceptional children; it does not occur naturally during the developmental process, as is the case with normal children.

Among the activities requiring the integration of gross and fine motor skills are balancing, rhythm activities, and movement of the body through space; laterality, directionality, and space-and-time orientation also require the integration of these skills.

EXAMPLE: Martha was an excellent runner. Her physical motions were smooth and fast. During assessment, she manifested *no* handicaps in gross and fine motor skills when these abilities were assessed independently. However, it was noted that her performance on the Purdue Perceptual Motor Survey activities requiring the integration of fine and gross motor abilities was below average. She had particular difficulty on the balance beam activities: walking forward, backward, and sideways. Observations during field sports indicated that she had difficulty dancing, stopping and changing direction while running, and completing the obstacle course without bumping into objects.

A training program requiring Martha to perform increasingly difficult skills designed to facilitate motor integration was prescribed. She practiced activities on increasingly narrower balance beams, foot and hand rhythm exercises, creative dances, and several obstacle activities of increasing complexity.

EXAMPLE: Penny, a 7-year old third grader, was diagnosed by her remedial reading teacher as a "nonreader." During assessment, it was found that Penny performed certain readiness skills inadequately. She appeared to have not established dominance (consistent preference and use of one side of the body over the other). She used both the right and left hands poorly in fine motor activities. She used her left foot for kicking and her left eye when sighting through a telescope. Remediation was therefore prescribed to encourage Penny to consistently use her left hand, eye, and foot.

In addition, Penny had difficulty in the area of directionality. She frequently confused *over* and *under, left* and *right, up* and *down, on* and *in,* and so on. Remediation was also implemented to improve these skills. The remedial program progressed from physical activities to pencil-and-paper activities similar to those utilized in reading readiness programs.

For further study on motor integration, see Barsch (1967); Cratty (1967); Frostig and Maslow (1969); Geddes (1974); Kephart (1971); Montessori (1965); Reger, Schroeder, and Uschold (1968); Valett (1967); Van Witsen (1967); and Wedemeyer and Cejka (1970).

Visual perception*

Visual perception includes five subskills: visual-motor coordination, figure-ground discrimination, form constancy, position in space determination, and spatial relationships determination (Frostig, 1964).

Many learning-disabled children enrolled in camp have visual-perceptual handicaps. It is generally agreed that both visual acuity and visual-perceptual skill are basic to most learning tasks in the classroom. In addition, the majority of the activities offered in a typical camping program require visual-perceptual skill.

Visual-motor coordination is the ability to coordinate vision with the movements of the body and its parts. This ability is required in field games, table games, arts and crafts, reading, writing, computing, and other activities.

In the vignette presented at the beginning of Chapter 2 (Making name tags), George and Paul had difficulty positioning and carving the letters of their names on the tags. The boys understood the objective of the project and attempted to complete it as directed. Their handicap was diagnosed as a visual-motor coordination problem.

Figure-ground discrimination is the skill of being able to visually differentiate an object of attention from other objects in the field of vision. This ability is necessary when a child

---

*In this discussion of visual perception, it is assumed that the child has normal visual acuity with or without corrective lenses. Visual acuity should be evaluated by the appropriate specialist before the child is admitted to camp.

desires to attend to a specific object or objects in his environment. Without highly developed figure-ground discrimination, it is difficult to bounce a ball, hit a ball with a bat or racket, or place and pick up objects. Children with inadequate ability in this area have difficulty coloring, drawing, reading, writing, and so on.

EXAMPLE: One of the games frequently played at camp was "find the secret object." In the afternoon, counselors would select an object in the environment. To win the game, the campers had to find and name the object. Counselors could only respond to questions with a yes or no answer.

During the game, the children would be seated on their cabin steps. The "secret object" would be clearly visible in front of them. Prizes would be awarded to those who found and named the object. After the object was found and named by several children, the remaining children would be asked, "Do you see it?"

Elsie was handicapped in figure-ground discrimination. Even when she knew the name of the object and it was pointed out to her by the counselor, she could not find it.

Form constancy is the ability to see an object as having unchanging properties—shape, size, and/or color—in spite of variability in the position of the object relative to the eye (Frostig, 1964). Generally, those with well-developed abilities in form constancy, see a "square" as a "square" regardless of its position: angles vertical, angles horizontal, large or small, near or far, and so on. We are all subject to periodic optical illusions, but normally we see objects such as cars, trucks, boxes, houses, shirts, and shoes as being what they are regardless of their position relative to the eye.

EXAMPLE: Nine-year-old Dolores was diagnosed as "learning-disabled." She had no difficulty recognizing things in their normal position. However, if her possessions—shoes, socks, and so on—were out of place, she could not find them. On field trips, Dolores would not recognize familiar scenes if she viewed them from a pathway or angle differing from the one she normally used to approach the location.

Position in space determination is the skill of perceiving an object as in or on, over and under, and so on. This ability is required to discriminate among visually different images such as letters, numbers, and words.

EXAMPLE: June had an obvious reading disability. She constantly confused p and b, d and b, 6 and 9, and was and saw.

With a remedial intervention progressing from three-dimensional to two-dimensional activities, June's handicap was remediated.

Spatial relationships determination involves skill in preceiving the position of two or more objects in space in relation each other and to the self. This ability is needed for arts-and-crafts activities, such as carving, lacing, leather tooling, and wood burning.

EXAMPLE: Keith, a 12-year-old perceptually impaired child, was very interested in arts and crafts. For his first project of the year, Keith selected leather tooling. He wanted to make a Western belt for his father. During the project, Keith became very frustrated; he had difficulty positioning his tools properly.

Observation indicated that Keith had adequate fine motor skills but was handicapped in spatial relationships determination. He had difficulty positioning the leather and tooling knife in relation to each other and to himself. It was observed that he frequently positioned his materials by using his tactile sense and head movements.

At camp, remediation of visual-perceptual handicaps includes various visually oriented games, such as "hide and seek" and "find the hidden object"; arts-and-crafts activities; and so on.

For further study on visual perception, see Bush and Giles (1968); Cratty (1971); Frostig and Horne (1964); Karnes (1968); Kephart (1971); Kirk and Kirk (1971); Reger, Schroeder, and Uschold (1968); Valett (1967); Van Witsen (1967); and Wedemeyer and Cejka (1970).

Auditory perception*

Some exceptional children have auditory handicaps even though their hearing acuity

---

*In this discussion of auditory perception, it is assumed that the child has normal hearing acuity. Hearing acuity should be assessed by a specialist before the child is admitted to camp.

is normal. There are a variety of auditory perceptual handicaps that can have a significant impact on the child's performance. Among these are difficulties in (1) locating sounds in space, (2) coordinating head and body movements when pursuing sound in space, (3) blocking out extraneous stimuli, (4) engaging in sustained listening, and (5) discriminating between similar and different sounds.

Auditory location is the ability to locate a sound in space. Children with this handicap are unable to locate a sound (that they hear) in the environment.

EXAMPLE: Jacob would frequently play "pass the ball" and "keep away" during the morning activity period. It was observed that, when the ball was not in his field of vision, he would have difficulty. Frequently, he would respond to a call from a teammate (not in his field of vision) by turning in the wrong direction. Further observation verified that, although Jacob heard sounds, he could not locate them in the environment.

Auditory-motor coordination is the ability to move the head and body in the direction of a sound. The inability of the body to respond smoothly and accurately to auditory stimuli can lead to difficulty in game activities.

EXAMPLE: When playing basketball, Jonathan would hear his teammates yell when he was to catch a pass. However, he would frequently "fall all over himself" trying to turn and position himself to catch the ball. His movements were awkward and slow. Jonathan frequently missed the ball.

Auditory figure-ground discrimination is necessary if the child is to respond appropriately to environmental sounds. Human beings, especially in today's world, must block out much of the auditory stimuli that simultaneously bombard the sense of hearing.

EXAMPLE: Tom enjoyed having conversations with his counselor in the evening. This time was "quiet time" in his cabin; the campers could talk and play table games, such as cards, checkers, and chess.

The counselor noted that although he could block out the whispers and giggles of the other boys during their discussions, Tom could not. The boy was constantly leaning forward to hear the counselor and shouting at the others to keep quiet.

Sustained listening involves the ability to listen to and process information received naturally for an extended period of time. Pre-school or kindergarten children would not be expected to be able to listen for a long period of time. However, older children should have the ability to listen to a story and repeat its salient points.

EXAMPLE: Each day at the end of the language development lesson, Ms. Jan would read the children a story. This was their reward for performing acceptably during class.

Usually, Paul would become fidgety within 2 or 3 minutes after Ms. Jan started to read. He could be observed drifting off into his own thoughts. When asked to repeat the story after it was read, he could not do so.

Some children lack skill in auditory discrimination. Auditory discrimination is the ability to differentiate between similar sounds. These differences are subtle. The Wepman Auditory Discrimination Test (see Chapter 3) is an excellent instrument for evaluating this ability. The Wepman test assesses the child's ability to discriminate between words having a single phoneme differing, such as *thread-shred*, *tug-tub*, and *toast-coast*. Poor skills in auditory discrimination are observed frequently in children who have difficulty following verbal directions.

EXAMPLE: Herman's counselor was an articulate, long-winded, individual who would give the campers lengthy and complex directions. Herman was frequently accused of not following directions. During formal assessment, it was determined that Herman had an auditory discrimination handicap.

Camp activities can be designed for remediation of auditory perceptual handicaps. Listening for, locating, recognizing, and interpreting sounds in nature during hikes, nature walks, and field trips can be of value in the remedial program. Singing and reciting camp songs, listening to adventure stories, and memorizing riddles can also help develop auditory skills.

For further study on auditory perception, see Barsch (1967); Bush and Giles (1968); Edgington (1968); Farrald and Schamber (1973); Karnes (1968); Kirk and Kirk (1971); Montessori (1965); Reger, Schroeder, and Uschold (1968); Valett (1967); Van Witsen (1967); and Wedemeyer and Cejka (1970).

Tactile perception

Tactile perception is the ability to discriminate among objects without seeing them, through the sense of touch. Although the tactile sense is infrequently used as an aid to learning, when systematically applied, it can have a significant impact on the development of the child's academic readiness skills.

In the tactile discrimination program, the child learns size (large-small), shape (square, circle, triangle, rectangle), texture (hard-soft, rough-smooth), weight (heavy-light), and other characteristics (hot-cold, silky, sticky). Through the sense of touch, he learns differences and similarities among objects.

For a child with a reading disability, the sense of touch can be used to facilitate reading readiness and beginning reading skills. This is accomplished with the use of sandpaper letters, block letters, and other three-dimensional aids. Although seldom used alone, tactile perception in combination with the visual, auditory, and kinesthetic senses is a powerful remedial tool.

EXAMPLE: John, a third grader, was a nonreader. During the first 3 years of school, he was exposed to a variety of reading approaches, such as sight reading and phonics. None were successful in helping him learn to read.

It was suggested that John's tactile sense be used to supplement his visual and auditory senses. John completed a series of lessons to improve his tactile skills. During the remedial reading program, John applied many senses. He not only saw and heard letters and words, he felt and motorically perceived them.

In a few short weeks, John learned to recognize some letters of the alphabet and a few words.

For further study on tactile perception, see Barsch (1967); Montessori (1965); Reger, Schroeder, and Uschold (1968); Valett (1967); Van Witsen (1967); and Wedemeyer and Cejka (1970).

Perceptual integration

In this section gross motor, fine motor, tactile, visual, auditory, and the other perceptual and perceptual-motor abilities have been presented as independent entities. However, it must be emphasized that these abilities are interrelated and interdependent. As the child explores his environment, he does so as a whole person, applying all or many of his perceptual skills to the tasks at hand.

For example, the "simple" act of successfully playing a game of handball requires the integration of gross motor skills (running, jumping), fine motor skills (hitting, catching, grasping), tactile skill (feeling where your hands and feet are in relation to the floor and walls, knowing when you hit the ball or a wall), visual perception (being able to visually pursue the ball in space, discriminating between the ball and the wall) and auditory perception (locating the ball when it hits the wall, responding to a teammate's "I got it" or "You get it").

For further study on perceptual integration, see Barsch (1967); Bush and Giles (1968); Johnson and Myklebust (1967); Karnes (1968); Kirk and Kirk (1971); Reger, Schroeder, and Uschold (1968); Valett (1967); and Wedemeyer and Cejka (1970).

AFFECTIVE LEARNING HANDICAPS

No group of handicapped children require more staff time, concern, and energy in the camp setting than those with behavior disorders. What can be done to decrease the incidence of stealing, fighting, bullying, swearing, and disobedience? What can be done to increase productive group participation, enthusiasm for activities, courtesy, friendliness, and acceptance of others?

Of the three learning domains discussed in this chapter, we know the least about affective learning. In this section 25 frequently observed affective learning behaviors are described and exemplified. Suggestions for remediation are presented for each behavior. These behaviors do not include all problems confronted by the staff in the camp for exceptional children. Often, it appears that there are as many unique behavior problems as there are behavior problem children enrolled in the camp.

Before the characteristics of the affectively handicapped child are described, an effort is made to differentiate "normal" from "abnormal" behavior.

All children and adults have social and emotional problems. No one can live many days during a lifetime in the happy blissfulness portrayed on the movie and television screen. We *all* have arguments, fights, disappointments, frustrations, anxieties, and so on. Occasionally, all of us emit behaviors similar to those of individuals labeled "abnormal," "emotionally disturbed," "socially maladjusted," and "mentally ill." Then, why are some of us classified as "deviant" whereas others of us are not?

The difference appears to be related to the *degree* of the behavior or behaviors emitted by the individual and observed by others. However, this statement, although correct, is an oversimplification. It ignores several relevant variables: age, sex, physical constitution, cultural background, race, religious experience, financial circumstances, family background, and immediate and past environment. Readers interested in pursuing a study of the theories for emotional disorders in children are encouraged to read Rhodes and Tracy (1972a).

When assessing the child with a behavior disorder, one must give consideration to the frequency, intensity, duration, and type of behavior emitted.

Frequency. Children are often referred to camp on the basis of one or two occurrences of an unacceptable behavior. Many times, the behavior itself is not of sufficient consequence to be classified as deviant. It is the normal deviation of an emotionally healthy child who, in the process of maturing, is experiencing and experimenting with his environment. Occasionally, a behavior that leads to the child's referral is the pet peeve of his parent or teacher and occurs infrequently.

EXAMPLE: Elmo was referred to camp by his mother for "never doing what he's told."

During the preadmission period, Elmo's mother kept a diary on his deviations. It indicated that 9-year-old Elmo did not "do what he was told" 4 times during a 2-week period. He did not take out the rubbish (one occurrence). He did not pick up his clothes in the morning before school (two occurrences). He did not dress for church on time (one occurrence).

Elmo was not admitted to camp. His mother was counseled.

Intensity. Some parents and teachers characterize a child's retort of "No, I won't" or a 1-minute verbal outburst as a temper tantrum. Frequently in these cases, it is found that the child is reacting normally to a person who is forcing him to relinquish his autonomy.

EXAMPLE: Lee was referred to camp by her teacher for having "severe tantrums." During the first week of camp, Lee had three tantrums. These occurred when she was asked to do assignments she did not enjoy (in this case, mathematics).

Her tantrums consisted of saying in a loud voice, "I hate it, and I ain't going to do it." Then she would slam her workbook on the desk, sit down in her seat, and sulk. If the behavior was ignored, Lee would begin the assignment in 2 or 3 minutes.

Lee's behavior was a normal reaction for a child who had failed mathematics for the past 3 years.

Duration. Often, parents and teachers panic when a child emits a behavior that differs from his usual response. They become anxious and immediately proceed to "do something" about it.

EXAMPLE: Tilly is a 2½-year-old only child. Her parents were very concerned because Tilly seemed to say "no" constantly. She would say "no" when asked to go to bed, to get up, to eat her lunch, to drink her milk, and so on.

Tilly's mother and father had never heard of the "terrible twos": the age when most children have an inordinate, but normal, desire to assert their independence. Tilly's negative behavior was discussed with her parents, and they were given behavior management suggestions. Tilly was not admitted to camp. Her parents learned to cope with the behavior.

During an interview 6 months later, the parents indicated that Tilly's negativism was no longer a problem.

Type. There are behaviors that, although observed infrequently, necessitate immediate action. Among these behaviors are intense physical abuse of self and others, severe, unexplained, and unpredictable withdrawal, and attempted suicide. If these behaviors occur, the child is probably in extreme emotional discomfort and requires immediate help if he is to be prevented from harming himself or others.

EXAMPLE: Benji was referred to camp because, according to his principal, he "went crazy in school." Benji is described as a "very nice, quiet, hard-working seventh grader."

One day Benji had a fight with a classmate on the playground. Benji seemed to explode for no apparent reason. He was so angry it took both the principal and the custodian to break up the fight and remove Benji to the office.

Benji was so angry that a full half hour was required to calm him down. In a discussion with the principal, Benji could not explain his actions. He appeared unremorseful and unconcerned about the serious physical injuries he had inflicted on his classmate.

Benji was referred for psychiatric help and was later admitted to camp.

On the opposite end of the continuum are behaviors that, although bothersome, do not usually require intervention. Among these behaviors are restlessness after sitting 3 or 4 hours in a classroom, gum chewing, long hair on boys, saying "no," swearing, and stealing small change.

EXAMPLE: Elmer's father arrived at a parent meeting in a very distressed state. He said, "Now he (Elmer) is stealing. He took a dime from the cup on the kitchen counter. What are we going to do?"

The following exchange took place between Elmer's father and the discussion leader:

L. Why is the change there?

F. So it will be handy when needed.

L. Do others in the family take change from the cup without permission?

F. Yes.

L. Who?

F. Me, the missus, the big boys.

L. Has Elmer ever taken money from the cup before?

F. Yes, but he always asked.

L. Has Elmer, to your knowledge, ever stolen anything else?

F. No, I don't think so.

L. Did Elmer understand he could not take money from the cup without permission before he got caught?

F. I thought so.

L. Did you discuss the missing money with Elmer?

F. Yes. He said he was sorry.

L. I would suggest you do nothing unless the behavior recurs. Then we can discuss it further.

Anxiety

Anxiety is observable behavior indicative of apprehensiveness, tension, and uneasiness. This behavior may be the result of an anticipated danger whose source is unknown or unrecognized by the individual. The anxious child is fearful, fidgety, shy, withdrawn, and uninvolved in a productive manner. He appears to be equally anxious about success and failure, meeting new friends and bidding farewell to old friends, and beginning new activities and ending familiar activities. If the anxiety increases to a high level, it may immobilize the child for all practical purposes.

Remediation includes (1) a failure-proof program; (2) sequenced activities carefully graded in degrees of difficulty; (3) short activity periods; (4) the elimination of all competition with others and against the clock; (5) the use of puppetry, role playing, and psychodrama as a media for self-expression of fear and concerns; and (6) involvement in activities reducing preoccupation with self: helping others, games, humor, music, and skits.

EXAMPLE: Tommy, a 6-year-old emotionally disturbed child, was the last of the children in the tribe to arrive for the evening campfire. He walked into the circle cautiously, holding his counselor's hand.

As the group sat down near the roaring fire, Tommy sat very close to the counselor. He held the counselor's shirt sleeve. Tommy situated himself behind the counselor, out of direct view of the fire and the skit area.

The evening skits were on the topic of "cowboys and indians." With each loud and exciting skit (which was thoroughly enjoyed by the other campers), Tommy moved closer to the counselor and finally ended up sitting on his knee.

When his group presented their skit, Tommy's role was to hold the cards announcing the scenes and introducing the characters. During his performance, Tommy held the cards in front of his face and mumbled the words he was to speak. He kept his head down during the entire time. Tommy's counselor accompanied him to the skit area and stood behind him with his hand on Tommy's shoulders throughout the performance.

For further study on anxiety, see Bakwin and Bakwin (1960); Blanco (1972); Rhodes and Tracy (1972b); Rubin, Simson, and Bettwee (1966); and Siegel (1969).

Attention-seeking behavior

Attention-seeking behavior is an action (verbal or nonverbal) that the child uses to inappropriately gain the attention of peers and adults. This behavior is inappropriate for the activity in which the child is involved.

Attention seekers arrive at camp with a broad range of behavior designed to glean attention. These include shouting, boisterousness, clowning, showing off, running away, and having the last word in all verbal transactions. Other, more subtle, attention seekers engage in foot tapping, finger snapping, hand waving, shyness, tattling, and whining.

The attention seeker is often confused with the hyperactive child. However, it is generally found that, unlike the hyperactive child, the attention seeker's level of activity decreases rapidly immediately after attention is received.

EXAMPLE: George, a 12-year-old socially maladjusted camper, considered himself an excel-

lent canoeist. He frequently bragged to the members of his tribe about his great skill and about his experiences canoeing the previous summer.

George frequently ran to the dock when the tribe was having an activity in the lake area. He would grab a paddle and launch a canoe. This behavior was in violation of the camp rules.

George would proceed about 30 feet into the lake, repeatedly shouting to his peers and counselor to watch him. His attention-seeking behavior included much dangerous clowning, such as standing up and rocking the canoe.

Remediation of attention-seeking behavior includes (1) a structured activity program, (2) the giving of immediate attention for appropriate behavior, and (3) ignoring inappropriate attempts to get attention. In severe cases, isolation or timeout is implemented, and in all cases, many opportunities are provided to obtain attention from counselors, instructors, and peers for appropriate behavior.

For further study on attention-seeking behavior, see Blanco (1972), Siegel (1969), and Woody (1969).

Disruptive behavior

Disruptive behaviors are actions that interfere with the activities of an individual or a group. In the camp setting, disruptive behaviors interrupting ongoing activities include inappropriate talking, laughing, clapping, stamping, shouting, singing, and whistling. Also included in this classification are noncooperation during activities and the use of vulgarity and sarcasm.

EXAMPLE: Mary, a 7-year-old camper, disliked "school-like" activities, such as reading, language, and arithmetic. She applied a variety of techniques to disrupt the group and escape from lessons.

Techniques she used in Mr. Calm's study center during reading lessons included (1) interrupting the instructor while he was giving instructions; (2) dropping books, workbooks, and pencils; (3) laughing at other children's efforts to read; (4) singing, groaning, and whistling during individual study time; and (5) arguing and contradicting the instructor.

Disruptive behavior can be modified by negative and positive interventions. A remedial intervention that includes some punishment or deprivation for emitting disruptive behavior can be imposed. This negative strategy will decrease the frequency of the behaviors.

A more effective approach is to ignore disruptions and reward the child's nondisruptive behaviors. When instructors, counselors, and other children ignore the disruptions, the child's acceptable behaviors will increase. The acceptable behaviors must be consistently rewarded.

For further study on disruptive behavior, see Bakwin and Bakwin (1960), Blanco (1972), and Woody (1969).

Physical aggression

Physical aggression is hostile physical actions against self or others to harm or create fear. Physical aggression against the self is characterized by self-distructive behaviors such as hitting, biting, scratching, and throwing oneself against hard surfaces: doors, walls, floors, and ground. The goal of such behavior is to inflict physical damage on the self.

EXAMPLE: David, an 8-year-old, was diagnosed by his psychiatrist as "psychotic." David exhibited a variety of self-injurious behaviors. Whenever any of David's self-stimulating (ritualistic) behaviors—fondling himself, rapid finger flicking, and so on—were interrupted, he would engage in the following activities: biting his arm, beating himself on the head, or pulling and scratching his face.

Outwardly directed physical aggression is characterized by fighting, hitting, and bullying others—peers and adults. Also included are more subtle forms of physical abuse, such as pinching, scratching, tripping, and roughhousing.

EXAMPLE: Michael, a stocky 8-year-old, was referred to camp because of his frequent fighting and bullying. Michael assaulted children younger, smaller, and incapable of defending themselves.

Michael would hit and kick other children without observable provocation several times each day. He had to be physically restrained on these occasions. Michael would attack if the unsuspecting child walked in front of him, accidently bumped him, or asked him a question.

Physical aggression includes damaging and destroying personal property and the property of others.

Generally, physical aggression cannot be ignored in the camp setting. It is dangerous to the child emitting the behavior as well as to others. Active steps must be taken to prevent damage to property. Punishment and deprivation of privileges are frequently effective in reducing aggressive behaviors. However, physical punishment should be avoided.

Interventions that will decrease the frequency of aggression if applied consistently include (1) time-out, or isolation; and (2) sitting-out, but observing, an activity that is highly desirable, such as swimming, campfire, and field trips. Tangible items that may be taken away for a brief period of time without physical discomfort to the child are favored toys and games, snacks, and desserts.

Punishment of unacceptable behaviors is *always* accompanied by the consistent reinforcement of acceptable behaviors.

For further study on physical aggression, see Bakwin and Bakwin (1960), Berkowitz and Rothman (1969), Blanco (1972), and Hamblin (1971).

Verbal aggression

Verbal or nonphysical aggression is hostile action against self or others to harm or create fear. Verbal aggression against self is characterized by self-distructive statements, such as "I'm stupid," "I'm dumb," "I'm bad," and "God made me a no-good." The goal of this behavior appears to be the inflicting of psychological damage on the self.

EXAMPLE: David (see previous example) was also given to verbal aggression. This aggression was directed at himself. When frustrated, David would say, "David is stupid," "David will go to Hell," or "David is going to hurt you."

Outwardly directed verbal aggression is characterized by swearing, name calling, and put-downs designed to hurt others. Subtle forms of outwardly directed nonphysical aggression are tattling, jealousy, gossiping, and making derogatory comments about another's race, sex, religion, physique, and so on. The purpose of this behavior is to inflict hurt or make the other person fearful.

EXAMPLE: Larry, an 11-year-old camper, was extremely verbally aggressive. However, he feared and avoided physical aggression. He was constantly provoking the members of his tribe by calling them names such as "turkey" and "craphead." Naturally, this would anger the other boys, and they would attack him. When attacked, Larry would quickly run to his counselor or instructor for protection.

The control or management of aggression, both physical and verbal, is the most difficult problem confronting the camp staff. Aggression, expressed inappropriately, has a direct negative effect on the members of the group. Extreme physical aggression in the camp setting cannot be ignored; it causes great discomfort in others. Aggression causes aggression or withdrawal in others, inhibiting their functioning. External control must be initiated if the physical aggression could cause physical harm to the individual, the other children, the staff, or camp property.

Verbal aggression is less threatening to others than physical aggression; yet, in extreme forms it must be externally controlled. It not only causes psychological hurt, it also has the effect of taunting others to aggressive actions.

Some subtle forms of inappropriate aggression should be ignored; constructive aggression should be positively reinforced.

The suggestions for remediation of verbal aggression are similar to those recommended for the control of physical aggression.

For further study on verbal aggression, see Bakwin and Bakwin (1960), Berkowitz and Rothman (1969), Blanco (1972), and Hamblin and others (1971).

Inflexibility

Inflexibility is characterized by a limitation in the quantity of defense or adjustment mechanisms and in the quality of the application of available adjustment mechanisms. The inflexible child repeatedly uses a behavioral response that is inappropriate for the task at hand. His responses are compulsive. These conditions severely limit the variety of his reactions to the environment.

The inflexible child is characterized by compulsiveness, aloofness, restricted interests, overinhibition, and overcriticalness of self and of his productions. His life is devoid of joy, excitement, interest, and variety.

EXAMPLE: Ralph enjoyed attending camp on weekends and participated in the activity program. He exhibited maladaptive behaviors when a planned activity was modified or rescheduled.

Ralph insisted on personal perfection. If he noticed a simple mistake on a math or reading work sheet, he crumbled it and threw it in the wastebasket. If he made an error while braiding "boondoggle" or during a wood-burning session, he threw the entire project away and began again.

Ralph became very disagreeable if the rules of a game were changed or a field trip was canceled because of inclement weather.

Remediation includes (1) a failure-proof program to encourage personal risk taking, (2) a variety of activities presented in structured, logical sequences, (3) tolerance by others of the child's errors, (4) positive reinforcement for all "new" and "different" behaviors the child exhibits, and (5) minimal competition and evaluation.

Discipline should be avoided until the child grows in self-confidence. If necessary, discipline must be mild, positive, and constructive. Harsh discipline must be avoided; a single occurrence can instantaneously erase the child's progress.

Remediation is highly dependent on positive interpersonal relations between the child and his counselor and instructors. *He must feel* wanted, acceptable, safe, and secure.

For further study on inflexibility, see Blanco (1972), Farrald and Schamber (1973), and Hewett and Forness (1974).

Instability

Emotional instability (also referred to as emotional lability) is characterized by unstable moods, which are accompanied by rapid and frequent changes in observable behavior. Mood-behavior shifts may be from happy to sad, from withdrawal to acting out, from aggressive to submissive, from cooperative to noncompliant, and so on. These shifts occur without apparent and sufficient cause.

Emotionally unstable children are frequently described by counselors and instructors as irritable, uptight, and unpredictable.

EXAMPLE: Christine, a 5-year-old emotionally disturbed child, was emotionally unstable. Her mood swings were rapid and unpredictable. The counselors and instructors were seldom able to predict when she would be happy or sad, or cooperative or uncooperative.

One minute she was a happy, cheerful, outgoing child; the next minute, and without apparent reason, she was sad, grouchy, and withdrawn.

Christine's reactions to various activities, such as arts and crafts, swimming, and boating, varied from day to day. One day she would joyfully run to the lake and practice her swimming strokes; the following day she would physically resist attending the swimming session.

To remediate these problems, it is necessary to stablize and structure the child's environment. Undesirable behaviors should be ignored and desirable behaviors continuously and consistently reinforced or rewarded. It is absolutely necessary that the instructor's reactions to the child's behavior remain consistent and predictable throughout the intervention. The child should be provided opportunities to express his feelings through physical activities, such as dancing, skits, and games, and in a variety of two-dimensional arts, such as drawing and painting.

For further study on instability, see Blanco (1972); Haring and Phillips (1962); and Reger, Schroeder, and Uschold (1968).

Deficient awareness of cause-and-effect relationships

Deficient awareness of cause-and-effect relationships is characterized by a lack of awareness of the dependency existing between personal actions and their effects on others.

Occasionally, a child attending camp is unaware of the effects of his behavior on others. The child says (and believes) "It wasn't my fault," "I didn't know it would happen," or "I didn't do anything." His lack of awareness is especially noticeable in interpersonal transactions with peers and adults. He is surprised when his profanity, sarcasm, or aggressiveness is responded to negatively by others. This type of child is often described as irresponsible or hostile.

Remediation includes techniques designed to alert the child to the effects of his actions on others. The life-space interview and reality therapy, described in Section Three, are effective remedial interventions.

EXAMPLE: One morning, while Hermie and Benji were playing basketball, Benji hit Hermie in the face with his fist for no apparent reason. Hermie chased Benji across the playing field toward the fence near the cabin area. Benji, in his effort to escape, climbed a fence. As he was scrambling over the fence, his shirt caught in the wire and a large hole was torn in the front of it. Hermie gave up the chase. Benji went to his counselor, complaining that Hermie had ripped his shirt and was responsible for his plight.

Applying the life-space interview technique, the counselor helped Benji explore the incident. Benji related the chain of events in proper chronological order. However, during the discussion that followed, he was unable to relate his initial behavior (punching Hermie) to his present plight (going home with a torn shirt).

For further study on deficient cause-and-effect relationships, see Kessler (1966); and Reger, Schroeder, and Uschold (1968).

Overcompetitiveness

Competitiveness is action, verbal or nonverbal, designed to overcome competition; that is, to be "first" or "best" in an activity or task. This competition may be with self or with others.

In modern American society, a spirit of competition is instilled in the citizenry from childhood. This spirit is observed frequently in the school. Competition is found in athletic events, quiz shows, spelling bees, popularity contests, and the academics. Children learn that they must be "first," "best," or "most popular" to be worthwhile; nothing less is acceptable.

I have seen children (even students and professional colleagues) devastated to the point of tears, tantrums, and suicide because they were "second" or "third" on a test, in a game, in a contest, or in competition for a position.

Overcompetitiveness can deeply scar the child's psyche, especially when the competition is unrealistic. Not everyone can run a 4-minute mile, read and comprehend a historical novel, spell 10-syllable words, or be the handsomest or the prettiest.

Overcompetitiveness in the camp is made manifest by (1) adverse and inappropriate reactions to not being "number one" in an activity, (2) adverse and inappropriate reaction to failure in an activity, (3) inordinate excitement and frustration in unfamiliar activities, (4) overconcern with rules and regulations, (5) insistence on changes in rules and activities for personal advantage, (6) aloofness (apparent unconcern), and (7) unwillingness to engage in new activities.

EXAMPLE: Nine-year-old Howard liked to play field games with the members of his tribe. He was skilled in most of the required motor abilities, such as running, throwing, and catching, and usually won any competition he entered.

However, when he lost a race, did not make a touchdown, or dropped the ball, he became very angry at his teammates; he lost control of his behavior and cried.

For remediation to take place, first, competition should be minimized or eliminated in activities. The child should be encouraged to participate in various physical and mental activities for the enjoyment derived from the activity. Second, if the child is required to compete, he should only compete in activities he is capable of performing with success. Third, the child should not be required to compete against more skilled children. Fourth, all the children involved in the com-

petition should be winners. This can be accomplished by having a "first winner," "second winner," "third winner," and so on. Fifth, the meaning of winning and losing should be discussed with the child. The child should be urged to express his feelings openly on these issues. Finally, the child should be prepared to lose as well as to win. The socially appropriate responses to winning and losing should be discussed with him.

For further study on overcompetitiveness, see Berkowitz and Rothman (1969); Reger, Schroeder, and Uschold (1968); and Woody (1969).

Inattentiveness

Inattentiveness is an inability to focus on a perceived stimulus situation for sufficient time to purposefully engage in and complete a task. The inattentive child is characterized by an inability to complete given tasks within the alotted time. His behavior includes (1) not attending to the task; (2) not attending to instructions given by the counselor; and (3) wandering about the immediate environment, touching and inspecting item after item without apparent purpose. At times, the inattentive child appears to be preoccupied or daydreaming.

EXAMPLE: When Tommy arrived at camp, the staff initially diagnosed his handicap as hyperactivity. The boy was incapable of remaining in an assigned position or at a task for as brief a time as 3 or 4 minutes. Although he was physically present during the required time, he became restless and focused his attention elsewhere.

When questioned about the instructions for an activity, Tommy could repeat the counselor's initial statements but would be unable to repeat all of the instructions.

Tommy could not remain involved in individual activities, such as table games, arts-and-crafts projects, and jigsaw puzzles, for the 15 or 20 minutes required to complete them.

Counselors and instructors can help the inattentive child learn attending skills by (1) providing him limited quantities of highly stimulating tasks; (2) using instructional methods that include a game format; (3) minimizing nonstructured time before, during, and after activities; (4) reducing extraneous and nonverbal stimuli in the environment; (5) providing clear, precise directions; and (6) providing instruction for brief units of time and opportunities for physical activity between the instructional periods.

For further study on inattentiveness, see Blanco (1972); Farrald and Schamber (1973); Haring and Phillips (1962); Rubin, Simson, and Betwee (1966); and Siegel (1961, 1969).

Impulsivity

Impulsivity is characterized by an instantaneous response to stimulation. The response appears to lack thoughtfulness and planning. It is extremely rapid, inappropriate, and often ends in error.

The impulsive child is often described by counselors as "not thinking" or "not looking before he leaps."

EXAMPLE: Jeri was diagnosed by the school psychologist as impulsive.

Jeri's impulsivity during the camp program was made manifest by an obvious lack of thought before beginning an activity. Jeri would often run to the playing field to begin a game before it was decided what game would be played. She would frequently begin a project before she had obtained directions and the needed materials and equipment. She seldom completed an activity.

In addition, Jeri would change and revise projects several times during each activity period. In the academic areas, Jeri's impulsivity resulted in errors in arithmetic and reading.

Remediation necessitates (1) a structured program, (2) brief activity periods, and (3) the reduction of extraneous stimuli. Each assigned task must be appropriately responded to and/or completed before the child is permitted to engage in another activity. During physical activities a "buddy" (counselor or nonimpulsive peer) is frequently helpful in keeping the impulsive child at a task.

Discipline should be firm but kind.

For further study on impulsivity, see Blanco (1972); Farrald and Schamber (1973); Hamblin and others (1971); Haring and Phil-

lips (1962); Rubin, Simson, and Betwee (1966); and Siegel (1961).

Perseveration

Perseveration is the tendency to continue an action after it is no longer appropriate for the task at hand. The perseverative child has difficulty changing from one activity to another. His repetitions do not appear to be goal directed.

Perseveration can be either verbal or physical. For example, the child may continue to laugh at a joke long after everyone else has stopped laughing. He may respond to a question long after it is appropriate. He may continue to write until he writes off the edge of the paper and across the top of the desk. He may continue repeating a word, number, or letter until he is stopped. He may jump rope or dance after the activity has been terminated.

The perseverative child is like a scratched phonograph record; lacking self-control, he must repeat actions until his "needle" is lifted by an external force and his set is modified.

EXAMPLE: Scott, a severely emotionally disturbed child, was diagnosed by a psychiatrist as autistic. Scott's perseveration inhibited his ability to receive information and engage in productive activities that would allow him to learn and experience new things.

If Scott became involved in an activity, he would repeat it again and again until he was physically removed from the environment and another activity was forced into his awareness. For example, Scott would continue to sing, dance, run, and jump after the time assigned for this activity had ended.

If permitted, he would watch water run from a faucet or a phonograph record spin. He would sift sand or rework a jigsaw puzzle for hours unless he was forced to stop and his attention directed elsewhere. Scott physically resisted these attempts to change his activity.

Remediation includes providing (1) external signals alerting the child to stop, (2) activities requiring a variety of responses rather than a simple response, and (3) activities using multiple sensory learning methods. In severe cases, a counselor must accompany the child and initiate changes in his set as required by the activities.

For further study on perseveration, see Farrald and Schamber (1973); Reger, Schroeder, and Uschold (1968); and Siegel (1961).

Poor self-concept

Poor self-concept is the perception of oneself as a person (son, daughter, student, friend, learner) who is unacceptable in comparison with the idealized self. Many children perceive themselves as inadequate and inferior. A poor self-concept is made manifest in statements and actions communicating the message "I can't do it," "He's better than me," "I'll never win," or "I'm no good."

The child with a poor self-concept (1) lacks self-confidence, (2) fears the unfamiliar, (3) expresses feelings of inferiority, (4) is hypersensitive to criticism, (5) resists independent functioning, and (6) is reluctant to attempt a wide range of activities. In some cases of inferiority, the child is given to self-injury. He is frequently immobilized when confronted with "new" or "different" problems and situations.

EXAMPLE: George perceived himself as a "loser." This 12-year-old boy had established a pattern of failure in academic and extra-curricular activities throughout his 7 years of school. George received *D*s and *F*s on his report cards, and these grades reinforced his belief that he was a "loser."

George seldom entered into an activity with a positive attitude. He was constantly putting himself down by saying, "I can't do it," "It won't be right," or "I'll never get it."

Remedial interventions include (1) failure-proof tasks and activities during the initial stages of remediation; (2) frequent and consistent positive reinforcement with social praise and, if necessary, tangible rewards; (3) avoidance of punishment or negative value statements concerning the child and his products; (4) direct appeal to peers and adults to build the child's self-concept; (5) assigning of special jobs and tasks that are meaningful, visible, and rewardable; and (6) close physical contact and proximity with an accepting adult during the initial stages of remediation.

For further study on poor self-concept, see Kessler (1966); Reger, Schroeder, and Uschold (1968); Siegel (1969); and Woody (1969).

Negativism

Negativism is extreme and consistent verbal opposition to the suggestions, advice, and directions of others. The oppositional child is characterized as "disliking everything and liking nothing," "agreeing to few activities," "enjoying a limited variety of things," and "always saying no."

If questioned, the oppositional child will indicate displeasure with camp, the program, instructors, counselors, peers, food, bed, and so on. He appears to receive little pleasure from life.

This mode of responding may be a learned pattern of behavior resulting from experiences of having the things the child liked taken from him arbitrarily and capriciously.

EXAMPLE: Dennis was negative in all of his interactions with peers and authority figures during the backpacking trip.

He was against walking, carrying his pack, studying nature (flowers, birds, trees), erecting and taking down his tent, and so on. He would become extremely negative with his peers when the group was planning evening activities. The only time he would willingly participate in any activity was when he was "the boss" and exercised total control over the others. Even then, he would be dissatisfied with the final outcome of the activity.

Although most of his negativism was ignored and "laughed off" by the counselors to avoid conflict, his behavior frequently resulted in physical conflict with his peers.

As seen in the above example, much of the oppositional child's negativism is meaningless and can be ignored. Ignoring the behavior but insisting on participation renders negative responses nonfunctional. If a response is rendered nonfunctional, that is, not rewarded, it decreases in frequency and is eventually eliminated from the child's behavior repertoire.

For further study on negativism, see Bakwin and Bakwin (1960); Blanco (1972); and Reger, Schroeder, and Uschold (1968).

Hyperactivity

Hyperactivity is heightened, persistent, sustained physical motion. This behavior is characterized by disorganization, disruption, unpredictability, and apparent nongoal directedness. The hyperactive child overreacts to stimuli in the environment. Such a child's behavior can be described as restless, jittery, nervous, impulsive, and uninhibited. Counselors and instructors describe hyperactive children as being "in constant motion" or "unable to stay still."

EXAMPLE: Marty, a 5-year-old hyperactive child, was described by his counselor as being in "constant, frenetic motion."

If not physically confined to a specific area of the camp, he would run about, hitting, touching, and grabbing everyone and everything. There were no apparent purposes or directions to his activities. Marty would engage in one activity after another with great rapidity. If forced to sit and attend to a task, Marty would jump and wiggle about in his seat.

Remedial interventions should include (1) a reduction in extraneous environmental stimuli, both visual and auditory; (2) a structured remedial program including limited tasks and precise directions; (3) firm, positive discipline; (4) frequent opportunities for physical activity; and (5) positive reinforcement for activities attempted and completed. Initially during programming, emphasis should be on *learning to learn* rather than on *learning specific knowledge or skills.*

For further study on hyperactivity, see Farrald and Schamber (1973); Haring and Phillips (1962); and Reger, Schroeder, and Uschold (1968).

Hypoactivity

Hypoactivity is characterized by slow, lethargic, and/or insufficient motor activity in response to stimulation. The hypoactive child is described as lacking interest and being sluggish, lazy, drowsy, and uncon-

cerned. The behavior may be related to the child's energy level or to an inability to perceive the environment accurately and react to its demands appropriately. Hypoactivity may be a symptom of anxiety or fear that has immobilized the child.

EXAMPLE: Darryl was referred to camp because of hypoactivity. After several physical and neurological examinations, his physicians concluded that there was no physical reason for his behavior. Darryl was aptly described as "a child in slow motion."

The boy functioned in all areas at approximately 25% of the normal rate for a child of his age and size. He ate slowly, talked slowly, and walked slowly. For example, it would take Darryl 20 minutes to complete the 5-minute walk from his cabin to the dining room. It took him 30 minutes to climb two flights of stairs.

Darryl appeared to have to concentrate on processes that are automatic in most children and adults, such as walking, running, or moving an arm.

Remediation includes several strategies. First, an activity program in which the child must participate should be provided. This program should include activities requiring the expenditure of more energy than is normal for the child. Second, activities that are desirable to the child should follow less desirable activities. The child is not permitted to engage in a desirable activity until he has participated in the less desirable activity. Third, the child should be rewarded for both appropriate behavior and approximations of that behavior. Fourth, demands on the child are increased slowly and systematically. Fifth, the child should participate in an exercise program to increase his muscular strength and tonus. Sixth, it is frequently helpful to use a timer against which the child competes in his effort to complete an activity. If this device is used, care must be taken not to make the time allowed to complete the activity so brief that success is impossible. The time requirement is systematically decreased from the child's average time to the desired time. Finally, the child should not be forced into activities or punished for not participating in activities that he fears. The counselor's primary function is to provide a secure environment, emotional support, and encouragement for the child.

For further study on hypoactivity, see Hamblin and others (1971).

Withdrawal

Withdrawal is the act of leaving or escaping from a life situation, which, in the perception of the child, may cause personal conflict or discomfort.

The behavior of the withdrawn child is characterized by isolation, preoccupation, daydreaming, drowsiness, shyness, coquettishness, fearfulness, and depression. Affective behavior is "flat," or unresponsive.

EXAMPLE: Shelia, a severely withdrawn 7-year-old child, was referred to camp because she did not speak in school, she frequently hid in closets and under tables, and she appeared unhappy and depressed.

In camp, Shelia would hide in her cabin all day unless accompanied by a counselor. With the exception of individual activities that she could complete without interacting with others, she seldom engaged in activities. During field games, Shelia would stand quietly on the side of the field. When she did participate in an activity, she manifested no satisfaction.

If urged to participate, Shelia would cry and run to her cabin.

Remediation includes (1) a failure-proof program of activities, (2) personal comfort and a feeling of security, (3) the development of positive interpersonal relations with counselors and peers, (4) suggestions for alternative response patterns, (5) activities that necessitate a variety of responses, (6) an active, well-planned, program that discourages withdrawal, and (7) the avoidance of harsh discipline and physical punishment.

For further study on withdrawal, see Berkowitz and Rothman (1969); Kessler (1966); Reger, Schroeder, and Uschold (1968); and Rubin, Simson, and Betwee (1966).

Passive-suggestible behavior

Passive-suggestible behaviors are actions that an individual emits at the request of another without apparent personal forethought. The passive-suggestible child is frequently

described as "irresponsible," "easily-led," "overcompliant," and a "follower."

The passive-suggestible child is insecure. He adopts a "leader" to direct him and uses this person as an excuse for personal actions. He will do almost anything to please others. His behavior may be positive or negative, productive or nonproductive. The passive-suggestible child is unskilled in the processes of problem solving, decision making, and selecting activities.

EXAMPLE: Horace, a very quiet, reserved 11-year-old camper, was referred to camp as a "slow learner." Horace had adequate psychomotor and cognitive abilities, although he required more time and drill to learn a concept than is normally anticipated of a boy in his age group.

Horace's primary problem at camp was made manifest in social situations. At the request of his counselor, Horace would engage in any activity without question.

This overcompliance caused Horace to be assigned the most distasteful work in the camp: cleaning restrooms, scraping garbage from trays, and scrubbing pots and pans. In an effort to be accepted, Horace misinterpreted jokes and humor as commands to perform.

Horace also followed the directives of his peers without question, and this frequently resulted in conflicts with counselors, instructors, and other children.

Remediation includes helping the child to (1) solve problems, (2) make decisions, and (3) select appropriate activities. The child should be encouraged to function independently. Discipline should be firm but nonpunitive. The child should be afforded many opportunities to participate in group and individual decision-making activities.

For further study on passive-suggestible behavior, see Blanco (1972); and Reger, Schroeder, and Uschold (1968).

Social immaturity

Social immaturity is age-inappropriate behavior, that is, the exhibiting of behaviors that are typical of a person of a younger chronological age. This behavior is frequently observed when the child is in unfamiliar and/or stressful situations. The socially immature child lacks skill in age-appropriate behavior. The variety of social response mechanisms he has available for immediate use is limited, requiring him to use available, but less mature, responses.

Described as "a baby," "a sissy," and "immature," the socially immature child characteristically prefers the company of younger or older children and adults to peers. Occasionally, in a familiar, nonstressful situation, he will exhibit adult behaviors. He selects toys, games, and activities below his age level.

EXAMPLE: Ralph, a 14-year-old maladjusted camper, was extremely immature. When he was under emotional stress, his behavior more closely approximated that of a 5- or 6-year-old child than that of an adolescent boy.

Ralph exhibited these age-inappropriate behaviors when he failed or did not get his way during an activity. On these occasions, he cried, pouted, engaged in temper tantrums, and used baby talk.

Remedial interventions include (1) provisions for a variety of enriching experiences at the appropriate age level, (2) direct instruction for appropriate behavior during new activities, (3) consistent rewarding of age-appropriate behavior to improve the self-concept, (4) increased peer contacts in structured activities, and (5) direct instruction and discussion of alternative ways of reacting in specific situations.

For further study on social immaturity, see Haring and Phillips (1962); Hewett and Forness (1974); Kessler (1966); Rubin, Simson, and Betwee (1966); Siegel (1969); and Valett (1967).

Inefficient interpersonal relations

Interpersonal relations include the child's actions and reactions to peers and adults, and the actions and reactions of peers and adults to the child. In this volume emphasis is focused on transactions between the child and others. These transactions may be appropriate or inappropriate, positive or negative, productive, nonproductive, or counterpro-

ductive, personally satisfying or dissatisfying, and acceptable or unacceptable.

The child with inefficient interpersonal relations (1) may not know the appropriate behavior; (2) may not be able to perform the behavior; (3) may not be able to perceive or comprehend the behavior of others and therefore cannot respond appropriately; (4) may lack experience in specific interpersonal situations; or (5) may respond pathologically as a result of fear, insecurity, or frustration.

EXAMPLE: Jack was referred to the summer school-camp because of extreme shyness, withdrawal, and refusal to attend school. Jack, an underachiever, had experienced repeated failure in school. He perceived himself as an unworthy person.

Among Jack's handicaps was the inability to interpret facial expressions. Jack was unable to differentiate happy (smiling) faces, angry (frowning) faces, and emotionally neutral expressions in pictures and drawings. Consequently, Jack frequently misinterpreted the facial expression of his teachers and peers. He reacted to others on the basis of his perceptions rather than on the basis of their intent.

Jack attended a sixth-grade class for social studies. One day, he arrived in the classroom while a lesson was in progress. Immediately after Jack had taken his seat, a boy in the front row turned toward him, smiled, and gave the peace sign. Jack immediately opened the top of his desk, put his head inside, pulled the top down on his neck, and began to cry.

The teacher removed Jack from the room, and they discussed the incident. Jack said, "That kid was making fun of me. He hates me."

Remediation includes providing an environment in which the child feels secure and comfortable. Counselors must encourage positive interpersonal transactions by showing friendliness, helpfulness, and overt concern. Life-space interviewing and reality therapy techniques are most productive in developing the child's interpersonal skills. These techniques are discussed in Section Three.

For further study or inefficient interpersonal relations, see Farrald and Schamber

(1973), Hewett and Forness (1974), and Kessler (1966).

Sexual deviations

Sexual deviations are acts with sexual denotations and connotations that are at variance with accepted practice in the culture. Sexual deviation creates a unique problem when an effort is made to define the behavior.

First, it is generally agreed that accepted sexual behavior varies among the American subcultures. Thus, the evaluation of a specific behavior is highly dependent on both the subculture of the person acting out the behavior and the subculture of the person perceiving the behavior.

Second, because of more open information on all aspects of sexual behavior, accepted standards for sexual behavior in society are extremely difficult to determine (if a universal standard exists).

In addition, we must recognize that the taboos on sex and sex-related expressions enforced during the last generation have made sexuality an extremely personal, emotional, and explosive issue in many segments of society.

A small group of children are referred to camp each summer for sexual deviations. These generally include (1) autoerotic activities, voyeurism, and fondling of other children or animals; (2) sex-inappropriate behavior, that is, behavior different from that of like-sex peers; and (3) verbalizations and gestures with sexual implications.

The majority of children referred for sexual deviations do not demonstrate these behaviors in the camp environment. The reason for their referral may be oversensitivity to sexuality among the general population (parents and teachers, in particular).

Sex-inappropriate behaviors are frequently observed in children who lack a strong like-sex identification figure in the home. Steps are taken at camp to provide these children with an acceptable like-sex identification figure.

The frequent use of sexual characterizations, profanity, and gestures, especially among older children, is generally an attention-seeking device. Children who use this device are aware of the impact of their behavior on others; their use of unacceptable behavior makes them the center of attention. Many young children, in all probability, have little understanding of the meaning of the words they say or of the gestures they make. They are only aware of the effectiveness of their words and gestures.

EXAMPLE: Calvin, a 13-year-old socially maladjusted camper, was a prolific user of profanity and double meanings. It was difficult for the counselors to complete even the most innocent of statements without Calvin projecting sexual meaning onto it. On these occasions, Calvin would laugh and rephrase the statement in very precise, descriptive sexual language. His peers would join in the "fun," and the activity would be disrupted. The purpose of Calvin's behavior was to disrupt the activity, to gain his peers' attention, and shock the counselors—especially the female counselors. Calvin's technique was very effective.

The intervention imposed was to reward appropriate use of language, including nonprofane substitutes for profane words and phrases, and punish, by deprivation of privileges, the use of profanity. The intervention was effective; the frequency of profanity decreased significantly within a few days.

Efforts to remediate sexual deviations are highly dependent on the counselor's and instructor's personal attitudes and/or hang-up about sex and sexual behavior. Many counselors project their personal feeling about sex onto the innocent behaviors of children; that is they perceive the behavior they anticipate perceiving rather than the behavior that occurs.

Many behaviors of a sexual nature can be decreased by simply ignoring them, that is, not responding to them. This technique renders the behavior nonfunctional.

Many so-called sexual behaviors are learned and acceptable responses in the child's noncamp environment. If a child comes from a home or subculture in which sexual profanity, swearing, and gestures are common occurrences, he should not be punished for it. Often, direct *private* instruction and discussions will decrease the behavior. The child's noncamp environment should not be derogated in these discussions. The counselor should simply emphasize the appropriate behavior for camp. Behaviors that can be decreased by this technique are swearing, profanity, double meanings, gestures, and nudity. The child will need frequent reminders and encouragement to change his behavior.

A severely disturbed child will often exhibit pseudomasturbatory behavior. This behavior is unconscious. In all probability, it has no sexual meaning to the child. He is simply stimulating himself. He could have chosen other, more damaging, means, such as head banging. The child should never be punished for this behavior. Continuously and consistently interfering with the behavior by engaging the child in another activity should eliminate it.

Finally, it should be remembered that curiosity about self and others is a part of growing up. Children at the preschool age have a tendency to engage in sexual play. Although it is not desirable at camp, it should not be punished.

The most valuable and effective technique available for controlling sexual deviation is prevention through the provision of an environment that is interesting and exciting enough that self-stimulation is not necessary. All camp personnel should have an opportunity during in-service training to discuss their personal opinions, attitudes, and standards concerning sexual deviations and normal sexual behavior. This personal awareness permits them to monitor their response to similar behaviors among the campers.

For further study on sexual deviations, see Bakwin and Bakwin (1960), Berkowitz and Rothman (1969), and Kessler (1966).

Psychosomatic complaints

The term *psychosomatic* denotes the interdependence of the physical and psychic human systems. This adjective is used to describe psychic conflicts made manifest in physical symptoms. The symptoms may be a result of real or imagined physical disturbances. It should be kept in mind that the fact that a physical disturbance does not exist in no way makes the symptom less real to the complaining individual. In stress situations, many people develop headaches, upset stomachs, nausea, stomach cramps, and so on.

Psychosomatic complaints are made manifest by children who excuse themselves from activities because they "don't feel good," "they hurt," "they are tired," and so on. Some will affect limps to avoid participation. They are often described by peers and counselors as "quitters," "cop-outs," and "constant complainers."

The hypochondriac child can be programmed for remediation *after it has been determined that a physical disturbance does not exist.* (In Chapter 3 it is recommended that each child admitted to camp receive a complete physical examination.)

The remedial intervention includes (1) an interesting, physically active program; (2) firm, nonpunitive discipline, that is, insistence on participation in scheduled activities; (3) nonresponse to complaints and distraction (through humor, for example) to help the child forget his aches and pains; and (4) positive reinforcement for participation—the child should be reminded and praised for overcoming his physical symptoms.

EXAMPLE: Randolph, a 14-year-old junior high school student, was referred to camp as a hypochondriac. Before he was admitted, he was given a comprehensive physical examination. According to the physicians, the results were negative; that is, no abnormalities could be found to account for his complaints.

During a backpacking trip, Randolph complained of aches and pains in his arms, legs, and shoulders. After meals, he would declare that his stomach was upset and that his bowels were cramped. He complained of dizziness and headaches. His complaints were frequent (40 or 50 a day).

After a 3-mile walk, he crawled into the camping site screaming, "You're trying to kill me! You don't care about me! I'm a sick boy!"

With an intervention similar to the one described above, Randolph completed the 5-day, 25-mile trip without adverse effects.

For further study on psychosomatic complaints, see Bakwin and Bakwin (1960).

Chronic disobedience

Disobedience is action contrary to the directives of an authority figure. The chronically disobedient child is characterized as "constantly" involved in activities contrary to the rules of the camp and the directives of the counselors and instructors.

Many preadolescent boys admitted to camp are chronically disobedient. They aggressively challenge the authority of the staff rather than obey the simplest of rules.

Remediation can be effected by making the camp's rules, "their rules," that is, by permitting them to discuss and establish rules of behavior.

The *few* rules that are necessary to ensure the health, safety, and comfort of everyone at camp must be discussed with these children before conflicts arise. These discussions should focus on the rationale for the rules.

The chronically disobedient child should not be confronted with his unwillingness to comply with a rule or be forced to obey, if possible. Such confrontations are not only nonproductive, they tend to reinforce disobedience. As an alternative strategy, the child may be given two or more courses of action from which to choose. In this way, a conflict is avoided and the child learns to respond positively.

Counselors and instructors should avoid the use of "you will" statements. However, they must be prepared to enforce via strict discipline, including deprivation of privileges and isolation, those few rules that must be obeyed for the sake of everyone at the camp.

EXAMPLE: Counselors and instructors learned very quickly that they should never give Michael a direct command. If they did, he would disobey. If they chose to enforce their order, there would be a physical conflict. Michael frequently won these conflicts.

Michael would disobey even the simplest order, such as "Make your bed before you go to breakfast," "Pick up your clothes," "Eat your spinach," or "Complete your math." Michael would even refuse to participate in activities he enjoyed if he was given a direct command, such as "Michael, hurry up and dress for swimming," or "Michael, prepare for arts and crafts."

The staff did not wish to reinforce Michael's disobedience or physically force him to obey. Consequently, an intervention that consistently provided Michael with an alternative course of action was designed. For example, his counselor would say, "Michael, you can go swimming *or* remain in our cabin," or "Michael, you can complete your reading *or* math first—which do you prefer?"

This intervention was effective.

For further study on chronic disobedience, see Blanco (1972) and Kessler (1966).

Motivational problems

Motivation is the process of having or developing a reason for participation in an activity. Most adults and children are self-motivated. However, some children do not comprehend the reason for participation in activities and are described as unmotivated.

Very few children are unmotivated to participate in camp activities. The reasons for this lack of motivation include failure to understand the activity, fear of the "new" or "different," and a lack of self-confidence.

Before implementing a remedial intervention, the staff must evaluate the appropriateness of the activity for the child. Criteria for evaluation include age, sex, handicap, previous experience, and the activity, itself.

Children tend to imitate their counselors. If counselors are disinterested, unmotivated, and unwilling to participate, the child will respond in kind.

Children who are not motivated by the counselor, their peers, or the activity, itself, must be externally motivated. Rewards for the children can be established and given to them for participating in activities. The rewards selected for the child must be rewarding to him. Rewards can be determined through observation of the child and notation of the activities he prefers. During remediation, the child is given his reward only after participation. This technique helps the child overcome his reservations about "new" activities.

EXAMPLE: According to the instructor, Mary was unmotivated to participate in physical education. She "half-heartedly" dressed for PE and remained uninvolved unless she was forced to participate. She escaped from the gym as soon as possible after class.

Observations conducted at camp agreed with the PE teacher's perception. In addition, it was observed that Mary lacked many of the skills required for successful participation in PE.

The intervention included adapting the activities to increase Mary's probability to success, rewarding Mary's efforts to participate, and implementing a training program in gross motor skills.

For further study on motivational problems, see Blanco (1972); Kessler (1966); and Reger, Schroeder, and Uschold (1968).

Hyperresilience

Redl (1971) describes hyperresilient children as "youngsters who are perfectly healthy —as normal, clinically speaking, as anyone might want a youngster to be" (see The healthy hyperresilient child, Chapter 1, p. 8). Rather than being a symptom of a pathological condition, the abnormal behaviors of these children are "desperate means to ward off danger from without."

The hyperresilient child selects a defense or adjustment mechanism that he applies in an effort to live in a state of relative comfort in an unacceptable and/or unaccepting environment. This defensive behavior is characterized by either overt aggression designed to keep others away or withdrawal designed to prevent others from entering into the child's life-space.

In a positive, exciting, and accepting camp environment, no specific interventions are recommended for these children. Generally, within a matter of days, they settle into the environment and become productive campers. Counselors will ask, "Why is he here?" or indicate that the child is "normal," "OK," or their "best child."

EXAMPLE: Nine-year-old Ted was referred to camp as a chronic truant. He was absent from camp approximately 2 days each week during the year. When he attended school, Ted was shy and quiet. He always obeyed his teachers.

At camp. Ted was designated as "the outstanding camper." He eagerly participated in all activities and was "a great conversationalist" according to his counselors and instructors. Ted was liked by the members of his tribe.

The staff could not find any reason for his withdrawal in school or his truancy.

When Ted was asked why he liked camp, he said, "They don't paddle you here. The teachers are nice."

For further study on healthy hyperresilience, see Redl (1971).

COGNITIVE LEARNING HANDICAPS

The majority of children attending camps for special populations are referred because of cognitive learning handicaps: problems of comprehension, memory, or an inability to manipulate knowledge productively. Before a program of remediation can be implemented for these children, the complex cognitive learning skills must be assessed (see Chapter 3).

During the assessment and remediation processes, counselors and instructors should remain aware of the interrelatedness of psychomotor, affective, and cognitive learning.

In this discussion of cognitive learning handicaps, it is assumed that the child is not deficient in the basic learning abilities presented at the beginning of this chapter: awareness of the environment, attentiveness to stimulation from the environment, responsiveness to stimulation, and organization of responses in a systematic and meaningful manner.

General knowledge

Frequently, educational personnel erroneously assume that all children enter school with an extensive reservoir of general knowledge, that is, knowledge of persons, places, things, and processes. In theory, this knowledge is to be expanded and applied throughout formal education.

Unfortunately, many children arrive at

camp with an inadequate knowledge reservoir. It is not unusual to find children who lack readiness training in numbers, letters, colors, shapes, and the like. Nor is it surprising to discover children who are unaware of common concepts, such as *man, woman, boy, girl, car, truck, flower, tree, house,* and so on.

A few children show evidence of knowledge gaps. For example, a child may be able to add and multiply but not subtract or divide, even though he is past the grade in school in which these skills are learned. Or a child who is a superior "word reader" may not comprehend what he reads.

Sometimes children possess erroneous knowledge that confuses them in their efforts to learn and apply new knowledge. For example, a child may believe that certain people are innately inferior, dishonest, or stingy. Such erroneous knowledge must be corrected if the child is to productively discuss social studies topics with his peers and instructor.

Occasionally, as a result of cultural experiences, a child has knowledge that is unacceptable or inappropriate when applied in certain environments. For example, a child may think that thrift is foolish or that stealing another person's property is acceptable.

The child with inadequate general knowledge must be encouraged during formal and informal camp activities to explore his environment and expand his knowledge of himself and his world. During the initial weeks of camp, counselors and instructors should make very few assumptions concerning the child's general knowledge reservoir.

EXAMPLE: Charlie, a severely experiencially deprived 6-year-old, had great difficulty functioning efficiently at camp because of a lack of common knowledge. Charlie was unfamiliar with the purpose and names of a broad range of persons, places, and things.

He had never seen or used an indoor bathroom and did not understand its purpose. He was unfamiliar with the names of many things, such as *towel, shower, sheet, plate, desk, knife, nurse, cook, cabin, ball, bat,* and *bus.* Charlie had never seen a television set, typewriter, or tape recorder.

He spent a productive summer exploring a new environment.

For further study on general knowledge, see Meeker (1969); and Meeker, Sexton, and Richardson (1970).

Specific knowledge

Frequently, a child lacks specific knowledge in a variety of subject areas and this lack prohibits progress commensurate with that of his peers. This type of child lacks the knowledge to function with even minimal effectiveness in the academic setting. Formal assessment indicates that he has a limited vocabulary and inadequate information about specific dates, places, and things. These deficiencies are the primary reason for his poor performance on standardized intelligence and achievement tests.

The child with inadequate specific knowledge either does not know, or is unable to recall, specific information. He may not know colors, shapes, letters, or numbers. He may be unfamiliar with common items such as pencils, crayons, scissors, paper, and paint. His limited vocabulary makes it difficult for him to understand instructors' verbal communications. He has difficulty communicating with others.

EXAMPLE: David was 7 years old before he was enrolled in school. He lived with his grandfather in an isolated rural area.

Although David responded intelligently to manual problems and was eager to learn, he had difficulty understanding verbal communications.

David was very knowledgeable about the rural environment. He could name many animals, trees, flowers, and so on. However, he was unfamiliar with the school environment and its emphasis on verbal language, reading, writing, and computing. He did not recognize the letters of the alphabet, numbers, colors, or shapes. Although he was familiar with and could use many common items, he was unfamiliar with their names, such as *desk, pencil, work sheet, pencil sharpener, scissors,* and the like.

For further study on specific knowledge, see Meeker (1969); and Meeker, Sexton, and Richardson (1970).

Knowledge application

Although they have adequate knowledge reservoirs, some children have difficulty applying their knowledge effectively. Their handicap is evident in speech usage, writing forms, spelling, and grammar. They have difficulty sequencing knowledge. Consequently, they have little understanding of cause-and-effect relationships and problem solving processes.

These children are unable to classify newly acquired knowledge with the appropriate previously learned knowledge. Although they know and can verbalize the rules of a game, they are unable to apply the rules in practice. This handicap is most evident in their ineffective attempts to apply the rules of grammar in verbal and written communications.

The ability to generalize the application of universals and abstractions from one situation to another is a complex skill. The child may know the rules for self-care, safety, or conservation in the classroom setting, but he cannot generalize this knowledge to other settings, such as home or camp.

EXAMPLE: A group of educable mentally handicapped 12- and 13-year-old boys and girls attended a special purpose camp to study outdoor safety. During the 2-week session, a series of classroom lessons and correlated outdoor laboratory experiences were presented to teach the outdoor safety rules.

It was noted by the instructor and counselors that several of the adolescents could verbalize the safety rules in the classroom but were unable to apply them during laboratory experiences.

Remediation demanded repeated and varied experiences for learning to take place.

For further study on knowledge application, see Meeker (1969); Meeker, Sexton, and Richardson (1970); Reger, Schroeder, and Uschold (1968); Valett (1967); and Wedemeyer and Cejka (1970).

Analysis, synthesis, and evaluation of knowledge

To function effectively in today's changing society, the individual must be capable of analyzing vast amounts of information. Some children, however, lack the ability to analyze the knowledge they receive and classify it as either relevant or irrelevant, or useful or useless for specific purposes.

These children respond to all information as absolute truth that is to be acted on regardless of its irrelevance. They do not recognize obscurities or jokes, nor do they comprehend sarcasm. They are unable to compare new information with previous experiences. It appears that they simply store knowledge without analyzing and comparing it with existing knowledge.

Synthesis requires that the child manipulate and communicate previous experiences and thoughts in an understandable manner. Synthesis may involve retelling a story that was read or heard or relating an event in which the child participated. The child who cannot do this is unable to develop strategies for solving problems. He is incapable of communicating information to others, either through verbal or written communications.

When a person is confronted with a problem, he must evaluate the available knowledge and the adequacy of that knowledge to solve the problem. Some children frequently attempt to solve problems before the necessary information is available.

EXAMPLE: Jackie, a 12-year-old mentally handicapped child, had great difficulty manipulating and associating new information with old information to solve problems.

All humor was lost on Jackie. She would believe and act on the most absurd data. She was frustrated by her abortive attempts to solve everyday problems. When questioned about what she was doing or how she intended to solve the problem, she was unable to communicate a logical plan. In addition, Jackie proceeded to solve problems without the appropriate materials and equipment.

When an evening treasure hunt was scheduled for her cabin group, Jackie would eagerly participate. However, she frequently proceeded to seek out the treasure before it was described and before being informed as to where it was located. She would listen to the counselor's clues but frequently proceeded in the wrong direction or just randomly walked about the camp, looking at the ground. Often,

Jackie would begin the treasure hunt without a flashlight. She had to be reminded repeatedly that she could not see in the dark.

Jackie continued her unsuccessful problem solving efforts throughout the summer.

Camp is an excellent environment in which to remediate this handicap by means of problem-solving activities, and the like.

For further study on analysis, synthesis, and evaluation of knowledge, see Meeker (1969); Meeker, Sexton, and Richardson (1970); Reger, Schroeder, and Uschold (1968); Valett (1967); and Wedemeyer and Cejka (1970).

Comprehension

Some handicapped children are incapable of comprehending information. These exceptional children can pronounce the words and series of words making up the sentences of a story; however, they have little understanding of the meaning of the story. They can solve simple mathematical problems using mechanical skills but have no understanding of the meaning of the results.

They are incapable of paraphrasing and interpreting stories, problems, and directions, even though they may be able to repeat them verbatim.

EXAMPLE: Kyle, an 8-year-old third-grade student, was an excellent word reader. He could recognize and pronounce words about the level anticipated for a child in his grade. Often, Kyle was selected to read ghost stories to his cabin group.

However, if he was asked to paraphrase, interpret, or explain the story in his own words, he was unable to do so. The stories he read had no meaning to him.

Kyle had difficulty following verbal directions. He could repeat the instructions verbatim, but he was unable to explain them.

At camp, the child can read a story and then apply its lesson in role-playing activities, psychodrama, and the like.

For further study on comprehension, see Della-Piana (1968); Meeker (1969); Meeker, Sexton, and Richardson (1970); Reger, Schroeder, and Uschold (1968); Valett (1967); and Wedemeyer and Cejka (1970).

Memory

Memory is the ability to recall previously learned knowledge and experiences. Many children who attend camp have poor memory skills. They cannot remember where they put their personal belongings, the location of their cabin, the camp song, activity directions, or camp rules.

EXAMPLE: Billy, an 11-year-old camper who liked to sing and enjoyed the evening campfires, was unable to remember the camp song.

Billy's counselor noted that the child had great difficulty recalling the words of songs, riddles, and jingles. In addition, Billy was always hunting about the camp for his personal belongings.

Camp is an excellent environment for improving long-term and short-term memory. Memory can be improved by means of songs, cheers, salutes, recalling and discussing recent and distant experiences, and memorizing the names of artifacts, equipment, and groups.

For further study on memory, see Bush and Giles (1968); Kirk and Kirk (1971); Lerner (1971); Meeker (1969); Meeker, Sexton, and Richardson (1970); Reger, Schroeder, and Uschold (1968); Valett (1967); and Wedemeyer and Cejka (1970).

SUBJECT MATTER AREAS

Frequently, the exceptional child's cognitive, psychomotor, and affective handicaps are manifested in his inability to successfully master school subjects.

The child's overall achievement in subject matter areas can be accelerated in the camp setting, either in the camp classroom or in the common camp environment. In this section, several subject matter areas that can be incorporated with little difficulty into the camp program are reviewed and exemplified.

Language

Language is basic to living successfully in modern society. The language skills that the child must learn if he is to communicate effectively and comprehend the communications of others are many and varied. These skills include vocabulary (the ability to understand and say a variety of words), the ability to express oneself verbally, and the ability to speak clearly.

Remediation of language handicaps in the camp setting includes (1) providing a secure environment in which the child can express himself without fear of derogation from instructors, counselors, or peers; (2) providing opportunities to hear and say a variety of words relative to the persons, places, and things in the camp; and (3) providing opportunities to express new or unfamiliar words in appropriate ways. The child's verbal fluency can be developed by encouraging him to use complete sentences and by permitting him to relate stories, jokes, and personal experiences.

EXAMPLE: Leonard's verbal communication during the initial week of camp was negligible. He mumbled his responses, spoke in incomplete sentences, and called many common items "the thing."

During the remainder of the summer, a concerted effort was made to increase his language skills.

Many items in Leonard's cabin and camp were labeled with cards on which were written the names of the items. Leonard and his counselor played a game that involved naming those items. If on two consecutive days Leonard named an item correctly, he was permitted to keep the card. At the end of the week, Leonard was rewarded on the basis of the number of "new" words he had learned. Leonard was encouraged to describe the items named and explain their use. He was encouraged to speak distinctly and in complete sentences.

Leonard's language skills were remediated in other situations, such as story-telling circles, skits, dramatic plays, and puppet shows.

For further study on improving language skills, see Bush and Giles (1968); Cratty (1971); Johnson and Myklebust (1967); Lerner (1971); Smith (1968); and Wedemeyer and Cejka (1970, 1971, 1972).

Individualized instruction.

Reading

A child cannot succeed in school without reading, that is, without the ability to analyze, comprehend, and verbalize the printed word. Reading skills include the language skills previously discussed, word-attack skills, comprehension, spelling, and the ability to verbalize the printed word.

EXAMPLE: With Leonard (see preceding example), increasing his receptive and expressive vocabulary and accelerating his verbal expressive abilities were in effect an effort to develop his reading readiness skills.

The word game played by Leonard and his counselor was extended to include repeating a word correctly when the word was read to Leonard from the card, and recognizing and pronouncing the word when he saw it in written form.

As Leonard's game evolved, he learned to read stories containing "his words." He would dictate a story to his counselor, who would type it. Then Leonard would read and explain the story to the counselor.

Helping a child develop reading skill in the camp setting requires (1) that the child read about interesting and exciting events, (2) that the reading material be composed of words the child can read and would like to read, (3) that the environment be nonthreatening, and (4) that the child's efforts and accomplishments be rewarded.

For further study on developing reading skill, see Brueckner and Bond (1955); Bush and Giles (1968); Cratty (1971); Della-Piana (1968); Edgington (1968); Ferald (1943), Johnson and Myklebust (1967); Lerner (1971); Taylor (1972); and Trela (1968).

Writing

Writing, the skill of expressing oneself in written communications, is highly correlated with fine motor coordination, visual perception, language, and reading. A child with any of these handicaps may have difficulty learning to write.

Camp activities beneficial in preparing the child to write include arts-and-crafts projects, drawing, copying and tracing, painting, and other activities requiring the coordination of eye-hand movements.

EXAMPLE: Six-year-old Ellen had an observable fine-motor handicap. She had difficulty drawing, tracing, constructing with blocks, and the like. Ellen was at the age that most children begin to write. However, she was obviously unable to do so without additional readiness experience.

Remediation included a series of activities that required Ellen to manipulate small objects with increasing precision. She played with Lincoln Logs and Leggo, worked jigsaw puzzles, and engaged in arts-and-crafts projects requiring stringing beads, lacing with boondoggle, and sewing. Ellen also engaged in scribbling, freehand drawing, finger painting, tracing, and copying.

For further study on improving writing skills, see Edington (1968), Johnson and Mykelbust (1967), and Smith (1968).

Spelling

Spelling is the ability to state, in proper sequence, the letters representing the written form of a word. Spelling may be verbal or written.

Spelling requires that the child have skill in writing, reading, and language. This complex skill is developed over a considerable time and requires practice. Normally, it is wise to begin remediation with familiar words and progress from simple to complex words.

EXAMPLE: Kenny, a 10-year-old learning-disabled child, was involved in a remedial spelling project at camp. Kenny was encouraged to learn to spell four new words each day. He was allowed to select his own words but was encouraged to select words that represented things in the camp environment, such as *tree*, *cabin*, *mop*, and *cook*.

Each morning, Kenny and his instructor discussed and selected his "words of the day." Each word was printed by the instructor on a sheet of paper. Kenny copied each word on a 3 × 5 inch practice card. He kept the cards with him throughout the day and practiced in his spare moments.

The sheet of paper on which the instructor wrote the words was given to Kenny's counselor. During the day, the counselor pointed out the items that Kenny's words represented.

The counselor and Kenny practiced the words during rest periods and in the evening.

The boy was praised for all his efforts. Spelling errors were corrected by asking Kenny to spell the word while reading from the card.

The instructor tested Kenny each day before he selected "new words." If Kenny did not spell the words from the day before correctly, they were retained. If he knew two of the four words from the previous day, two "new words" were selected, and so on.

For further study on developing spelling ability, see Edington (1968), Ferald (1943), Learner (1971), and Mann and Suiter (1974).

Arithmetic

Proficiency in arithmetic requires skill in counting, using numbers to represent quantities, adding, subtracting, multiplying, dividing, and applying the basic computational processes to reasoning problems.

The camp can provide a variety of formal and informal opportunities to develop computational skills. Children can learn their numbers and the quantities they represent by counting, sorting, and quantifying things in the environment, such as, trees, flowers, children, adults, and buildings.

Basic addition, subtraction, multiplication, and division skills can be learned in number games such as bingo and lotto. Arithmetic reasoning can be taught by means of real problems. The children can solve problems concerning *how far, how tall, how much, how many,* and so on.

EXAMPLE: Six-year-old Beverly had negligible skill in numbers. She did not recognize the number symbols, nor could she rote count past the number three.

Using a game format, Beverly learned to count to 25 during the summer. Her instructors used number songs and jingles to accelerate learning.

Toward the final days of the session, Beverly began playing number bingo and lotto in an effort to further improve her skill.

For further study on improving computational skills, see Blanco (1972); Brueckner and Bond (1955); Cratty (1971); Mann and Suiter (1974); Smith (1968); Taylor, Artuso, and Hewett (1970b); and Wedemeyer and Cejka (1971).

Creative arts

The camp is the ideal setting for creative art activities. Creative arts encourage and permit children to express their feelings and emotions in an acceptable manner. The child can manifest, without fear of punishment or criticism, his likes, dislikes, fears, anger, and hurt.

Creative arts help the child improve his psychomotor, cognitive, and affective abilities in interesting, stimulating activities. He can learn many skills he failed to learn in the more structured environment of the school.

Among the creative activities that can be incorporated into the camp program are (1) creative dance and movement; (2) skits, psychodramas, plays, and puppetry; (3) arts-and-crafts projects, (4) two-dimensional arts, such as painting and drawing using a variety of media; and (5) three-dimensional arts, such as modeling, casting, and carving in wood, clay, plastic, and sand.

EXAMPLE: Shelia, a 7-year-old camper, seldom showed excitement or interest in camp activities. She went through her days quietly attending to her work. She was not a behavior problem. Shelia's counselor and instructors described her as "emotionally flat"; that is, she never cried or laughed, or appeared excited or sad.

To help her express her emotions more openly, Shelia's counselor encouraged her to participate in puppetry and psychodrama with the members of her cabin group. When Shelia became involved in these activities, she appeared to be a "different" child. Frequently, she would become extremely aggressive; she would get very excited and would attempt to dominate the activity. Initially during the remediation program, she preferred to play the parts of "mean, nasty witches and villians." However as the summer progressed, she began to select roles that involved laughing and clowning.

For further study on the use of creative arts with handicapped children, see Berkowitz and Rothman (1969), and Berlin and Szurek (1965).

Music

Although one of the creative arts, music is singled out here because it has a very special place in the camp. It is this media that is used to develop camp spirit and group cohesion. Music is an excellent behavior management tool.

Children receive great pleasure from learning new songs and from singing around the campfire and in the bus on field trips. They like sentimental songs and humorous songs.

Some children find their "place in the spotlight" during a songfest when they are called on for a solo. They must be helped, praised, and encouraged by an audience.

EXAMPLE: The weekly sing-along and parade with Ms. Carol and Mr. Hart is an exciting time for all the children. They enjoy designing costumes, applying funny faces with grease paint, making musical instruments, and practicing songs.

For further study on the use of music with handicapped children, see Reichard and Blackburn (1973).

Social studies

Many children, not only exceptional children, fail to develop an appreciation for geography and history. Some of the children served in the special camp have never ventured more than a few miles from their city, town, block, or farm. They are unfamiliar with common places, such as the police station, firehouse, post office, zoo, museum, and so on. They are unaware of historically significant places within a few miles of their home.

The special events and field trip programs of the special camp can help these children find answers to the questions "Who am I?" "What is my heritage?" "Where do I live?" and so on.

EXAMPLE: John, the product of an urban ghetto, seldom ventured far from his home or school. He was an intelligent and curious child with a great interest in his racial heritage. John was proud to be black, but he did not know why. The special events program was used to increase John's knowledge and understanding of his racial heritage.

Trips were arranged for John and his friends to visit successful American Blacks in the community. The group visited a judge, fireman, police captain, business man, medical doctor, contractor, and politician. On another trip, the boys saw an exhibit of Black art and sculpture. They visited a museum display depicting Black history. A visit was made to the courthouse in which the famous Dred Scott Decision was made.

Science

The outdoor environment is ideal for increasing a child's knowledge and understanding of his physical environment. At camp, a child can study in a natural environment. He can learn the basic principles of conservation, ecology, and earth science. He learns to observe, explore, and appreciate nature and develops a clear understanding of the life cycle and benefits of flowers, plants, trees, and animals.

The principles of ecology become clear to the child as he explores the washed-out banks of a river or the shore of a dead lake. Conservation of America's natural resources becomes clear to those who walk over a single mile of burnt-out forest. The abstract concepts presented in the classroom take on new meaning and life in the natural environment.

EXAMPLE: Ms. Anne and her children decided to study animal care. The topic was chosen because several of the classroom pets were not being cared for and were occasionally abused by the children. The classroom pets included a rabbit, two turtles, six goldfish, four hamsters, and three baby chicks.

The animal care study unit consisted of (1) a classroom phase, during which the principles of animal care were presented in lectures, discussions, slides, and movies; (2) a laboratory phase, during which the children visited a zoo to observe, hold, pet, brush, and feed the small animals; and (3) a review and summary phase, during which the children applied their skills with the classroom pets and demonstrated their knowledge through projects: skits, plays, collages, drawings, paintings, movies, and scrapbooks.

For further study on teaching science, see Taylor, Artuso, and Hewett (1973).

REFERENCES

Arena, J. (Ed.). *Teaching educationally handicapped children.* San Rafael, Calif.: Academic Therapy Publications, Inc., 1966.

Ashlock, P., and Stephen, A. *Educational therapy in the elementary school*, Springfield, Ill.: Charles C Thomas, Publishers, 1966.

Bakwin, H., and Bakwin, R. M. *Clinical management of behavior disorders in children* (2nd ed.). Philadelphia: W. B. Saunders Co., 1960.

Barsch, R. *Achieving perceptual-motor efficiency*. Seattle: Special Child Publications, 1967.

Berkowitz, P. H., and Rothman, E. P. *The disturbed child: recognition and psychoeducational therapy in the classroom*. New York: New York University Press, 1969.

Berlin, I., and Szurek, S. (Eds.). *Learning and its disorders: clinical approaches to problems of childhood* (Vol. 1). Palo Alto, Calif.: Science & Behavior Books, 1965.

Blanco, R. *Prescriptions for children with learning and adjustment problems*. Springfield, Ill.: Charles C Thomas, Publisher, 1972.

Bloom, B., and others. *Taxonomy of educational objectives: handbook I: cognitive domain*. New York: David McKay Co., Inc., 1956.

Brueckner, L., and Bond, G. L. *The diagnosis and treatment of learning difficulties*. New York: Appleton-Century-Crofts, 1955.

Bush, W., and Giles, M. *Aids to psycholinguistic teaching*. Columbus, Ohio: Charles E. Merrill Publishing Co., 1968.

Conover, D. Physical education for the mentally retarded. *Focus on Exceptional Children*, 1972, **3** (8), 1-10.

Cratty, B. J. *Developmental sequences of perceptual-motor tasks*. Baldwin, N.Y.: Educational Activities, Inc., 1967.

Cratty, B. J. *Motor activity and the education of retardates*. Philadelphia: Lea & Febiger, 1969.

Cratty, B. J. *Active learning: games to enhance academic abilities*. Englewood Cliffs, N.J.: Prentice-Hall, Inc., 1971.

Cruickshank, W. M., Bentzen, F., Ratzeberg, G., and Tannhauser, M. A. *Teaching method for brain-injured and hyperactive children*. Syracuse, N.Y.: Syracuse University Press, 1961.

Della-Piana, G. M. *Readings: diagnosis and prescriptions*. New York: Holt, Rinehart and Winston, Inc., 1968.

Edgington, R. *Helping children with reading disabilities*. Chicago: Developmental Learning Materials, 1968.

Epps, H. O., McCammon, G. B., and Simmons, Q. D. *Teaching devices for children with impaired learning*. Columbus, Ohio: Columbus State School, 1958.

Farrald, R. R., and Schamber, R. G. *A diagnostic and prescriptive technique: handbook I: a mainstream approach to identification, assessment and amelioration of learning disabilities*. Sioux Falls, S.D.: ADAPT Press, 1973.

Ferald, G. *Remedial techniques in basic school subjects*. New York: McGraw-Hill Book Co., 1943.

Fitzhugh, K. B., and Fitzhugh, L. *The Fitzhugh Plus Program*. Galien, Mich.: Allied Education Council, 1966.

Frostig, M., and Horne, D. *The Frostig Program for the Development of Visual Perception: teacher's guide*, Chicago: Follett Corp., 1964.

Frostig, M., and Maslow, P. *Frostig MGL: Move-Grow-Learn: movement education activities*. Chicago: Follett Corp., 1969.

Frostig, M., and Maslow, P. *Movement education: theory and practice*. Chicago: Follett Corp., 1970.

Geddes, D. *Physical activities for individuals with handicapping conditions*. St. Louis: The C. V. Mosby Co., 1974.

Getman, G., Kane, E., Halgren, M., and McKee, G. *Developing learning readiness: teacher's manual*. New York: McGraw-Hill Book Co., 1968.

Goodman, L., and Hammill, D. The effectiveness of the Kephart-Getman activities in developing perceptual-motor and cognitive skills. *Focus on Exceptional Children*, 1973, **4** (9), 1-10.

Hamblin, R., and others. *The humanization processes*. New York: John Wiley & Sons, Inc., 1971.

Haring, N. G., and Phillips, E. L. *Educating emotionally disturbed children*. New York: McGraw-Hill Book Co., 1962.

Harrow, A. J. *A taxonomy of the psychomotor domain: a guide for developing behavior objectives*. New York: David McKay Co., Inc., 1972.

Harvat, R. W. *Physical education for children with perceptual-motor learning disabilities*. Columbus, Ohio: Charles E. Merrill Publishing Co., 1971.

Hewett, F. M. *The emotionally disturbed child in the classroom*. Boston: Allyn & Bacon, Inc., 1968.

Hewett, F. M., and Forness, S. R. *Education of exceptional learners*. Boston: Allyn & Bacon, Inc., 1974.

Johnson, D. J., and Myklebust, H. R. *Learning disabilities: educational principles and practices*. New York: Grune & Stratton, Inc., 1967.

Karnes, M. B. *Helping young children develop language skills*. Arlington, Va.: The Council for Exceptional Children, 1968.

Kephart, N. C. *The slow learner in the classroom* (2nd ed.). Columbus, Ohio: Charles E. Merrill Publishing Co., 1971.

Kessler, J. W. *Psychopathology of childhood*. Englewood Cliffs, N.J.: Prentice-Hall, Inc., 1966.

Kirk, S. A. *Diagnosis and remediation of psycholinguistic abilities*. Urbana, Ill.: University of Illinois Press, 1966.

Kirk, S. A., and Kirk, W. D. *Psycholinguistic learning disabilities: diagnosis and remediation*. Urbana, Ill. University of Illinois Press, 1971.

Krathwohl, D. R., and others: *Taxonomy of educational objectives: handbook II: affective domain*. New York: David McKay Co., Inc., 1956.

Kugelmass, N. I. *The autistic child*. Springfield, Ill.: Charles C Thomas, Publisher, 1970.

Lerner, J. W. *Children with learning disabilities: theories, diagnosis, and teaching strategies*. Boston: Houghton Mifflin Co., 1971.

Madsen, C. H., Jr., and Madsen, C. K. *Teaching discipline: a positive approach for educational development* (2nd ed.). Boston: Allyn & Bacon, Inc., 1974.

Madsen, C. K., and Madsen, C. H., Jr. *Parents/children/discipline: a positive approach*. Boston: Allyn & Bacon, Inc., 1972.

Mann, P. H., and Suiter, P. *Handbook in diagnostic teaching: a learning disabilities approach*. Boston: Allyn & Bacon, Inc., 1974.

Meeker, M. N., *The structure of intellect: it's interpretation and uses*. Columbus, Ohio: Charles E. Merrill Publishing Co., 1969.

Meeker, M. N., Sexton, K. M., and Richardson, M. O. *SDI abilities workbook*. Los Angeles: Loyola University Press, 1970.

Montessori, M. *Dr. Montessori's own handbook*. New York: Schocken Books, Inc., 1965.

Myers, P. I., and Hammill, D. D. *Methods for learning disorders*. New York: John Wiley & Sons, Inc., 1969.

Redl, F. Foreword. In N. Y. Long, W. C. Morse, and R. G. Newman (Eds.), *Conflict in the classroom: the education of emotionally disturbed children*. Belmont, Calif.: Wadsworth Publishing Co., Inc., 1971.

Reger, R., Schroeder, W., and Uschold, K. *Special education: children with learning problems*. New York: Oxford University Press, Inc., 1968.

Reichard, C. L., and Blackburn, D. B. *Music based instruction for the exceptional child*. Denver: Love Publishing Co., 1973.

Rhodes, W. C., and Tracy, M. L. *A study of child variance* (Vol. 1): *theories*. Ann Arbor: The University of Michigan Press, 1972 (a).

Rhodes, W. C., and Tracy, M. L. *A Study of child variance* (Vol. 2): *interventions*. Ann Arbor: The University of Michigan Press, 1972 (b).

Rubin, E. Z., Simson, C. B., and Betwee, M. C. *Emotionally handicapped children and the elementary school*. Detroit, Wayne State University Press, 1966.

Siegel, E. *Helping the brain injured child*. New York: Association for Brain-Injured Children, 1961.

Siegel, E. *Special education in the regular classroom*, New York: The John Day Co., 1969.

Smith, R. M. *Clinical teaching: methods of instruction for the retarded*. New York: McGraw-Hill Book Co., 1968.

Strauss, A. A., and Lehtinen, L. *Psychopathology and education of the brain-injured child*. New York: Grune & Stratton, Inc., 1947.

Taylor, F. D., Artuso, A. A., and Hewett, F. M. *Creative art tasks for children*. Denver: Love Publishing Co., 1970 (a).

Taylor, F. D., Artuso, A. A., and Hewett, F. M. *Individualized arithmetic instruction*. Denver: Love Publishing Co., 1970 (b).

Taylor, F. D., Artuso, A. A., and Hewett, F. M. *Exploring our environment: science tasks*. Denver: Love Publishing Co., 1973.

Taylor, F. D., and others. *Individualized reading instruction: games and activities*. Denver: Love Publishing Co., 1972.

Trela, T. M. *Fourteen remedial reading methods*. Palo Alto, Calif.: Fearon Publishers, 1968.

U.S. Office of Education. *Physical education and recreation for handicapped children: proceedings of a study conference on research and demonstration needs*. Washington, D.C.: U.S. Office of Education, 1969.

Valett, R. E. *The remediation of learning disabilities: a handbook of psychoeducational resource programs*. Belmont, Calif.: Fearon Publishers, 1967.

Valett, R. E. *Programming learning disabilities*. Belmont, Calif.: Fearon Publishers, 1969.

Van Witsen, B.: *Perceptual training activities handbook*. New York: Teacher's College Press, 1967.

Walker, J. E., and Shea, T. M. *Behavior modification: a practical approach for educators*. St. Louis: The C. V. Mosby Co., 1976.

Wallace, G., and Kauffman, J. *Teaching children with learning problems*. Columbus, Ohio: Charles E. Merrill Publishing Co., 1973.

Wedemeyer, A., and Cejka, J. *Creative ideas for teaching exceptional children*. Denver: Love, 1970.

Wedemeyer, A., and Cejka, J. *Learning games for exceptional children: arithmetic and language development activities*. Denver: Love Publishing Co., 1971.

Wedemeyer, A., and Cejka, J. *Language instruction activities*. Denver: Love Publishing Co., 1972.

Wing, J. K. (Ed.). *Early childhood autism: clinical, educational and social aspects*. New York: Pergamon Press, Inc., 1966.

Wing, L. *Autistic children: a guide for parents*. New York: Brunner/Mazel, Inc., 1972.

Woody, R. H. *Behavioral problem children in the schools*. New York: Appleton-Century-Crofts, 1969.

Young, M. A. *Teaching children with special learning needs: a problem-solving approach*. New York: The John Day Co., 1967.

SIX MODEL CAMPS

In Chapters 5 to 8, six model camps for exceptional children are described in detail. The models are the day camp (Chapter 5), the evening/weekend camp and the preschool day camp (Chapter 6), the residential camp for special populations and the special purpose residential camp (Chapter 7), and the wilderness camp (Chapter 8).

Starting in 1967, I have operated the camps described in this section with the financial and logistic assistance of many organizations and groups: United States Office of Education; Illinois Office of Education; Illinois Department of Mental Health; Southern Illinois University at Carbondale and Edwardsville; Roxana (Ill.) Public Schools; Tri-County Special Education District, Murphysboro, Ill.; and others. I have received financial and moral support from many community service clubs: Optimists' Club, junior chambers of commerce, Veterans of Foreign Wars, Lion's Club, Kiwanis Club, and student councils for exceptional children.

These model camps have served many groups of exceptional boys and girls, including those who are severely emotionally disturbed, educable mentally retarded, socially maladjusted, learning disabled, or slow learners. Enrollees have included preschool,

elementary, and junior high age children and, occasionally, children excluded from public school service. The degrees of the children's handicaps have ranged from mild to severe; the majority of the handicaps have been in the moderate-to-severe range.

Following the prescriptive teaching strategy presented in Chapter 3, each camp program has been designed to facilitate the individual camper's development in the psychomotor, affective, and cognitive skill areas. However, in the implementation of each of the programs, primary emphasis has always been focused on the therapeutic benefits of camping for the children.

It can be stated without equivocation that the children enrolled in these programs have been primarily engaged in (1) learning how to learn, regardless of the subject matter content; (2) learning to enjoy and receive satisfaction from learning; and (3) improving their perceptions of themselves as individuals worthy of acceptance and love through growing self-awareness.

The camps have ranged from simple to complex, from a community or school–based recreation camp operated by volunteers on weekends and evenings during the school year to a 6- or 8-week residential camp operated by specialized personnel in permanent physical facilities. Specific programs selected for implementation have been determined by the availability of personnel, funds, materials, equipment, and facilities, as well as by the innovativeness of those responsible for planning.

The camps have also ranged from inexpensive to costly. The evening/weekend camp (Chapter 6) has operated for as little as 50 cents a session per child. The residential camp for severely emotionally disturbed children (Chapter 7) has cost approximately $45.00 a week per child. The day camp (Chapter 5) has been approximately $5.00 a week per child.

Financial assistance, volunteers, facilities, and materials can be obtained for the asking, in most communities, from individuals, service clubs, schools, and public and private children's service agencies. The lack of immediate availability of resources is not a deterrent to planning.

Each of the camps described in this volume has advantages and disadvantages for the children who attend. It is generally true that more intense and extensive experiences (such as those provided by residential camps) have more advantages for the child from a therapeutic point of view than do less intense and extensive experiences (such as those provided by the evening/weekend camp).

It is difficult to initiate the concept of camping for the exceptional child in a community with an expensive and complex model such as the residential camp. Most communities are unwilling to commit substantial sums of money and support to unfamiliar and unproved (to them) programs. Consequently, those interested in camping for the handicapped may find it necessary to implement the less expensive evening/weekend or day camp initially. As the community grows in awareness of the benefits of camping for their exceptional children, more comprehensive programs can be implemented. Of course, regardless of the model introduced into the community, it is to be designed primarily for the benefit of the children.

For reader convenience, a common format is used in Chapters 5 to 8. The following topics are discussed for each camp:

Camp title
Purposes and objectives
Population
    Number of campers
    Age range
    Characteristics
    Classifications of exceptionality
Administration
    Organizational pattern
    Staffing pattern
    Manpower requirements
Physical facilities, equipment, and materials
Personnel training program
Program description
    Hourly, daily, and weekly activities
    Forms, schedules, and calendars
Advantages and disadvantages

Special friends.

CHAPTER 5

The day camp

"I don't understand Martin. Why does he do these things? He should know better," says Mr. Louis, the juvenile officer.

The camp director, looking toward the ball field where a group of boys are playing softball, replies, "Perhaps he's found something he likes—a place he is accepted—and it was worth the chance to him.

"You know, we have many boys and girls at camp who are community and school misfits. But for some reason, they come here every day all summer. Perhaps 2 hours of reading, mathmatics, writing, and obeying are worth it to them when they know they are wanted, can play games, make friends, and go on field trips.

"His isn't an unusual case for us. There are many others—although not as dramatic. Nevertheless, each child communicates to us in some way that he wants to attend camp."

The juvenile officer and camp director are discussing Martin, a 12-year-old camper who arrived at camp a half hour ago, driving a 60-passenger school bus.

Martin's difficulties began during his preschool years when his father disappeared and his mother, in an effort to provide for her children, moved to the city. She worked long hours as a domestic to keep food on the table and had little time for the children.

Martin's school problems started in kindergarten. After 7 stormy years, he was excluded

from school in the fourth grade. During the next year, Martin was sent to the city hospital psychiatric clinic, to the children's center for the severely disturbed, and, finally, to the state hospital. He was discharged from the hospital as "normal but maladjusted" after a 6-week evaluation.

Martin returned to the fifth grade, and the problems began again. In a last desperate effort, public school personnel enrolled Martin in the special day camp. They hoped that during the summer he could be prepared academically and socially to reenter the fifth grade in the fall.

Originally, Martin was reluctant to attend camp. However, he agreed to make the 30-mile round trip journey each day. The first week at camp, Martin was an ideal camper. However, the next 3 weeks were very difficult. Martin had fights and arguments with campers and counselors daily. On these occasions, he was physically restrained and isolated from the group. Discipline was strict, and many demands were made on him.

But he kept coming. Every morning, the boy would get himself out of bed, prepare his breakfast, and catch the 7:30 bus for camp.

On Tuesday morning of the fourth week, Martin had a fight with the bus driver. The driver refused to transport the boy again. The camp director and the driver discussed the problem and agreed that Martin should be excluded from camp for 1 day as punishment. Martin was told that he could not attend camp on Wednesday but should catch the bus on Thursday morning as usual.

On Wednesday morning, the bus arrived without Martin. However, at 9:30 AM, Martin arrived on a bicycle and joined the group. His mother was called at work to pick up Martin and "his" bicycle.

His mother said, "I'll have to call Mr. Louis, the juvenile officer. Martin doesn't have a bike."

Mr. Louis came to the camp and returned Martin and the bicycle to the city. Martin was excluded from camp for an additional day.

The next morning at 10:15, Martin arrived driving a school bus that he had appropriated from the public school garage. He had driven the 15 miles from the city without difficulty. Martin parked the bus and joined his group at the arts-and-crafts center.

The day camp model presented in this chapter is based on Camp R & R (recreation and remediation), a special 6-week day camp that I operated at Southern Illinois University at Edwardsville from 1970 to 1975, and is the result of observations of the actions and reactions of over 250 exceptional boys and girls who attended during that 5-year period.

PURPOSES AND OBJECTIVES

The main purpose of the day camp is to render educational assessment, remediation, recreation, and socialization services to elementary school age emotionally disturbed, socially maladjusted, learning-disabled, and experiencially handicapped children. This purpose is attained through the individualized programming of each child's psychomotor, affective, and cognitive abilities and disabilities.

The day camp is composed of three distinct yet complementary units: an educational assessment and prescriptive programming unit, a remediation unit, and a recreation-socialization unit.

The objectives of the educational assessment and prescriptive programming unit are:
1. To obtain from each child enrolled in the camp a sampling of test results in each of the learning domains: psychomotor, affective, and cognitive. The results of this formal assessment are translated into a tentative individual prescription for learning.
2. To familiarize the child with the assessment or test setting, reduce his anxiety surrounding testing, and instruct him in productive test-taking behavior.
3. To conduct systematic observations of the child's performance during camp activities. The results of this informal assessment are applied to the child's prescription for learning.
4. To transmit the results of the assessment and the tentative prescription for learning to remediation and recreation-socialization personnel for implementation into the child's camp program.
5. To develop and transmit, in cooperation with remediation and recreation-socialization personnel, the child's prescription for learning to the referring agent: parent, teacher, physician, psychologist, or social worker.

The objectives of the remediation unit are:
1. To implement, via planned program activities, the tentative prescription for learning proposed for the individual child by assessment personnel. Implementation focuses primarily on school-related subject matter in the cognitive learning domain.
2. To integrate new data derived from the systematic observations by assessment personnel into the child's prescription for learning.
3. To systematically observe and evaluate the effectiveness of the prescription for learning. Information derived from this function is used to modify the prescription and is transmitted to assessment personnel.
4. To design effective classroom behavior management interventions for the individual child. These interventions are to be included in the prescription for learning.
5. To cooperate with assessment and recre-

ation-socialization personnel in the development of the individual prescription for learning to be transmitted to the referring agent.

The objectives of the recreation-socialization unit are:

1. To implement, via planned program activities, the tentative individual prescription for learning proposed by assessment personnel. Implementation focuses primarily on recreation and socialization activities related to the psychomotor and affective learning domains.
2. To integrate new data derived from systematic observations by assessment personnel into the child's prescription for learning.
3. To systematically observe and evaluate the effectiveness of the prescription for learning. Information derived from this function is used to modify the prescription and is transmitted to assessment personnel.
4. To design and implement effective behavior management interventions for the individual child. These interventions are to be included in the prescription for learning.
5. To facilitate the development of individual and group recreation and socialization skills, via planned activities that are appropriate and meaningful to the child.
6. To plan opportunities for the child to engage in personally rewarding and enriching activities, such as field trips, projects, and games.
7. To cooperate with assessment and remediation personnel in the development of the individual prescription for learning to be transmitted to the referring agent.

POPULATION

The number of exceptional children enrolled in the summer day camp ranged from 35 to 72 during the 5-year period of 1971 to 1975. This number was primarily determined by the severity of the handicapping conditions among the population and by the availability of staff and facilities. It is generally true that a direct ratio exists between the severity of the handicapping conditions represented among the children and the number of staff members required to operate the program efficiently.

Forty appears to be the most manageable number of children for the model presented in this chapter.

Care should be taken to ensure that the overall camper-to-counselor ratio does not exceed 5:1 when mildly to moderately handicapped children are admitted to the day camp. If severely handicapped children attend camp, the camper-to-counselor ratio must be no greater than 3:1. In those special circumstances where autistic and/or psychotic children attend camp, the camper-to-counselor ratio is reduced to 1:1.

These are the maximum ratios allowable if the children are to benefit significantly from their camping experience.

The day camp population is divided into groups of five or six children. Each group is supervised by one or two counselors, depending on the severity of the handicapping conditions.

The children are grouped by age. However, within the age groups, the children are grouped heterogeneously according to skills, ability, sex, handicap, and so on. For example, during the summer of 1975, the 12 children in the 9- to 11-year age group were organized into 2 groups of 6 children. Each group was organized homogeneously according to age (each group was composed of 9-, 10-, and 11-year-old children) and heterogenously according to sex, handicap, degree of handicap, interests, and abilities. No group contained a single boy or a single girl. There must always be a like-sex child in each camper group.

The children admitted to the day camp range in age from 6 to 11 years. Experience indicates that younger children do not have the skills required to participate productively in the camp's activities, older boys and girls are bored with the activities, which they consider "baby stuff."

There are few restrictions on the classifications of exceptional children admitted to the day camp. Experience indicates that learning-disabled, educable mentally retarded, and experiencially handicapped children benefit most from remedial activities, special events, and field trips. Emotionally disturbed and socially maladjusted children benefit greatly from socialization and recreation activities, especially small-group activities.

ADMINISTRATION

Camps for the handicapped do not offer full-year employment for staff personnel. Consequently, the day camp is mainly staffed by part-time, inexperienced personnel who are unfamiliar with policies and procedures. In addition, precamp training periods are usually brief—4 or 5 days at most.

The camp coordinator is confronted with still another problem on the first day of camp: he must coordinate and develop cohesion among 2 or 3 assistant coordinators, several counselors, several volunteers, and 40 or more children who are not only unfamiliar with policies and procedures but are unknown to one another.

As a result of this problem, a centralized administrative organization is recommended for the day camp. In this administrative organization one person, the coordinator, is responsible for all final decisions. In this way, the probability of confusion and dissension among the staff concerning children, programs, supervision, employment, and behavior management is minimized.

The camp coordinator is responsible for all final decisions and delegates his authority to two assistant coordinators, who, with the coordinator, make up the administrative team. One assistant is responsible for the educational assessment and prescriptive programming unit and for the remediation unit. The other assistant coordinator is responsible for the recreation-socialization unit. If the maximum population of 70 children is admitted to the day camp, a third assistant coordinator is employed, who is responsible, under the coordinator's supervision, for purchasing, transportation, clerical staff, field trip and special events planning, and health care. The assistants coordinate their activities with the coordinator and one another during daily administrative team meetings.

Each group of five of six children is supervised by one or two full-time counselors, depending on the characteristics of the campers. Group counselors are responsible to the assistant coordinator within whose jurisdiction they fall during a specific activity period. For example, during remediation they are responsible to the assistant in charge of the remediation unit; during field games they are responsible to the assistant in charge of the recreation-socialization unit.

Other counselors, called special counselors, are assigned specific duties, such as remediation, assessment, special events, camp store operations, arts and crafts, and so on. These special counselors are responsible to the assistant coordinator within whose jurisdiction they function.

Volunteers are responsible to the counselor or special counselor to whom they are assigned.

Children are the responsibility of their counselor. In situations where both a counselor and a special counselor are working with a group of campers, they share the responsibility of the children. However, if a disagreement arises, the counselor's decision is final; his decision overrules that of the special counselor.

The coordinator, assistant coordinators, and clerical personnel should be full-time, paid employees. These individuals must be qualified for their duties and responsibilities by either training, experience, or both.

Assistant coordinators can often be recruited from among the ranks of recreation specialists, physical education teachers, special education teachers, and psychologists seeking summer employment. The assistant coordinators must be experienced in the functions of the units to which they are assigned.

Counselors and special counselors can be recruited from universities, colleges, community colleges, and high schools in the vicinity of the camp. Frequently, young people seeking employment as counselors are studying to be recreation specialists, physical education teachers, special education teachers, or social service personnel. Some colleges and universities grant academic credit to students participating in special camps. The granting of credit is frequently contingent on the student's paying tuition, attending lectures and seminars, and being supervised by personnel approved by the credit-granting institution. Although counselors' wages are minimal, they should be paid employees of the camp.

Community volunteers are helpful additions to the camp staff. Many volunteers have unique skills that can be beneficial to the children. At a minimum, volunteers must be interested in helping handicapped children and willing to contribute their time consistently throughout the summer.

PHYSICAL FACiLITIES, EQUIPMENT, AND MATERIALS

Extensive physical facilities, equipment, and materials are not required for the day camp. However, the facilities, equipment, and materials available must be compatible with the purposes, objectives, and programs of the camp.

The basic physical facilities and equipment needed are:

A large play area for field sports. This must be of adequate size for three or four activities to be going on simultaneously, such as baseball, volleyball, badminton, and kickball.

A shaded area with adequate picnic tables and benches for all campers and staff. This area is to be used for several activities going on simultaneously, such as arts and crafts, dramatic play, table games, and lunches.

A sheltered area of adequate size for all campers and staff on rainy days. This area must be large enough for several activities to be going on simultaneously.

Enough outdoor and indoor classrooms containing desks, tables, and chairs of appropriate adult and child sizes to provide for at least 50% of the campers and staff at one time. These areas are for assessment and remediation activities and must be located so as to minimize visual and auditory distractions.

Sanitary facilities. If indoor sanitary facilities are not adequate, portable chemical facilities can be rented for a reasonable fee.

Water. Hot and cold water must be available for washing and drinking and for the arts-and-crafts projects. At least one outdoor faucet is needed.

Office space and equipment. Among the basic office needs are desks, chairs, typewriters, file cabinets, amd duplicating equipment.

Telephone service. Adequate and immediately available telephone service is necessary for both routine and emergency communications.

Storage facilities for equipment and materials.

Swimming facilities. Either a pool or designated beach area must be available for swimming. This area must be designed to facilitate close and constant supervision of the campers.

Time-out or isolation facilities for severely disturbed children.

Among the materials and equipment needed for efficient operation of the camp are:

Record player
Cassette player-recorder
16-mm movie projector and screen
35-mm slide projector and screen
Educational and entertaining films and filmstrips
Language Master (specialized player/recorder used in language development)
Tachistoscope (specialized filmstrip projector used in visual perceptual and visual memory training)
Overhead projector

A wide variety of assessment, remediation, and recreation materials and equipment are needed for the effective and efficient operation of the day camp. However, instructional materials should be compatible with those used by the schools referring children to the camp.

PERSONNEL TRAINING PROGRAM

All camp personnel (coordinator, assistant coordinators, counselors, special counselors, and volunteers) attend the personnel training program.

Staff training and supervision are continuous processes beginning 1 week before the arrival of the campers and terminating 1 week after the children depart. The training program discussed here assumes that the primary staff (coordinator and assistant coordinators) are professionals in the fields of recreation, physical education, education, special education, social service, or mental health and that they are responsible for the supervision of all other staff members.

Phase 1: precamp orientation workshop

A 1-week precamp workshop is conducted before the arrival of the campers. The workshop is conducted by the primary staff and consultants and adheres to the following schedule:

DAY 1 Overview of the day camp (purpose, objectives, policies, procedures, schedules, and activities)

DAY 2 Assessment (training in the administration, scoring, and interpretation of the basic assessment instruments to be used at the camp)

DAY 3 Prescriptive teaching (procedures, methods, and materials available for preparing prescriptions for learning in the cognitive, affective, and psychomotor learning domains)

DAY 4 A day at camp (Playing the roles of counselor, special counselor, volunteer, and camper, the entire staff actually participates in a typical day at camp)

DAY 5 Planning (Using preadmission data, the staff plans a tentative 1-week activity program, including formal assessment, for each child)

Phase 2: on-the-job training

On-the-job training and supervision is conducted by the primary staff on a daily basis throughout the session. The coordinator and assistant coordinators review lesson plans and observe campers, counselors, and volunteers during activities.

Opportunities for individual counselor-supervisor discussions are scheduled throughout each day at the counselor's convenience. These supervisory discussions are conducted daily, if possible, during the initial days of the camp session; as the session progresses and the counselor's skill increases, they are held less frequently. Supervisory discussions are of greatest benefit to the counselor if they focus on his *real* concerns relative to individual campers and the activity program.

Daily planning, coordination, and evaluation meetings are conducted by the individual counselors for the volunteers assigned to them. At these sessions, the plans for the day are developed, reviewed, discussed, and evaluated by the staff members directly responsible for the campers.

Phase 3: postcamp evaluation workshop

The week after the children are dismissed from camp is devoted to the program evaluation and to the preparation of individual teaching prescriptions.

The following tasks are accomplished:

1. Organization, writing, and reproduction of a final prescription for learning for each child on the basis of his formal and informal assessment and camp performance. This prescription is transmitted to referring personnel for implementation during the school year.

2. Evaluation of the entire camp program, in writing, as it was conducted and experienced by the staff.

3. Inventory and storage of all materials and equipment.

The primary purposes of the training program are the transmission of knowledge and skills to the individual staff members concerning camp policies and procedures and the coordination of activities.

An equally important but less obvious purpose of the training program is its effect on the personal affective behavior (feelings and frustrations) of the individual staff members. During daily sessions, the members are encouraged to express their feelings about themselves, their effects on the children, the children's behavior, and so on. These sessions provide an opportunity for the staff members to reduce their anxiety. The primary staff members must accept the feelings of those under their supervision and offer them support, encouragement, and most important, practical suggestions for change.

PROGRAM DESCRIPTION

Variations of the materials and program presented here were utilized during the summers of 1971 through 1975. The model should be modified according to the needs of the children in the specific situation.

Assessment and prescriptive programming unit

The formal assessment instruments administered by unit personnel are:

Auditory Discrimination Test (Wepman, 1958)
Developmental Test of Visual-Motor Integration (Beery, 1967)
Purdue Perceptual-Motor Survey (Roach and Kephart, 1966)
Slosson Intelligence Test for Children and Adults (Slosson, 1963)
Wide Range Achievement Test (Jastak, Bijou, and Jastak, 1965)

These instruments are administered to each child during the first week of the session unless they have been recently administered by referring agency personnel and the results have been forwarded to the camp. Approximately 4 hours are needed to complete the formal assessment.

Formal assessment data are supplemented by the information of the preadmission forms discussed in Chapter 3. If the completed forms are not available before the child arrives at camp, they are completed by recreation-socialization and remediation personnel during the initial week of the session.

Assessment personnel continue the child's evaluation, in cooperation with other camp personnel, throughout the session by means of observation and specialized assessment instruments as needed.

All assessment data are incorporated into the final prescription for learning. The child's prescription for learning is developed from the results of the formal and informal assessment according to the prescriptive teaching model described in Chapter 3.

Remediation unit

All children attending camp participate in remedial programs for a minimum of 2 hours daily during the 6-week session. The program includes individual instruction in school-related, preacademic and academic skills.

Among the subjects presented to the children are:

Language development and communications skills
Conceptualization skill development
Memory training
Tactile discrimination skill training
Visual-perceptual training
Auditory-perceptual training and listening skills
Fine motor coordination
Reading
Writing
Arithmetic
Spelling
General and specific information enrichment
Social studies
Physical sciences

The children's time with remediation personnel is divided about equally between individual and small-group activities. During individual activities, emphasis is on achievement and/or mastery. During small-group activities, in addition to achievement emphasis is focused on group participation, the development of interpersonal skills, and the use of social amenities.

Recreation-socialization unit

Recreation and socialization activities are planned to respond to the child's functional level and individual needs. This program includes individual and group activities. Although the children participate in group activities, minimal emphasis is placed on interchild competition. The children are encouraged to develop their personal skills and to compete with themselves. Among the activities presented by unit personnel are:

Gross motor training
   Walking
   Crawling
   Running
   Skipping
   Hopping
   Jumping
   Rolling

Gross motor training—cont'd
 Throwing
 Catching
 Hitting
Tumbling
Balance beam activities
Swinging
Field and circle games
Foot races
Obstacle course and relay races
Tug-of-war
Creative dance and creative movement
Swimming
Softball
Tag
Volleyball
Badminton
Hiking
Camp-outs and Cookouts
Fishing
Nature study
Arts and crafts
Dramatics and puppetry
Woodwork
Finger and water color painting
Sand and clay sculpturing
Singing
Food preparation
Outdoor safety

Also included in the recreation-socialization unit's responsibilities are various special activities:

Interpersonal skill development: Emphasis is focused on the development of interpersonal and group skills by means of group discussions, cooperative camper-counselor planning and evaluation of activities, and individual camper-counselor discussions.

Movies: Educational and entertaining movies are viewed by the campers during the summer. This activity is offered (1) after unusually tiring physical activity, (2) to prepare children for field trips, and (3) on rainy days.

Table games: Checkers, chess, Tip-it, cards, and so on, are scheduled daily immediately before or after lunch. This provides the children a time to relax while developing skills that can be used in the noncamp setting.

Special events: Fridays at camp are reserved for the special events program, which in-

cludes visits to places of historical and educational interest, parties, carnivals, and special athletic events.

Lunch: The lunch period is a planned activity. Frequently, children are enrolled who must be trained in proper eating habits and table manners.

All activities not specifically assigned to the other two units are the responsibility of recreation-socialization personnel.

Weekly and daily planning

All remediation and recreation-socialization activities are preplanned for each child and/or small group of children to be involved in the activity. Instructors and counselors use a variety of forms to facilitate the organization of the program.

Form A (Fig. 7) is used in the weekly planning of activities. Instructors and counselors are requested *not* to select more than six objectives per week. The same objective or objectives may remain the focus of the program for more than 1 week. Objectives are written in specific behavioral terminology. They may be selected from the cognitive, affective, or psychomotor learning domains.

The objectives utilized for the planning activities for week 1 are determined by the prescription for learning prepared during the fifth day of the precamp orientation workshop. However, after the initial week of the session, objectives are determined by the child's responses to the week's activities plus any additional assessment data derived by assessment unit personnel.

Form B (Fig. 8) is used to assist the instructor and counselor in converting the weekly objectives into time periods, specific activities, and locations for the activities. It is also helpful to the coordinator, assistant coordinators, and assessment personnel, who must observe the child during the week, provide supervision for counselors and instructors, and facilitate the availability of the needed personnel, equipment, materials, and space.

Form C (Fig. 9) is used to facilitate the planning of specific activities. Instructors and counselors complete Form B for all activities

Text continued on p. 109.

FORM A

Child or group _____

Instructors, counselors, assessors _____

_____

Dates: from _____ to _____

Assessment objective 1 ___(With all objectives, state in behavioral terms what will be done to

attain the objective.) _____

Subobjectives:

a. _____

b. _____

c. _____

d. _____

e. _____

Comments _____

_____

Remedial objective 1 _____

_____

Subobjectives:

a. _____

b. _____

c. _____

d. _____

e. _____

Comments _____

_____

Remedial objective 2 _____

_____

Subobjectives:

a. _____

b. _____

c. _____

d. _____

e. _____

Comments _____

_____

Continued.

Fig. 7. Weekly plan for the day camp.

FORM A—cont'd

Recreation-socialization objective 1 _____

_____

Subobjectives:

a. _____

b. _____

c. _____

d. _____

e. _____

Comments _____

_____

Recreation-socialization objective 2 _____

_____

Subobjectives:

a. _____

b. _____

c. _____

d. _____

e. _____

Comments _____

_____

Other objectives _____

_____

Subobjectives:

a. _____

b. _____

c. _____

d. _____

e. _____

Comments _____

_____

Fig. 7, cont'd. Weekly plan for the day camp.

FORM B

Child or group _____

Instructor, counselors, assessors _____

_____

Day of week _____ Date _____

Time segment	Activity	Equipment and location
9:00-9:30 AM	(Briefly describe the activity.)	(Be as specific as possible.)
9:30-10:00		
10:00-10:30		
10:30-11:00		
11:00-11:30		
11:30-12:00		
12:00-12:30 PM		
12:30-1:00		
1:00-1:30		
1:30-2:00		

Fig. 8. Daily record for the day camp.

FORM C

Child or group _____

Instructor or counselor _____

Day of week _____ Date _____

Specific objectives	Equipment and materials		
(State the specific objective to be emphasized in this activity in specific behavioral terminology and in terms of camper performance.)	(State the type and quantity of equipment and materials needed for the activity.)		

Time and location	Procedure	Formation	Teaching points
(State where and when the activity is to be conducted.)	(Describe the activity to be conducted to attain the objective. Explanation should focus on activity sequence, group formations, motivation techniques, and behavior management techniques.)	(For recreation activities, present a diagram of the formation.)	(State points to be stressed reviewed, and/or discussed with the individual or group after the activity.)

Evaluation (Evaluate the activity relative to (1) attainment of the objective, (2) camper interest and behavior, (3) efficiency of method, and (4) level of active participation.)

Fig. 9. Activity plan for the day camp.

FORM D

Child or group _____

Instructor or counselor _____   Date _____

Target behavior	Intervention	Comments
Behaviors to be increased 1. (In specific behavioral ter- 2. minology, state the three 3. behaviors the child or group is to increase.)	1. (In specific behavioral ter- 2. minology, describe the in- 3. tervention to be applied to change the target be- havior.)	1. (Note information on the 2. characteristics of the be- 3. havior before the imposition of the intervention: type, in- tensity, duration, and frequency. Note informa- tion on methods to be used to evaluate the effects of the intervention.)
Behavior to be decreased 1. (In specific behavioral ter- 2. minology, state the three 3. behaviors the child or group is to decrease.)	1. (In specific behavioral ter- 2. minology, describe the in- 3. tervention to be applied to change the target behavior.)	1. (Note information on the 2. characteristics of the be- 3. havior before the imposition of the intervention: type, in- tensity, duration, and frequency. Note informa- tion on methods to be used to evaluate the effects of the intervention.)

Fig. 10. Behavior intervention plan.

Time	Monday				Tuesday				Wednesday				Thursday				Friday			
	AB	CD	EF	GH	AB	CD	EF	GH	AB	CD	EF	GH	AB	CD	EF	GH	AB	CD	EF	GH
8:00-9:00	Preparation—planning time for counselors and instructors →→→																			
9:00-9:30	S	R	S	R	SW	R	SW	R	S	R	S	R	SW	R	SW	R		R		
9:30-10:00	S	R	S	R	SW	R	SW	R	S	R	S	R	SW	R	SW	R		R		
10:00-10:30	R	S	R	S	R	SW	R	SW	R	S	R	S	R	SW	R	SW		R		
10:30-11:00	R	S	R	S	R	SW	R	SW	R	S	R	S	R	SW	R	SW		R		
11:00-11:30	S	R	S	R	S	R	S	R	S	R	S	R	S	R	S	R		SE		
11:30-12:00	L	R	L	R	L	R	L	R	L	R	L	R	L	R	L	R		SE		
12:00-12:30	TG	L	TG	L	TG	L	TG	L	TG	L	TG	L	TG	L	TH	L		SE		
12:30-1:00	R	TG	R	TG	R	TG	R	TG	R	TG	R	TG	R	TG	R	TG		SE		
1:00-1:30	R	S	R	S	R	S	R	S	R	S	R	S	R	S	R	S		SE		
1:30-2:00	Quiet time, singing, special activities, and all group meetings																			
2:00-3:00	Evaluation of day's activities and planning time for counselors and instructors																			

R, remediation; *S*, recreation-socialization; *L*, lunch; *TG*, table games; *SE*, special events; *SW*, swimming.

Fig. 11. Weekly schedule for the day camp.

directly correlated with the weekly objectives stated on Form A.

Form D (Fig. 10) is used to facilitate planning, organization, orderly implementation, and evaluation of the behavior management interventions to be applied to change the behavior of a child or group. (See Chapter 9 for a detailed discussion of a variety of behavior management techniques applicable in the camp setting.)

Weekly activity schedule

The weekly activity schedule presented in Fig. 11 was used in the summer of 1973 with a group of 48 handicapped children. During that summer, the available physical facilities prohibited indoor activities for more than 50% of the population at one time.

The 48 campers were divided by age and functional ability into 4 sections of 12 campers. Each section of 12 children was divided into 2 tribes. These tribes were titled A (Arapaho), B (Braves), C (Chicksaw), and so on. The two tribes in each section were programmed on the same schedule to facilitate intertribe and large-group activities.

The schedule provided the camper with a 5-hour daily activity program, including 2 hours of remediation activities and 3 hours of recreation-socialization activities (1½ hours of recreation-socialization, ½ hour for table games, ½ hour for quiet time and large-group activities, and ½ hour for lunch).

Not presented on the schedule but included in the daily program were a 15-minute preparation and planning session from 9:00 to 9:15 AM to familiarize the children with the day's activities, a 10-minute recess during midmorning for a snack (juice and cookies), and a 15-minute evaluation and planning session at approximately 1:15 to 1:30 PM.

The 1:30 to 2:00 PM period was devoted to group singing, skits, projects, and planning of future events.

Calendar of events

The calendar of events presented here was used for the same (1973) 6-week summer day camp session. Week 1 was used for the pre-

camp orientation workshop; the postcamp evaluation workshop was held during week 8. The campers were in attendance from weeks 2 through 7.

WEEK 1	Precamp orientation workshop
MONDAY	Overview of camp
TUESDAY	Assessment program
WEDNESDAY	Prescriptive teaching model
THURSDAY	Day at camp
FRIDAY	Planning of children's program for week 2

WEEK 2	
MONDAY	Regular schedule
TUESDAY	Regular schedule
WEDNESDAY	Regular schedule
THURSDAY	Regular schedule
FRIDAY	Remediation; day at the lake (fishing, boating, swimming, and picnic)

WEEK 3	
MONDAY	Regular schedule
TUESDAY	Regular schedule
WEDNESDAY	Regular schedule
THURSDAY	National holiday
FRIDAY	Thursday schedule

WEEK 4	
MONDAY	Regular schedule
TUESDAY	Regular schedule
WEDNESDAY	Regular schedule
THURSDAY	Regular schedule
FRIDAY	Remediation; day at St. Louis Children's Zoo and picnic in the park

WEEK 5	
MONDAY	Regular schedule
TUESDAY	Regular schedule
WEDNESDAY	Regular schedule
THURSDAY	Regular schedule
FRIDAY	Remediation; day in the park and picnic (visit to St. Louis Art Museum or Museum of Science and Natural History)

WEEK 6	
MONDAY	Regular schedule
TUESDAY	Regular schedule (camp-out, Tribes E, F, G, and H)
WEDNESDAY	Regular schedule (camp-out, Tribes E, F, G, and H)
THURSDAY	Regular schedule
FRIDAY	Remediation; special athletic events and picnic

A daily planning session.

WEEK 7

MONDAY	Regular schedule
TUESDAY	Regular schedule
WEDNESDAY	Regular schedule
THURSDAY	Regular schedule
FRIDAY	Carnival day (9:00 AM to noon, parents and guests invited); campers dismissed at 12:30 PM; staff party (1:00 to ?)

WEEK 8	Postcamp evaluation workshop
MONDAY	Assessment and prescriptive programming unit evaluated
TUESDAY	Final prescriptions for learning begun
WEDNESDAY	Remediation unit evaluated; final prescriptions for learning continued
THURSDAY	Overall camp program, including administration and supervision, evaluated; recommendations for change written; final prescriptions for learning continued
FRIDAY	Equipment and materials inventoried and stored; final prescriptions for learning completed

Special events scheduled for Fridays are determined by the needs of the campers, the availability of transportation, and the location of the camp. The special events included on the calendar of events presented here are only suggestions.

Among the special events that have been scheduled over the past 5 years at Camp R & R, which is located near St. Louis, are:

Visits to:
  Art Museum
  Museum of Science and Natural History
  St. Louis Medical Museum
  National Museum of Transport
  Old Courthouse
  Jefferson Memorial
  Inner-city business district
  Missouri Botanical Garden
  St. Louis Zoo and Children's Zoo
Picnics at several city and county parks, which included swimming, fishing, boating, and field games
Visits to university campuses

At the creek: a place to hope.

Carnival days
Special athletic events
Theatrical productions
Concerts
Baseball games
Camp-outs in state, county, and private parks

The list of special events is limited only by the imagination of those responsible for program planning, the availability of transportation, and the needs of the campers.

During week 6 of the 1973 session, an overnight camp-out was scheduled for four of the tribes (the older campers). The counselors and instructors assigned to the younger campers (ages 5, 6, and 7 years) did not think that their groups were ready to participate in an overnight campout.

Details for planning and executing the camp-out are presented in Chapter 8.

ADVANTAGES AND DISADVANTAGES

The advantages of the day camp for handicapped children are:

1. Preadmission data about the child are easily obtainable from parents, teachers, physicians, and others in the community.
2. Campers can be assigned to small groups to facilitate the individualization of their assessment and activity programs.
3. The probability of developing productive communications with parents, teachers, therapists, and physicians is enhanced.
4. A 6-week session assures that the child will be in attendance for sufficient time to complete the assessment program and to plan and implement a viable prescription for learning.
5. The 6-week session facilitates the actual remediation of some of the child's handicaps in the mild-to-moderate range of severity.
6. Many volunteers, counselors, and instructors are available in the community.
7. The needed physical facilities are minimal.

8. The organization and administration is simple in comparison with other models.
9. It is inexpensive.
10. It is visible to the community and consequently receives excellent support.

The disadvantages of the camp are:

1. It is not the most effective model presented in this volume for the remediation of severe behavior and learning handicaps.
2. Transportation to and from camp is often difficult to arrange and administer. Transportation, especially voluntary transportation, is frequently unreliable.
3. Transportation for special events is expensive.
4. Facilities for self-care, behavior management, and recreation, such as showers, isolation facilities, and swimming facilities, are often unavailable.
5. Absenteeism among campers, staff, and volunteers is high.
6. Parental concern often inhibits the implementation of desirable interventions with consistency.
7. A 24-hour-a-day therapeutic milieu cannot be established; thus, much of the program's potential impact on the child may be diluted in the home and community during noncamp hours.

REFERENCES

Bain, M., and Grosso, C. A. Little bit of everything. *Parks and Recreation*, February 1974, pp. 42-55.

Beery, K. Developmental Test of Visual-Motor Integration. Chicago: Follett Corp., 1967.

Evry, A. A summer program for culturally deprived children. *Art Education*, 1967, **20**(7), 24-27.

Hammontree, J. L., and Monkman, J. A. Development of summer day camps for the mentally retarded in a rural community. *Journal of Health, Physical Education, and Recreation*, 1973, **44**(5), 59-62.

Hilsendager, D. R., Jack, H. K., and Mann, L. The Buttonwood Farms Project: a physical education-recreation program for emotionally disturbed and mentally retarded children. *Journal of Health, Physical Education, and Recreation*, 1968, **39**(3), 46-48.

Jastak, J. F., Bijou, S. W., and Jastak, S. R. *Wide Range Achievement Test.* Wilmington, Del: Guidance Associates of Delware, Inc., 1965.

Oliver, J. M. Add challenge with variety in activities. *Journal of Health, Physical Education, and Recreation*, 1966, **37**(4), 30-32.

Pugh, S. A. Psychiatric experiment. *Recreation*, 1960, **53**, 222-223.

Roach, E., and Kephart, N. C. The Purdue Perceptual-Motor Survey. Columbus, Ohio: Charles E. Merrill Publishing Co., 1966.

Ryan, P. J. Playground plans for the mentally retarded. *Recreation*, 1955, **48**, 166-167.

Scheer, R. M., and Sharpe, W. M. Social group work in day camping with institutionalized delinquent retardates. *Training School Bulletin*, 1963, **60**(3), 138-147.

Shipp, R. E. Expanding program services. *Parks and Recreation*, 1968, **3**(10), 43-56.

Slosson, R. I. *Slosson Intelligence Test for Children and Adults.* East Aurora, N.Y.: Slosson Educational Publications, 1963.

Stockhamer, R. Day camp for the mentally retarded. *Recreation*, 1963, **56**, 236-237.

Wepman, J. M. *Auditory Discrimination Test.* Chicago: Language Research Associates, 1958.

Yeates, J. C. Playground programs for handicapped children. *Recreation*, 1954, **47**, 280-281.

Time to be alone.

CHAPTER 6

Special purpose day camps

In this chapter two special purpose day camps are described: the evening camp and the preschool day camp.

These programs are designed to meet the needs of handicapped children within the confines of their communities. It has been my experience that ongoing compensatory and enrichment programs for handicapped children do not exist in the vast majority of towns and cities.

In addition, many of the cognitive, psychomotor, and affective disabilities of the handicapped child cannot be responded to in the present-day special education programs offered by the schools. This is largely because of a lack of time, personnel, and community and administrative support. However, it is generally recognized that if the handicapped child is to receive an equal opportunity to compete successfully in the school and community with his nonhandicapped peers, he needs additional assistance.

In most communities, afterschool, evening, and weekend activity programs for handicapped individuals are not available as frequently as are similar programs for the nonhandicapped population. Seldom do we find a variety of programs for the handicapped offered by organizations such as the YMCA, the YWCA, Boy Scouts, Girl Scouts, the Catholic Youth Organization, or 4-H. The handicapped child, as a result of the community's lack of responsiveness to his needs, spends much of his free time in-

113

volved in pursuits of questionable value. He occupies himself by hanging around his house or a street corner, watching television, listening to the radio, or going to the movies. The child has scant opportunities to develop satisfying and meaningful leisure-time skills.

The evening camp presented in this chapter responds to these unmet needs.

Preschool programs for handicapped children other than the culturally disadvantaged are now beginning to receive national attention in the United States. However, many severely handicapped preschool children continue to be deprived of the compensatory educational experiences they need to prepare them to enter kindergarten, first grade, or a special education program.

Without a "head start," these young children begin school unable to compete with their nonhandicapped peers. The preschool day camp presented in this chapter is designed to facilitate the child's development of the skills he needs to enter a formal school program.

THE EVENING CAMP

"Mary, where are you going?"

"To school, Mom. It's camp night."

"I don't understand you kids. You whine and complain about going to school every day; yet you insist on running over there at night. What's going on, anyway?"

"Aw, Mom, this is really great. You ought to see it. We have counselors; mine's Ms. Sandi. They're like teachers, but we call them counselors.

"Anyway, while some of the parents are talking in the other room with our 'real' teachers and some man, we get together with the counselors and Mr. George to plan activities. Mr. George is in charge of everything.

"We can do almost anything we want, but we have to agree to bring our homework and study for about an hour. But that's not too bad, because we have fun, too."

"Sounds pretty good, Mary. What do you do besides homework?"

"Lots of things. We get to choose whatever we want. We can do things like play cards and games, put puzzles together, do woodburning, cook or bake, and play outdoors. I like to help make the snack with Ms. Sandi and our group.

"The boys play basketball and do tumbling, wrestling, and things like that. At the end of the night, we all get together to talk, sing, or play games. I like it.

"I'm making a penholder to give Dad for Father's Day. Don't tell him. Mr. Tom, the arts-and-crafts guy, is helping me.

"And in a couple of weeks, we're having a barbecue for all the families—kids and all.

"It's really fun, Mom. You ought to come with me. You don't need a babysitter. The little kids can stay with me. Mr. George says it's OK. They can play with us."

"I'm really busy tonight, Mary. I have to finish this ironing and wash my hair for work tomorrow. Maybe next week. Remind me."

"OK, Mom. See you in a couple of hours. Don't worry about me. I'll be with Lois."

PURPOSES AND OBJECTIVES

The evening camp is designed to supplement the instructional program provided the exceptional child in the regular and/or special classroom and to facilitate the development of his leisure-time activity skills.

Although described here as an independent entity, the evening camp is most beneficial to the child when it is coordinated with his school program and with a parent education program.

More specifically, the camp provides the child opportunities to engage in activities to (1) increase his fine motor, gross motor, and perceptual skills (psychomotor learning domain); (2) develop his recreational skills and a positive attitude toward the use of his leisure time; (3) increase his emotional self-control and develop appropriate social skills; and (4) increase his competency in pre-academic and academic learning, as prescribed by his regular teacher, under the supervision and with the assistance of a trained counselor.

The evening camp can be a valuable supplement to the child's remedial program in each of the three learning domains: psychomotor, affective, and cognitive. However, the program's effectiveness is highly dependent on the level of cooperation given by the child's regular teacher and other school personnel.

The teacher, in discussions with the camp

staff and by assigning the child appropriate home-study projects on camp nights, guides efforts to remediate the child's specific disabilities. School personnel transmit assessment data to the staff on the child's functional abilities and disabilities. This information is used as a basis for an individual prescription for learning.

The camp is of assistance to school and community psychological and social service personnel responsible for the child's assessment, diagnosis, and remediation. During camp, the child is available to authorized personnel for observation, interviewing, and formal assessment. The camp staff may be trained to collect the diagnostic data needed by noncamp professionals for the child's case study.

When the camp is conducted in concert with parent group activities, information about the child's functioning can be shared with the coordinator of the parent education program. The reverse is also true; many times, information obtained during parent group sessions can be of value in planning the child's camp activities.

In addition, the camp staff provides supervision for the siblings of the handicapped child during parent meetings. Frequently, parents are prevented from attending the parent education program because they are unable to employ a responsible person to supervise their children.

If appropriate facilities are available, parents can observe their children during camp activities. Parent group personnel must supervise these observations, which can be instrumental in stimulating discussion.

The evening camp includes a formal assessment program of limited scope. Usually, neither trained personnel nor time is available to conduct a comprehensive assessment of the child's cognitive, affective, and psychomotor abilities and disabilities. The camp staff depends primarily on school and community personnel for assessment data in the cognitive and affective domains. To assess the child's psychomotor abilities, camp personnel administer the following instruments:

Purdue Perceptual-Motor Survey (Roach and Kephart, 1966)

Frostig Developmental Test of Visual Perception (Frostig, LeFever, and Whittlesey, 1961)
Developmental Test of Visual-Motor Integration (Beery, 1967)
An informal survey of the child's physical coordination skills (See appropriate sections of the preadmission form in Appendix A.)

The child's affective learning domain is usually assessed by noncamp personnel. However, if the assessment of this area of learning is to be supplemented with data collected by the camp staff, the following assessment instruments are recommended:

Direct observation of the child during a variety of camp activities
Devereux Elementary School Behavior Rating Scale (Spivack and Swift, 1967)
Devereux Child Behavior Rating Scale (Spivack and Spotts, 1966)

After assessment has been completed, the prescriptive learning processes are conducted as described in Chapter 3.

POPULATION

The number of campers enrolled in the evening camp ranges from 15 to 25 children per session. Because attendance is not mandatory, the number of participants varies from session to session.

A group this size (15 to 25) is adequate for team sports and other large-group activities, yet sufficiently small to allow each camper an opportunity to participate in all scheduled activities of his choice and to receive individual attention as needed.

The campers are elementary school children ranging in age from 7 to 11 or 12 years. Both boys and girls are enrolled in the camp. The ratio of boys to girls is usually three or four boys to each girl.

There are *no* restrictions on the classifications of exceptional children admitted to the program. The children may be attending either regular or special classes, or both. However, experience indicates that socially maladjusted, emotionally disturbed, and educable mentally retarded children are most responsive to this program.

If physically disabled and severely emotionally disturbed children are enrolled, special provisions for supervision and safety must be instituted.

When the evening camp is conducted in cooperation with a parent education program, the handicapped child's elementary school age brothers and sisters are encouraged to participate. This enlarges the group and necessitates additional supervisory personnel.

ADMINISTRATION

A centralized administrative structure is recommended for the evening camp. The camp coordinator is responsible for all final decisions concerning children, staff, and the activity program. This centralization of authority minimizes the probability of confusion and disagreement among camp personnel relative to admission, program, supervision, and behavior management.

The coordinator is assisted in the decision-making process by a policy board composed of community and school professionals and laymen.

Campers are organized into groups of five or six. An effort is made to ensure that each group is heterogeneous according to skills, sex, and handicapping conditions. The campers are grouped homogeneously by age: the 7-, 8-, and 9-year-olds are grouped together, as are the 10-, 11-, and 12-year-olds. In general, an effort is made to avoid establishing beginner, intermediate, and advanced groups.

If a handicapped child's brothers and sisters are attending camp, they are not assigned to a group that includes their siblings.

Two classes or types of counselors are needed to operate the evening camp: group counselors and special counselors. All counselors are directly accountable to the coordinator for their actions.

Each group counselor is responsible for five or six children. He accompanies and assists the children in his group during all activities throughout the session. The group counselor is responsible for all decisions concerning the child's program and behavior.

Special counselors are responsible for program activities. They are assigned to activity areas, such as arts and crafts, motor-coordination activities, music, sports, and table games. A special counselor may be assigned to more than one activity area. These counselors plan, prepare, and present lessons. They are assisted by the group counselors. The special counselor remains at his assigned center throughout the session and attends to each group scheduled into the center.

Excluding the coordinator and special counselors, a camper-to-counselor ratio of 5:1 is recommended. This ratio ensures proper supervision of the children, yet avoids adult domination of activities. The camper-to-counselor ratio must be reduced to 3:1 or 2:1 when physically handicapped and severely emotionally disturbed children are in attendance.

Except for the coordinator, manpower requirements are met by volunteers. The coordinator should be a professional who is trained in recreation, physical education, or special education. If feasible, the coordinator should be paid or granted college credit for his work.

Policy board members may include (1) public school and university instructors of recreation; (2) regular and special education teachers; (3) public school administrators and supervisors; (4) parent education program personnel; (5) parents of exceptional children; and (6) representatives of community service groups, such as the Lions Club, PTA groups, and the junior chamber of commerce.

Counselors, group and special, may be senior high school and college student volunteers. Other excellent sources of volunteer counselors are members of PTA groups, the Kiwanis Club, the Lions Club, and similar organizations.

PHYSICAL FACILITIES, EQUIPMENT, AND MATERIALS

Limited physical facilities are needed for the evening camp. The majority, if not all, of the needed facilities can be found in an elementary school. The facilities recommended are:

An outdoor play area for kickball, volleyball, badminton, softball, and other field games. This area should contain swings and seesaws for the younger campers and a picnic area.

A gymnasium or multipurpose room with standard physical education facilities and equipment. This area is used for basketball, wrestling, tumbling, and similar activities. It must also be available for activities on rainy and cold days, when the campers cannot play outdoors.

A meeting room including sufficient tables and chairs for the total group (about 45 or 50 persons). This area is used for meetings at the beginning and end of each session and for large-group activities. The room also serves as a study center. A large classroom is an excellent meeting room.

A shop or industrial arts area with the basic tools required for simple wood, metal, plastic, and leather craft activities.

A kitchen with the basic equipment for baking and cooking. This area is used by small groups to prepare snacks.

Sanitary facilities. These facilities must be easily accessible.

An emergency telephone.

A minimum of special equipment or materials is required for the evening camp. Scrap wood, metal, leather, and plastic for craft projects and foodstuffs for the cooking and baking program are essentially all that are needed.

If field trips are to be a part of the camp program, transportation is needed.

Remediation materials and equipment are requested from the child's teacher. The children bring their own home-study assignments, textbooks, paper, notebooks, and pencil or pen.

PERSONNEL TRAINING PROGRAM

A trained staff is needed for a successful camp. All personnel should attend and actively participate in training sessions.

The evening camp training program is composed of two phases: a precamp workshop and weekly pre- and postsession meetings.

Phase 1: precamp workshop

The precamp workshop familiarizes all personnel with the purpose and objectives of the camp, the individual roles and functions of the various staff members, and the characteristics of the campers. During the workshop, staff consensus is sought on program structure and behavior management techniques. An effort is made to integrate into the schedule various programs and activities in which individual staff members express interest and have expertise.

If a parent education program is conducted in concert with the camp, all personnel should be familiarized with its purpose, objectives, and procedures during the precamp workshop.

Visitors, consultants, and guest speakers are not invited to participate in the precamp workshop. Possible exceptions to this rule are members of the policy board.

The workshop is primarily a time for the staff members to get acquainted with each other and to actively participate in program planning.

Phase 2: pre- and postsession meetings

Fifteen- to 30-minute in-service training meetings are conducted before and after each session. These meetings are used to plan and evaluate the evening's activities. Announcements of general concern to the staff are made during presession meetings. Activities are reviewed, evaluated and criticized during postsession meetings. Program modifications are discussed at this time.

In-service meetings are conducted to encourage discussion among the staff members. Each week, staff members discuss individual children; they discuss the child's remedial program and his behavior.

The camp coordinator is responsible for in-service training. His role is facilitative, not directive. If the coordinator cannot function comfortably in this role, another staff member who is familiar with the children, the counselors, and the program's purpose is assigned to this leadership position.

PROGRAM DESCRIPTION

The model presented here is based on an evening camp program conducted in various communities in the St. Louis metropolitan area from 1970 to 1974. The camps were conducted in concert with parent education programs and in cooperation with community public schools.

On an average, 25 handicapped children and their nonhandicapped siblings attended the weekly 3-hour sessions. The campers were organized into groups of five or six. Each group was scheduled into the activity areas of their choice for 75 minutes (three 25-minute periods) during the evening.

Two 25-minute study periods were scheduled each evening. These sessions usually followed quiet activities, such as snack time, table games, and arts and crafts. This procedure minimized the time the campers required to settle down to study their remedial assignments.

The total group participated in 15-minute opening and closing activities. During opening activities, children and counselors scheduled the remainder of their evening. Closing activities included "show and tell," skits, singing, and planning of future activities.

The following is a description of the activity periods each camper participates in during each session of this model. The activity periods described here are only suggestions; they must be modified to respond to the needs of the campers and to the available facilities in a specific situation.

Opening exercises
   Time: 15 minutes
   Participants: all campers and staff
   Content
      Welcome
      Announcements
      Review of procedures
      Review of behavioral limits

A field game with friends.

Overview of activities available for the evening

Selection of group activities by campers and counselors

Arts and crafts

Time: 25 minutes (one or two periods per evening)

Participants: groups

Content

Woodworking (constructing birdhouses, magazine racks, shoeshine boxes) and wood-burning

Working with plastics (making jewelry, name tags, bookends, key chains)

Working with metals (making jewelry, penholders, wastebaskets, planters)

Cooking and baking (preparing the evening snack—baking cookies, brownies, and cakes)

Art (finger painting, cutting and pasting, painting with watercolors, drawing, coloring)

With the assistance of the group counselor, each group selects one activity per 25-minute period. All members of the group participate in the activity that the group selects. The exact time the activity is scheduled during the evening is determined by the coordinator, who maintains a master schedule of all activities.

Gross motor activities

Time: 25 minutes (one or two periods per evening)

Participants: groups

Content

Tumbling

Wrestling

Group games, including interception, "steal the ball," "quiet Indian," and the like

Races, including foot races, relay races, and and the like

Competitive games, including badminton, volleyball, softball, basketball, kickball, field hockey, and Ping-Pong

Playground activities, including swinging and playing on the seesaw or slide

Snacktime

Time: 10 minutes

Participants: all campers and staff

Content: beverage and snack

The beverages and edibles are prepared by one of the groups as an arts-and-crafts

Minutes	15	25	25	25	10	25	15	25	15
Time	6:00-6:15	6:15-6:40	6:40-7:05	7:05-7:30	7:30-7:40	7:40-8:05	8:05-8:20	8:20-8:45	8:45-9:00
Group name									
Arapaho	1	3	2	5	4	2 or 3*	6	5	8
Braves	1	3	2	5	4	2 or 3*	6	5	7
Crows	1	3	2	5	4	2 or 3*	6	5	7
Eagles	1	2	5	3	4	5	6	2 or 3*	7
Fawns	1	2	5	3	4	5	6	2 or 3*	7

*Group selects 2 or 3-type activity for this time period. 1, Opening; 2, arts and crafts; 3, motor activities; 4, snack time; 5, study; 6, table games; 7, closing.

Fig. 12. Activity schedule for the evening camp.

activity. The group is also responsible for serving the snack and for cleaning the area afterward.

Study periods
- Time: 25 minutes (two periods per evening)
- Participants: groups
- Content: remedial assignments of a preacademic and academic nature

Assignments are given by the handicapped child's teacher. However, remedial assignments may be prescribed by the camp staff as a result of assessment.

Table games
- Time: 15 minutes
- Participants: groups
- Content
  - Cards
  - Checkers, chess, Chinese checkers, dominoes
  - Pool, table hockey, football
  - Monopoly, Life, Scrabble, Risk

Closing exercises
- Time: 15 minutes
- Participants: all campers and staff
- Content
  - Review of evening's activities, including "show and tell"
  - Preview of next session
  - Discussion of special events
  - Songfest
  - Farewell

A sample camp schedule for five groups is presented in Fig. 12. On this schedule, each group participates in two 25-minute study periods, one 25-minute arts-and-crafts period, and one 25-minute gross motor activity period, as well as opening and closing exercises, snack time, and a 15-minute period for table games. An additional period of 25 minutes may be used for either arts-and-crafts or gross motor activities. Each group decides how to utilize this additional period.

Lessons to be presented at the various ac-

Activity center ______________________ Date ______________________
Group ______________________ Camper(s) ______________________

Counselor ______________________

Activity title ______________________

Overall purpose (State in general descriptive terminology.)

Instructional objective (State in specific descriptive terminology.)

Instructional methodology (State in specific terminology and present in sequence.)

Materials needed (State type or kind and quantity.)

Evaluation (Describe how the camper's performance is to be evaluated. What techniques are to be applied?)

Fig. 13. Camp activity plan for the evening camp.

tivity areas are preplanned, following the activity plan form presented in Fig. 13. The special counselor prepares the form in an original and one copy, filing the copy with the coordinator and retaining the original at his activity area. The counselor prepares a plan for each activity that is offered in his area.

Several times during the year, an entire camp session is devoted to a special event. The campers are actively involved in planning these sessions.

Special events may be conducted on both camp and noncamp evenings, on weekends, and on holidays. Examples of activities that can be scheduled are:

Attending a professional, college, or high school basketball, football, or baseball game
Cookouts and picnics
Camp-outs and float trips
Parent nights
Attending a movie, play, or demonstration in the community
Presenting a play or series of skits or a demonstration to an audience of parents, siblings, relatives, friends, teachers, and so on
Hay rides, sleigh rides, and bike rides
Hikes and nature walks
Visits to places of historical interest, such as museums
Visits to places of educational interest, such as businesses, factories, and stores
Visits in nature, such as to zoos, botanical gardens, and farms

ADVANTAGES AND DISADVANTAGES

The advantages of the evening camp are:
1. Remedial programs can be provided in the psychomotor and affective learning domains, which, because of limits on personnel, space, and time, are prohibited in the child's normal school program.
2. The handicapped child's remedial program in the cognitive learning domain can be supplemented in cooperation with his teacher via home-study assignments.
3. The camp program for the handicapped child and his siblings can be coordinated with a parent education program in cooperation with qualified school and community personnel.

4. The limits of the camp relative to personnel, time, and space encourages the structuring of activities. This characteristic is advantageous to children who are hyperactive or distractible, or who have difficulties selecting and completing activities.
5. The camp provides an excellent opportunity for cooperating school and community agency personnel to observe and evaluate the child. Their observations and evaluation are beneficial in the effort to design a comprehensive therapeutic prescription for the handicapped child.
6. The program provides many excellent opportunities to initiate enduring positive interpersonal relationships between handicapped children and acceptable and accepting adult identification figures.

The disadvantages of the camp are:
1. The brevity of the sessions limits the feasibility of initiating and completing many desirable activities.
2. The lack of availability of trained personnel, time, and specialized facilities prohibits many desirable activities.
3. Volunteer counselors, unless committed to handicapped children, are frequently unreliable. This increases the difficulty that the coordinator has in maintaining program consistency.
4. Personnel training is difficult because untrained counselors are generally overanxious about their competency to interact productively with exceptional children.
5. The camp is dependent on parent and volunteer transportation, which is frequently unreliable.
6. The camp shares equipment and facilities with school personnel. Great care must be taken to avoid damaging and/or losing or misplacing property belonging to the school or teachers.

THE PRESCHOOL DAY CAMP

It is a hot humid day in eastern Missouri, but Ms. Bonnie and her preschool campers do not appear to mind the weather. They are involved in an arts-and-crafts period scheduled for 10:15 each morning at day camp.

Ms. Bonnie's 4- and 5-year-old campers are in their second week of the 6-week summer program. The first week was devoted to assessing the children's abilities and disabilities. The teacher and her assistants evaluated each child's social-emotional (affective), perceptual-motor (psychomotor), and preacademic (cognitive) development. They utilized some formal child development screening scales and observed each child in a variety of activities throughout the initial week of camp.

The variety of potentially handicapping behaviors observed among the nine children was bewildering. However, Ms. Bonnie and her two assistants, after analyzing their assessment findings, designed an individual teaching prescription for each child.

Thus far, the prescriptions designed for Charlie, Tyrone, and Nancy appear to be ineffective. Last Friday, Ms. Bonnie and her assistants agreed that they needed additional help in programming these three youngsters. Ms. Bonnie called Mr. Mart, the camp's early childhood education consultant, for assistance. Mr. Mart has observed all of the children's activities this morning and is now observing them in arts and crafts. He is focusing his observations on only the three children Ms. Bonnie has called to his attention.

Although it is only midmorning, Mr. Mart's notes include several observations of each child:

CHARLIE

9:02 Charlie is taken from the minibus screaming and kicking. It takes Ms. Bonnie approximately 7 minutes to quiet him. She holds him. (The driver says, "Charlie was screaming when his mother put him on the bus.")

9:10 Charlie refuses to join the group. He does not participate in opening activities.

9:45 During free play, Charlie grabs a toy truck from George. He bangs on it with a wooden hammer.

9:50 Charlie refuses to leave the classroom. He is taken from the room screaming and kicking.

10:03 Charlie smashes his cookie into the ground with his foot. He throws his juice at Ms. Bonnie.

10:15 Charlie sits at his easel making random

designs on a large piece of paper with finger paint. He has many different colors of paint (red, yellow, orange, and green). While painting, he moves his hands in a rapid, circular motion, splashing paint on himself and others. He is smiling.

TYRONE

8:58 Tyrone jumps off the bus and runs to the registration table. He yells his name to Mr. Keith, throws his lunch into the wrong box, and races to the playing field. Ms. Bonnie brings him back to the registration table.

9:07 Tyrone sits in the group for opening activities. He is constantly wiggling. Tyrone is held in place by an assistant.

9:12 Tyrone participates in language circle. He is held in his assigned seat by an assistant. He grabs the puppet from Ms. Bonnie's hand and throws it into the corner of the room.

9:37 During free play, Tyrone runs from one activity and toy to another. He manipulates 12 or 13 games and toys during the 20-minute activity period.

9:45 While the group is preparing to leave the classroom, Tyrone runs out the door, leaving his toys scattered about the room. He is returned to the room by the assistant and picks up the toys.

10:01 Tyrone eats his cookie in one bite and gulps his juice. He drops the paper cup on the ground and runs to the playing field.

10:13 Tyrone grabs a sheet of paper, puts his hands in two pots of finger paint simultaneously, and runs them rapidly over the paper.

10:15 Tyrone, covered with finger paint from head to toe, runs to the playing field. He is returned to the arts-and-crafts area by an assistant.

NANCY

9:04 Nancy steps from her taxi, cautiously closes the door, and slowly walks to the registration table. She puts her lunch in the proper box and smiles at Mr. Keith, who is in charge of attendance. Mr. Keith says, "Good morning. Your name, please." Nancy smiles but does not respond. Mr. Keith says, "Say, 'Nancy.'" Nancy smiles, takes her counselor's hand, and walks to the classroom.

9:08   Nancy sits with her group during opening activities. She smiles, claps her hands, and walks in the play circle, holding hands with the other children. She does not recite the morning welcome, nor does she sing "Happy Birthday" to June with the other children.

9:13   Nancy sits and attends to the counselor during language period. She does not speak but points to the various animal picture cards when requested to do so by the counselor.

9:35   During free play, Nancy, playing alone in the corner of the room, completes four puzzles. The puzzles contain 15 to 20 pieces.

9:57   Nancy returns the puzzles to the bookcase when requested to do so by Ms. Bonnie. She leaves the classroom with the group.

10:03   Nancy sits at the picnic table with her group. She eats her cookie, drinks her juice, and drops her paper cup into the wastebasket. When Ms. Bonnie and the assistants question her about her new playsuit and compliment her on her behavior, Nancy smiles but is silent.

10:10   Nancy, dressed in a smock, sits at the table with a large piece of paper and a pot of finger paint. An assistant encourages her to finger paint, but Nancy does not respond except to move farther away from the table.

10:14   The assistant, holding Nancy's hand, moves it toward the paint pot. Nancy yanks her hand away and bursts into tears.

PURPOSES AND OBJECTIVES

The preschool day camp is designed to provide educational assessment and prescriptive teaching services to handicapped and potentially handicapped children. For children attending a formal preschool, the camp is used to accelerate their program. For children not enrolled in a preschool, the camp provides the experiences desirable for admission to a formal preschool or kindergarten.

The specific objectives of the preschool day camp are to help the child (1) develop a positive concept of self; (2) increase awareness of the environment via sensory experiences; (3) develop communications skills (listening, observing, and speaking) prerequisite to reading, computing, and writing; (4) develop psychomotor competencies needed to function successfully in the environment; (5) develop a recognition of his strengths and weaknesses, and the ability to overcome failure, cope with success, and challenge the difficult; (6) learn to express, verbally and nonverbally, positive and negative feelings in a socially acceptable manner; (7) develop group participation skills indicative of respect for the rights and property of others and self; and (8) become self-motivated, as made manifest in a willingness to explore the environment freely and productively.

The preschool day camp designed to respond to these objectives can be a valuable supplement to the individual's prescription for learning in each of the learning domains: psychomotor, affective, and cognitive. Emphasis at the preschool day camp is focused primarily on the psychomotor and affective domains. Less emphasis is placed on cognitive learning because of the preschool child's developmental level.

The standardized assessment instruments available in the marketplace for the evaluation of preschool handicapped children are extremely primitive. This is because of the only recent emphasis on preschool education for the handicapped and the resulting lack of research in this area of teaching.

Preschool day camp assessment procedures include the application of formal and informal child development surveys, checklists, rating scales, and anecdotal records. A few of these instruments have been standardized on quantitatively substantial populations.

Among the most useful techniques and instruments are:

Direct observation and the writing of anecdotal records (Cohen and Stern, 1958; Hendrick, 1975; and Rowan, 1973)

Checklists and surveys (see Chapter 3 of this volume and Hendrick, 1975)

Purdue Perceptual-Motor Survey (Roach and Kephart, 1966)

Devereux Child Behavior Rating Scale (Spivack and Spotts, 1966)

Vineland Social Maturity Scale (Doll, 1953)

Denver Developmental Screening Test (Frankenberg et al, 1970)

It can be readily understood that an excellent knowledge of child development is needed by practitioners entering into the field of preschool camping.

Prescriptive teaching processes for use in the preschool day camp are described in detail in Chapter 3.

POPULATION

The number of children admitted to the preschool day camp is restricted by the staff and facilities available for the program. It is suggested that camp enrollment not exceed 15, or a maximum of 20, preschoolers unless a well-equipped facility with adequate supervision is available.

Children admitted to the camp are ages 4 and 5 years. On occasion, severely handicapped 3-year-old children and very immature 6-year-old children are admitted to the program. If the recommended application and preadmission procedures are adhered to, the camp staff can readily determine if the proposed program is adequate to serve the child's needs.

The vast majority of preschoolers referred to the camp are moderately to severely handicapped. Mildly handicapped children are usually not identified until they enter a formal kindergarten or first-grade program.

Although some preschool age children are classified as behaviorally disordered, neurologically impaired, or socially maladjusted, the vast majority are undifferentiated atypical children. These youngsters appear to function abnormally but have not been formally assessed or classified. A few physically handicapped children are enrolled in the camp when physical facilities are adequate to meet their needs.

Characteristics most frequently observed among the preschool group include:

Combination of severe hyperactivity, distractibility, and/or impulsivity

Severe perceptual disorders of a visual order

Disruptive behavior: generally tantrums and unacceptable aggressive group behaviors

Adjustment difficulties due to traumatic physical injuries, such as loss or paralysis of a limb

Severe withdrawal from peers, adults, and the environment

Severe hearing impairment

Severe motor coordination problems

Severe vision impairment

Severe speech handicaps, including a total or near-total lack of verbal communications

ADMINISTRATION

A centralized administrative organization is suggested for the preschool day camp. A coordinator is responsible for all final decisions relative to the campers, the staff, and the program. The coordinator is assisted by one assistant coordinator for each ten children admitted to the camp.

Including the primary team—coordinator and assistant coordinator—an overall camper-to-counselor ratio of 3:1 is recommended. However, if severely handicapped and/or nonambulatory children are attending, the camper-to-counselor ratio should be 2:1.

There is a dearth of qualified preschool special education professionals. Consequently, it is suggested that the primary team members be trained in a combination of the following disciplines: child development, early childhood education, kindergarten/primary education, recreation, physical education, and special education. The coordinator must be a trained professional in one or more of these disciplines. Assistant coordinators should be either professionals or professionals-in-training. Primary team personnel should be paid employees of the camp.

Counselors and aides may be volunteers from the community and local high schools, community colleges, and universities. All staff members are required to attend and participate in the personnel training program.

PHYSICAL FACILITIES, EQUIPMENT, AND MATERIALS

The normal physical facilities required for a quality kindergarten or preschool program are needed for an effective and efficient special preschool day camp. Among the needed physical facilities are:

A large, well-lighted and well-ventilated classroom for group meetings, and readiness and prereadiness activities. The classroom should be carpeted. This area is also used for rainy day activities.

An outdoor play area with swings, seesaws, slides, a sandbox, and space for an obstacle course. A wading pool is desirable but not absolutely necessary. A source of water for drinking and for use in arts and crafts should be readily available.

Sanitary facilities. Facilities of the appropriate size must be readily accessible to the children.

A rest area with mats or cots (for the full-day camp).

Transportation for field trips.

Special physical facilities are needed when nonambulatory children are admitted to camp. In this situation, the physical facility must be devoid of architectural barriers, such as stairs, curbs, and narrow doorways. Sanitary facilities must not be designed so as to prohibit use by the nonambulatory child.

Special instructional materials and equipment are usually not required for the preschool day camp, except as discussed in Chapter 5 for the day camp. In the preschool program, emphasis is placed on three-dimensional rather than on two-dimensional materials.

PERSONNEL TRAINING PROGRAM

The personnel training program suggested for the preschool day camp is similar to that discussed in Chapter 5 for the day camp. Emphasis is focused on early childhood development and education.

PROGRAM DESCRIPTION

Prescriptive teaching procedures and forms utilized at the preschool day camp are the same as those described in Chapter 5 for the day camp and are not repeated here.

The preschool day camp model presented here is based on sessions conducted during the summers of 1972 and 1973 at Southern Illinois University at Edwardsville. This camp was a half-day program. However, an extended or full-day program schedule is also presented.

The camp admitted 20 children for the 6-week session. During the session, the preschoolers attended camp 3 hours a day, 5 days each week.

Sixteen to 18 children attended the daily sessions. They were organized into groups of eight or nine children. Each group's activities were supervised by an assistant coordinator and two counselors. If a severely handicapped child was a member of the group, an additional counselor or aide was assigned to assist him.

The daily activity program consisted of a series of 15- to 20-minute periods. Experience indicated that longer periods were not practical because of the children's relatively limited attention span. During longer periods, the children became bored and restless.

The activities suggested here for the preschool day camp are drawn from my experiences with the Edwardsville camp and from the available preschool literature. They are only a very small percentage of the possible activities preschool children can engage in at camp. Several excellent references are presented in the references at the end of this chapter. The reader is encouraged to review these for additional program suggestions.

Gross motor activities

Gross motor activities are conducted in the outdoor play area and are designed to increase the child's gross motor coordination. Among the gross motor activities included in the preschool program are:

Calisthenics
Walking at various rates and with various-size steps
Running in various ways, including races
Jumping; including both feet, right foot, left foot, over objects, forward, and backward
Hopping on both feet, left foot, and right foot
Balancing with and without balance beam
Kicking various-size balls
Throwing a ball, Frisbee, or other object—both overhand and underhand—at a target or for distance

Bounding and catching a ball

Hitting a target (stationary or moving, such as a ball or beanbag) with hand, bat, or racket

Running an obstacle course

Jumping rope

Team sports, such as tag, tetherball, badminton, kickball, and circle games

Wading, water play, and swimming when appropriate facilities are available

Wagon, scooter, and tricycle riding

Tumbling and roughhousing

Fine motor activities

Fine motor activities are conducted to develop the child's fine motor skills necessary for success in the school setting. Among the fine-motor activities included in the program are:

Constructing with blocks and similar objects

Manipulating knobs, locks, switches, buttons, zippers, and similar mechanisms

Disassembling and reassembling mechanisms

Using form boards, pegboards, and puzzles

Pouring liquids and solids into various-size containers

Manipulating objects with thumb and fingers

Using crayons, paintbrushes, and clay

Using thumb and fingers in bead stringing and sewing

Using a hammer, saw, and screwdriver; manipulating nuts, bolts, screws, and nails appropriately

Tearing and cutting paper

Lacing and tying

Tracing, copying, and drawing

Writing letters, numbers, and geometric symbols

Negotiating two- and three-dimensional mazes with crayon and fingers

Language development

Every child, if he is to function successfully in the environment, must develop language skill. Language is the basic tool of meaningful communications among humans. The child must have skill in both receptive and expressive language. Among the expressive language development activities suggested for the preschooler are:

Learning and verbalizing name, age, address, and telephone number

Learning and verbalizing letters, numbers, and names of objects, persons, and events

Stating needs and desires clearly and concisely

Telling stories and experiences in sequence

Creating and relating original stories

Engaging in spontaneous conversation with peers and adults

Expressing ideas in complete thoughts

Describing objects by purpose, size, weight, texture, color, and the like

Using declarative statements, questions, and exclamations appropriately

Expressing emotional states appropriately by such means as jokes, laughter, anger, and tears

Among the suggested development receptive language activities are:

Listening to stories, lyrics, riddles, and the like

Listening to and following simple and eventually multistep directions

Attending to peers and adults who are talking

Demonstrating comprehension of the words *over, under, behind, in front of, forward, backward, beside, in, outside of, in, on, out, around, above,* and *below*

Understanding and responding to statements implying positives, negatives, and opposites

Interpreting via personal language the main thought of a picture, story, or experience

Differentiating between fact, fantasy, and opinion

Responding appropriately to jokes, tricks, funny stories, and the like

Sensory development

Activities that are designed to develop the child's sensory skills are planned each day of the camp session. Such activities focus on (1) visual discrimination and memory, (2) auditory discrimination and memory, (3) tactile discrimination, or (4) taste and olfactory discrimination. Among the activities used in developing visual discrimination and memory are:

Matching objects by visual characteristics

Matching, recognizing, and naming colors

Identifying objects in pictures and in the environment, and identifying partially hidden objects

Sizing objects

Describing likenesses and differences

Recalling and describing known objects that have been removed from sight

Reproducing and completing objects

Identifying and naming the letters of the alphabet

Identifying and naming the numbers zero through ten

Practicing visual tracking exercises prerequisite for reading and writing: left to right, top to bottom, and front to back

Among the activities used in developing auditory discrimination and memory are:

Identifying familiar sounds and their source
Discriminating between high and low, loud and soft, and long and short sounds
Repeating sound rhythms
Using appropriate inflexions in speech
Repeating from memory a series of numbers, letters, and words
Memorizing and reciting simple songs, poems, and riddles
Following three- and four-step commands
Discriminating among phonemes
Playing word games when words are of a similar sound pattern

Among the activities used in developing tactile discrimination are:

Identifying objects by touch
Identifying objects as hard or soft; thick or thin; smooth, rough, or fuzzy; sharp or dull; dry or wet; and sticky or slick
Identifying objects as heavy or light, hot or cold, and the like

Among the activities used in developing taste and olfactory discrimination are:

Identifying tastes as sweet, sour, bitter, salty, or spicy
Discriminating between hot and cold foods and drinks
Recognizing familiar scents
Identifying substances by taste cues only

Science and number concepts

Children at the preschool day camp participate in many activities related to science and number concepts. These activities are concrete rather than abstract. Among the recommended activities in this area are:

Matching and identifying shapes (circles, squares, triangles, rectangles) and lines (straight, curved, slanted)
Recognizing size differences: describing an object as big, little, long, short, large, small, and the like
Identifying the numbers zero through ten
Using counting sticks and counting frames for number correspondence problems

Doing simple addition and subtraction
Measuring liquids and solids
Observing and studying the environment
Observing and studying nature (animals, plants, flowers, water)
Developing collections of objects of scientific relevance
Caring for pets
Preparing simple foods (cookies, cakes, snacks)

Creative arts

Preschoolers participate in a broad variety of creative activities. Every camp program should provide an abundance of opportunities for the child to engage in art, crafts, music, rhythm exercises, dance, puppetry, sociodrama, and similar activities. A few of the many creative activities of interest to the preschooler are:

Singing and listening to music
Playing simple instruments
Learning a repertoire of songs for group songfests
Clapping and playing rhythm instruments
Drawing, coloring, tracing, and cutting and pasting
Painting and drawing with various media (finger paints, water colors, crayons, chalk, felt pens)
Modeling with creative media (clay, sand, plaster, paper, yarn, burlap, chalk)
Marching and dancing
Participating in creative movement and dance
Weaving, knitting, and sewing
Constructing with various materials (wood, metal, paper, cardboard, plastic)
Engaging in puppetry
Creative play acting
Preparing programs for presentation to an audience
Dramatizing stories, songs, rhymes, and experiences

Table games and toys

The preschooler should be given opportunities to learn to play various table games. Among the games used at the preschool camp are:

Card games (old maid, bottle, kings)
Checkers
Puzzles
Candyland Game
Ring toss
Building blocks

Leggo
Jollycraft Mosaics
Tip-it
Pick-up-sticks
Trouble
Paper dolls

Free play

At least one free-play activity period is scheduled daily at the preschool day camp. During this period the children are encouraged to select games and toys that are not familiar to them. They are restricted to one or two selections during the period. This discourages the hyperactive, distractible child from attempting to play with all of the toys and games in the play area.

Field trips

Field trips and special events are an important part of the camp program. Counselors are encouraged to plan trips and events that are a logical part of the child's overall program and to conduct follow-up discussions and activities afterward. Among the field trips and events that are of educational value to the child are:

Visits to shopping malls, open markets, grocery stores, rummage sales, restaurants, snack bars, department stores, ice cream shops
Visits to bakeries, food-processing plants, meat and fish markets, dairies
Visits to train stations, airports, bus depots, subways, marinas
Visits to zoos, farms, museums, historical monuments, libraries, schools
Costume days; clown days
Athletic events; field days
Carnival days
Picnics and barbecues

Affective education

Affective education activities focusing on the child's intrapersonal feelings and interpersonal skills are scheduled each week. During these sessions, the children participate in activities designed to help them (1) express their emotional states appropriately, (2) discuss their likes and dislikes, (3) select alternative way of responding to difficulties, and (4) sensitize themselves to the observable characteristics of others.

Lunch time

Lunch time is a learning activity period. The counselor helps the child develop appropriate eating habits and manners, learn to eat his lunch, learn not to waste food and drink, and learn basic courtesy.

Opening and closing activities

Opening activities include a greeting, a group song, "show and tell," and planning for the remainder of the day. This is a small-group activity.

Closing activities are a total-camp activity. This time is reserved for announcements; planning; group singing; small-group presentations to an audience (the other campers and staff); awards, recognition, and cheers for special projects completed by individual campers and small groups; and "farewell."

Rest period

Most preschoolers are very curious, enthusiastic, and active. They play very hard and become quite irritable when tired. Consequently, a quiet time for naps and rest is scheduled frequently.

Weekly activity schedules

Two typical camp schedules are presented in Figs. 14 and 15. The first schedule was actually used in the preschool day camp at Edwardsville. This program was scheduled from 9 AM to 12 noon, Monday thru Friday for a 6-week session. Approximately 20 children participated in the program.

The second schedule is for an extended day and is designed for approximately 20 children who would attend from 9:00 AM to 2:00 PM.

ADVANTAGES AND DISADVANTAGES

Advantages of the special preschool day camp are:
1. The camp is located in the child's community; therefore, he is not removed from his home for lengthy periods of time. The community-based camp also encourages parent involvement in their child's program.
2. The camp is of therapeutic and remedial

Fig. 14. Weekly schedule for 3-hour preschool day camp.

Time	Minutes	Monday	Tuesday	Wednesday	Thursday	Friday
9:00-9:15	15	←————————————— Opening activities* —————————————→				
9:15-9:30	15	←— Language development (on occasion incorporates creative arts, sensory development, and affective education) —→				
9:30-9:50	20	←— Creative arts (on occasion incorporates fine motor activities) —→				
9:50-10:15	25	Fine motor activities	Science/ numbers	Fine motor activities	Science/ numbers	
10:15-10:45	30	←———————— Snack and quiet time* ————————→				
10:45-11:10	25	←——————— Gross motor activities ———————→				
11:10-11:30	20	Affective education	Sensory development	Affective education	Sensory development	Special events and field trips
11:30-11:45	15	Table games	Free play	Table games	Free play	
11:45-12:00	15	←———————— Closing activities* ————————→				

*All campers and staff.

Fig. 15. Weekly schedule for 5-hour preschool day camp.

Time	Minutes	Monday	Tuesday	Wednesday	Thursday	Friday
9:00-9:15	15	←————————————— Opening activities* —————————————→				
9:15-9:45	30	←————————— Language development —————————→				
9:45-10:15	30	←————————— Gross motor activities —————————→				
10:15-10:45	30	←————————— Snack and quiet time* —————————→				
10:45-11:45	60	←——— Creative arts and fine motor activities ———→				
11:45-12:30	45	←——— Quiet time, lunch, and table games* ———→				
12:30-12:50	20	←——— Science and number concepts ———→				
12:50-1:10	20	←————————— Sensory training —————————→				
1:10-1:30	20	Free play	Affective education	Free play	Affective education	Special events and field trips
1:30-1:45	15	←————————— Quiet time* —————————→				
1:45-2:00	15	←————————— Closing activities* —————————→				

*All campers and staff.

benefit to severely handicapped children. The camp program can be closely coordinated with the child's noncamp therapeutic program.

3. For the suspected handicapped child who has not been diagnosed, the camp is an excellent assessment and observation setting readily available to school and community agency diagnosticians.

4. For the experiencially handicapped child, the camp provides a variety of activities and experiences to prepare him to enter a formal school program.

5. For the child of the working mother, the camp provides a stimulating environment in which to participate in purposeful activities under the supervision of trained personnel.

Disadvantages of the camp are:

1. Enrollment in a special camp may result in premature classification as an exceptional child.
2. The child is removed from his home for several hours per day at a time or stage in his development when close associations with his mother are of greatest importance.
3. The day camp program is often not powerful enough or long enough to have a significant effect on the overall behaviors of severely handicapped children.

REFERENCES

Beery, K. *Developmental Test of Visual-Motor Integration.* Chicago: Follett Corp., 1967.

Bennett, J., and Lippold, J. Community program for exceptional children. *Recreation,* 1961, **54**(10), 536-537.

Cherry, C., Harkness, B., and Kuzma, K. *Nursery school management guide.* Belmont, Calif.: Fearon Publishers, 1973.

Cohen, D. H., and Stern, V. S. *Observing and recording the behavior of young children.* New York: Teachers College Press, 1958.

Crain, J. Early childhood education for diversely handicapped children. Washington, D.C.: U.S. Office of Education, 1974.

Dewey, M. A. *Recreation for autistic and emotionally disturbed children.* Washington, D.C.: National Institute of Mental Health, 1973.

Doll, E. A. *Vineland Social Maturity Scale.* Minneapolis: Educational Test Bureau, 1953.

Frankenburg, W. K., Fandal, A. W., and Dodds, J. D. *The Denver Developmental Screening Test.* Denver: University of Colorado, 1970.

Frostig, M., LeFever, W., and Whittlesey, J. R. B. *Developmental Test of Visual Perception.* Palo Alto, Calif.: Consulting Psychologists Press, 1961.

Handicapped Adventure Playground Association. *Adventure playgrounds for handicapped children.* London: The Association, 1973.

Hendrick, J. *The whole child: new trends in early education,* St. Louis: The C. V. Mosby Co., 1975.

Hilsendager, D., Jack, H., and Mann, L. The Buttonwood Farms Project. *Journal of Health, Physical Education, and Recreation,* 1968, **39**(3), 46-48.

Karnes, M. B. *Helping young children develop language skills.* Arlington, Va.: Council for Exceptional Children, 1968.

Lavker, J., and Rosett, N. Teenagers provide recreation for the mentally retarded. *Parks and Recreation,* 1966, **1**(6), 487.

Littlejohn, R. T. (Ed.). *What can I do now, Mommy?* Kansas City, Mo.: The Crippled Children's Nursery School Association, 1971.

Meyers, E. S., Ball, H. H., and Crutchfield, M. *The kindergarten teacher's handbook.* Los Angeles: Gramercy Press, 1973.

Missouri State Department of Elementary and Secondary Education. *Focus on early childhood education: resource guide for the education of children ages three to six.* Columbia, Mo.: University of Missouri Press (no date).

Montessori, M. *Dr. Montessori's own handbook.* New York: Schocken Books Inc., 1965.

Roach, E., and Kephart, N. C. *The Purdue Perceptual-Motor Survey.* Columbus, Ohio: Charles E. Merrill Publishing Co., 1966.

Rowan, B. *The children we see.* New York: Holt, Rinehart and Winston, Inc., 1973.

Shearer, M., and Shearer, D. The Portage Project: A model for early childhood education. *Exceptional Children,* 1972, **39**(3), 210-217.

Spivack, G., and Spotts, J. *Devereux Child Behavior Rating Scale.* Devon, Pa.: The Devereux Foundation, 1966.

Spivack, G., and Swift, M. *Devereux Elementary School Behavior Rating Scale.* Devon, Pa.: The Devereux Foundation, 1967.

Van Witsen, B. *Perceptual training activities handbook.* New York: Teachers College Press, 1967.

Woods, C. Recreation for the mentally retarded child. *Recreation,* 1962, **55**(7), 335-357.

Zimmerman, I. L., Steiner, V. G., and Evatt, R. L. *Preschool language manual.* Columbus, Ohio: Charles E. Merrill Publishing Co., 1969.

CHAPTER 7

Residential camps for handicapped children

In this chapter two residential camps for handicapped children are presented in detail: the residential camp for special populations and the special purpose residential camp. Both camps are designed to be a part of the child's ongoing therapeutic and remedial program rather than independent, unrelated programs.

The residential camp for special populations model is based on a camp conducted during the summers of 1967 through 1969 at the Little Grassy Outdoor Laboratory at Southern Illinois University at Carbondale. This 5-week camp served moderately to severely emotionally handicapped children ages 6 to 12 years. The children were enrolled in the Day School for Emotionally Disturbed Children at Southern Illinois University.

The special purpose residential camp model is based on a camp conducted during the winter and spring of 1969 at the Little Grassy Laboratory in cooperation with several public school districts in southern Illinois. This 2-week camp served educable mentally retarded children ages 10 to 15 years. Pre- and postresidential phases of the program were conducted by the children's classroom teachers in local public school classrooms in cooperation with camp personnel.

The Outdoor Laboratory, the setting of both residential camps, is part of the Southern Illinois University Little Grassy facilities and is located 10 miles south of the main campus in Carbondale, in the foothills of the Ozarks. The laboratory is a 6,500-acre tract of natural woodlands; it includes a large lake, fishery, conservation camps, experimental farms and forests, an animal farm, a stable, and three camping complexes.

Camp Akwesasne was the site of the residential camp for special populations. This camp has fair-weather living accommodations for approximately 120 persons. Campers and staff are housed in primitive, screened cabins. Modern cabins are used as offices and for severely handicapped campers. Food service personnel provide well-balanced meals in a screened dining hall with a modern kitchen. The dining hall is used as a common room. Also available in this complex are a medical clinic, several shelters for use as classrooms, an arts-and-crafts shelter, sanitary facilities, and a beach area with swimming, boating, and fishing facilities.

The Little Giant Camp was the site of the special purpose residential camp. This camp has year-round living accommodations for 180 persons. Campers and staff are housed in modern, electrically heated dormitory cabins. Food service personnel provide well-balanced meals in modern dining facilities. Also available in the Little Giant Camp complex are a large common room with a fireplace, several classrooms, arts-and-crafts rooms, an emergency medical clinic, a beach with swimming, boating, and fishing facilities, an outdoor chapel, and sanitary facilities.

Within walking and driving distance of both camps are many historical sites and natural phenomena, such as Giant City State Park, Crab Orchard National Wildlife Refuge, a restored pioneer village, and a living nature museum and animal farm.

In both camp complexes facilities are available for archery, arts and crafts, horseback riding, riflery, fishing, nature study, hiking, and field games. Inclement weather facilities are available for arts and crafts, songfests, dancing, movies, skits and shows, cooking and baking, table games, and similar activities. In season, campers participate in camp-outs, cookouts, and water activities: swimming, canoeing, boating, and fishing.

The Little Giant Camp complex is devoid of architectural barriers that would inhibit the mobility of campers who are physically handicapped and confined to wheelchairs.

THE RESIDENTIAL CAMP FOR SPECIAL POPULATIONS*

■ Edward is an extremely shy, unobtrusive, 9-year-old student. He has a severe speech

handicap: stuttering. Edward seldom speaks unless it is absolutely necessary. He is classified by the school psychologist as "a slow learner with emotional problems and a speech handicap."

■ Sharon has a history of ear and throat infections. Her hearing acuity has been evaluated and is within normal limits. However, Sharon appears to have a habit of not listening; consequently she is unable to follow directions. This results in repeated conflicts with her teachers, parents, and classmates.

■ Peter is from a disorganized home. This seems to have exacerbated his handicaps. Peter says repeatedly, "I miss my mother." He is presently living with his father, a younger sister, and a housekeeper.

Peter needs a secure, stable environment that will help him regain his self-confidence. He appears to be physically tired, lacking the energy to productively participate in games with his peers. In school, Peter is easily frustrated by unfamiliar tasks. On these occasions, he cries.

■ Larry is a socially maladjusted, immature 7-year-old student. He is not ready for the small-group work required for success in the second grade. He finds it impossible to sit in the group or to be confined to any area for more than 1 or 2 minutes. Larry moves and shifts his position constantly while sitting.

Larry has been diagnosed by the family's physician as "hyperactive or brain damaged."

■ David is seldom in contact with reality. He responds to few things in his environment with the exception of dolls and sticks. He destroys any doll he puts his hands on almost immediately. If permitted, David would spend hours collecting sticks and twigs from the trees and placing them neatly in a pile.

David's tantrums are frequently violent and unpredictable. He is nonverbal except for his screams.

■ Bobby has frequent temper outbursts. When requested to complete any task not to his liking, he will kick, bite, hit, scream, and yell. At these times he must be physically restrained or he will harm himself or others.

With these and similar descriptions, handicapped children are referred to the Day

---

*The description of the residential camp for special populations is based on articles published previously: (1) Shea, T. M., Ott, M. F., Overturf, E., and Phillips, T. L. The Little Grassy Outdoor Laboratory for emotionally handicapped children. Newsletter: Council for Children with Behavioral Disorders, 1969, **6**(4), 13-19. (2) Shea, T. M. and Phillips, T. L. Emotionally disturbed in camping experiment. Newsletter: Information Center—Recreation for the Handicapped, 1968, **3**(11), 1.

School for Emotionally Disturbed Children at Southern Illinois University. The Day School, like many public and private day care facilities for severely emotionally handicapped children, is responsible for the education and rehabilitation of its clients. Many of these institutions provide excellent services; however, their ability to help many severely handicapped children is limited by the nature of their services. They are primarily day care centers and are unable to provide the 24-hour-per-day services needed by some of their clients.

Our experiences at the Day School (Shea and Booth, 1968) and at an experimental camp (Shea and Phillips, 1968) indicated that a continuation and expansion of the 9-month-per-year day care service was desirable: a residential program would increase the probability of the children's total rehabilitation to normal functioning.

As previously indicated, the residential camp for special populations is an extension and broadening of the child's regular therapeutic program rather than an independent activity.

PURPOSES AND OBJECTIVES

The overall purpose of the residential camp for special populations is to provide each camper with a therapeutic milieu, a total environment (Redl, 1966), in which to develop and test his ability to function at increasingly more personally rewarding and socially acceptable levels. This environment is designed to encourage the camper to change while providing for him the emotional support he needs during the process of relinquishing old ways of functioning and learning new ways.

More specifically, the objectives of the camp are:
1. To initiate, extend, and/or complete each camper assessment and evaluation process
2. To develop intervention techniques for maintaining and increasing positive changes in each camper's affective, psychomotor, and cognitive development
3. To provide an environment in which handicapped campers, when properly prepared, can be integrated with their "normal" peers in recreation and socialization activities.
4. To facilitate the development of intervention techniques to modify certain specific behaviors that resisted change in the day care program

The first objective responds to the needs of children admitted to a day care program either at the beginning of or just before the camp session. The assessment and evaluation process is a continuous process and thus is logically extended through the camp session.

The second objective demonstrates a recognition and response to the relationships between the psychomotor, affective, and cognitive learning domains.

The third objective responds directly to the needs of children who appear, in the artificial environment of the special school and/or special class, to be ready to return to normal school and community functioning. The availability of a "normal" peer population for integration permits the handicapped camper to function in a normal, albeit artificial, environment while having a trained staff available for emotional support.

The final objective responds to certain specific behaviors that a child manifests but that have not responded to interventions previously imposed by his parents and/or school personnel. Among the behavior in this hard-to-modify category are bedwetting, soiling, eating habits (eating only with the hands and the like), food preferences (eating only candies, potato chips, pickles, and similar foods to the exclusion of all others), personal hygiene, and aggressive behaviors (tantrums, fights, cursing, swearing).

The residential camp includes several organizational units: an assessment and evaluation unit, a remediation unit, a recreation-socialization unit, and a residential unit. A social service program involving parents and community agency personnel is provided during the camp session.

The assessment and evaluation, remediation, and recreation-socialization units are similar to the ones discussed in detail in Chapter 5.

Assessment and evaluation unit

The camp assessment and evaluation unit has several objectives in addition to, and in coordination with, those discussed in Chapter 5.

The first of these involves the completion of the psychoeducational evaluations for campers who have not been administered a standard battery of tests during the previous academic year. Newly enrolled children are evaluated during the session to determine their levels of development and specific remedial needs.

The next objective is the detection and remediation of inadequate psychomotor skill development, one of the most frequently observed handicaps among the camp population. During the initial week of the camping session, an assessment is made of each child's psychomotor development: gross and fine motor coordination, visual-motor skills, directionality, body image, and the like. Children manifesting difficulties in one or more skills are assigned to remedial activities for the remainder of the session or until their handicap responds to remediation.

Assessment personnel are responsible for attaining a third objective, developing individual behavioral checklists for each camper. The checklists include behaviors from each of the three learning domains, and the observable behaviors included on the child's checklist are the program or instructional objectives selected for him during the session.

These checklists are completed daily by the instructors and counselors responsible for the child's program. The information derived from the checklists is used to evaluate the child's progress and to assist in making decisions concerning his future.

The final objective of this unit is the overall evaluation of the camp. Assessment personnel are responsible for observing a sampling of all camp activities and evaluating their effectiveness for the children. Personnel focus on the viability of the activities, on instructor and counselor competencies, and on health and safety factors. This information is used by the administration to modify the program to increase its effectiveness.

Remediation unit

The objectives of the remediation unit are similar to those discussed in Chapter 5.

Two hours each morning, 5 days per week, are devoted to small-group and individual preacademic and academic instruction. This program is a continuation of the child's school year instructional program. Remediation includes instruction in the basic skills (reading, writing, spelling, and computing); social studies, science and health; perceptual training; and language development.

During the camp session, an important innovation is made in the instructional program: whenever possible, subject matter content is modified to relate to the environment in which the camper is living. For example, reading and language development activities focus on subjects available in the immediate milieu, such as trees, flowers, animals, camp personnel and the like. To further this innovation, counselors are provided with information about the instructional topics. Thus, concepts discussed during formal remediation sessions are reinforced during the remainder of the day.

Special tutoring sessions are provided by remediation personnel for children attempting to catch up with their peers before they are reintegrated into regular classes in the fall.

Recreation-socialization unit

The objectives of the recreation-socialization unit discussed in Chapter 5 also apply at the residential camp.

In addition, unit personnel are responsible for integrating and supervising handicapped campers into the nonhandicapped population. (It is recommended that the camp be organized as a near-autonomous division of a camp for nonhandicapped children.) The decision to integrate a child is based both on staff judgment of the camper's readiness and on the child's personal perception of his readiness. Handicapped campers are integrated into nonhandicapped groups at a maximum ratio of 3:12. The period of integration may be as brief as 90 minutes (one activity period for nonhandicapped campers), or it may last the entire day. Children integrated for the entire day generally move from the handicapped children's unit to a nonhandicapped unit.

However, these campers are required to visit with their "old" counselor daily to discuss their program. The "old" counselor is required to confer daily with the camper's "new" counselor.

Residential unit

The residential unit is designed to provide an accepting, secure, consistent, small-group living environment for each child enrolled in the camp. Three or four campers, depending on the behavioral characteristics of the individual children, are assigned to each counselor. The counselor and his campers are companions 20 hours each day.

The specific objectives of the residential program are to help the camper:

1. Develop acceptable group-living skills. Counselors attempt to teach the children that fighting and arguing do not solve problems and that it is better (at least, less fatiguing) to discuss or prevent conflicts. Children learn that cooperative efforts (work) are necessary and can be satisfying.
2. Develop self-care skills and personal health habits. Children learn to care for their basic personal needs, such as eating properly, sleeping, and washing. Counselors are concerned with special health and hygiene problems, such as soiling and wetting.
3. Develop acceptable work skills. The campers are responsible for cleaning their cabins and the immediate environment, making their bunks, and keeping their personal possessions clean and in order. Frequently, campers are requested to do "special jobs" for the camp director, such as sweeping the dining hall, wiping tables, and helping the cooks, the grounds keepers, and the instructors.
4. Develop an appreciation (or at least a recognition) of the natural human life cycle of work, play, and rest.

Social service program

The major objective of the social service program during the camp session is to keep parents and community agency personnel informed about the child.

This is partially accomplished by means of weekly parent group sessions. These informational sessions are to review and discuss the camp program and to elicit from parents their perceptions of the program and concerns about their child.

Individual therapy sessions for parents and children with the social worker are continued throughout the summer.

Social service personnel are responsible for coordinating the activities of nonstaff community agency personnel involved with the campers. Provisions are made for nonstaff personnel to meet with their camper-clients for therapy sessions at the camp.

POPULATION

Because in this model the residential camp for special populations is part of a camp for nonhandicapped children, the number, age, characteristics, and classifications of the exceptional children attending is in large part dependent on the total camp population.

Experience indicates that it is desirable to maintain a ratio of approximately one exceptional child to every four or five nonhandicapped children. The residential camp on which this model is based had a population ranging from 8 to 40 exceptional campers and was established as a division of a camp serving 100 to 120 nonhandicapped campers.

The age range of the campers enrolled in this program varied each summer but was generally 6 to 12 years. At times, younger (5-year-old) and older (13- and 14-year-old) children were admitted to the program; however, many of the activities appeared to be inappropriate for these age groups unless the younger children were quite socially mature and the older ones, very immature. The camp served both boys and girls on a ratio of approximately 5 or 6:1. No child was excluded because of sex.

The camp served moderately to severely emotionally disturbed children. The children were diagnosed as autistic, schizophrenic, neurotic, brain damaged, and as having personality disorders. Some children had speech handicaps; some were nonverbal. The children as a group manifested the full range of behavioral characteristics: from severe withdrawal to acting out; from hypoactivity to hyperactivity; from overcautiousness to recklessness. Staff members were confronted with problems of soiling, wetting, refusal to eat, inability to sleep, and the like.

Although the camp on which this model is based served moderately to severely emotionally handicapped children, other categories of handicapped children could benefit from the program. The camp could serve speech-handicapped, learning-disabled, educable mentally retarded, and socially maladjusted children with little modification.

The nonhandicapped population of the camp was composed of children attending regular classes in the public schools. This population was unique because the majority of the children were wards of the State of Illinois, foster children, or residents of the inner city.

ADMINISTRATION

The director of the division for special populations is responsible for coordinating all camp activities for the exceptional children. In cooperation with the director of the division for nonexceptional children, he coordinates many activities: integration, special events, transportation, dining and living accommodations, and housekeeping services.

The director supervises all unit coordinators within the division for exceptional children; these unit coordinators are responsible for the campers and counselors and compose a policy team that assists the director in decision making.

Fig. 16 is a schema of the basic organizational pattern applied at the camp. This pattern varies with the size of the camp's population and the availability and competency of the staff.

The coordinators of the units are usually

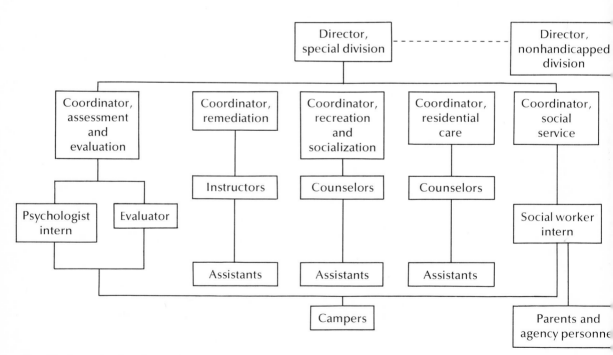

Fig. 16. Organizational pattern.

professionals, although, occasionally, advanced graduate students are employed. They are paid employees of the camp. The responsibilities of the coordinators are very demanding; consequently, untrained volunteers and/or students should not be employed in these positions.

The camp evaluator is a part-time employee. This individual must be an experienced camper, familiar with the activities and with the rules of safety and health.

Instructors are teachers of handicapped children. If possible, it is desirable to employ teachers familiar with the campers and their remedial programs.

Counselors and assistant counselors are graduate and undergraduate college students and advanced high school students. It is desirable to employ counselors and assistants interested in recreation, physical education, and special education. These young people are paid a minimum wage plus room and board.

All personnel are employed for the duration of the camping session and must participate in the training program.

On occasion, the nonhandicapped children's counselors are used as recreation activities instructors for the handicapped population. This is especially true when the special camp does not have qualified instructors available for activities of a specialized nature, such as swimming, archery, horseback riding, and canoeing.

PHYSICAL FACILITIES, EQUIPMENT, AND MATERIALS

All facilities available in the total camp, including dining facilities, classrooms, common rooms, health services, transportation services, living accommodations, recreation facilities, and water facilities, are used by the handicapped campers. However, separate lodging and classroom facilities are recommended for convenience in supervision and to enhance group cohesion.

Sanitary facilities should be easily accessible, especially between the hours of 9:00 PM and 7:00 AM.

Although the size of the cabins often dic-tates the number of campers per cabin, it is suggested that a ratio of three or four campers to each counselor be maintained. In special cases a camper-to-counselor ratio of 2:1, or even 1:1, may be necessary.

The special materials and equipment for recreation and remediation discussed in Chapter 5 for the day camp are also recommended for this program.

PERSONNEL TRAINING PROGRAM

Although the training program for the camp is similar to the one discussed in Chapter 5 for the day camp, modifications are made to ensure that the unit coordinators have sufficient opportunities to plan activities directly with the counselors and assistants assigned to their unit. In addition, the training schedule is modified to ensure that coordinators have adequate time to work with each other and with the director.

The counselors employed to work with the nonhandicapped populations should attend an orientation session to familiarize them with the purpose, objectives, program, and personnel employed for the special camp division. Of course, special population camp personnel must also be familiar with the purposes, objectives, program, and personnel of the nonhandicapped children's division.

The precamp training periods are conducted in residence. This arrangement permits personnel to familiarize themselves with the facilities and to begin forming positive working and living relationships.

PROGRAM DESCRIPTION

Variations of the program described here were used during the summers of 1967 through 1969. The program was modified annually as a result of the activities of the assessment and evaluation unit. The following is a brief overview of some of the unique features of the camp:

The camp is a 5-day-per-week residential program for approximately 40 moderately to severely emotionally disturbed children ranging in age from 6 to 12 years. The camping session is 5 weeks in duration. Children arrive early Sunday evening and remain at camp until Friday evening.

Individual and small-group preacademic and academic remedial instruction is conducted daily, Monday through Friday, from 8:30 AM to 10:30 PM. All campers are enrolled in these sessions. Special tutoring sessions may be scheduled at other times during the day.

Handicapped campers are integrated into activities with nonhandicapped campers throughout the day on a ratio of 3:12 (not all of the handicapped campers are integrated).

Community agency personnel continue individual therapy with their clients throughout the session in facilities provided at the camp.

The schedule is totally individualized to ensure that each child participates in the program at the level and to the degree possible for him.

The program is organized into the various units: assessment and evaluation, remediation, recreation-socialization, and residential.

A typical weekly schedule is presented in Fig. 17.

Assessment and evaluation unit

During the precamp personnel training workshop, the instructors and counselors are familiarized with the camp evaluation instruments. These instruments are administered under a psychologist's supervision during the first week of the session. The psychologist interprets the results of the tests.

Fig. 17. Weekly schedule for the residential camp for special populations.

Time	Sunday	Monday	Tuesday	Wednesday	Thursday	Friday	Saturday
7:00 AM		←		Wake-up time		→	
7:00-7:30		←		Personal care		→	
7:30-8:00		←		Breakfast		→	
8:00-8:30		←		Cabin cleanup		→	Staff meeting
8:30-10:30		←		Remediation		→	
10:30-12:00		←		Activity period 1 †		→	
12:00-1:00 PM		←		Lunch		→	
1:00-2:00		←		Rest/free play		→	
2:00-3:30	Staff meeting	←		Activity period 2		→	
3:30-5:00	Campers arrive	←		Activity period 3		→	
5:00-5:30	Supper	←		Supper		→	
5:30-6:30	Free time	←		Free time		→	
6:30-7:00	Visit to campus	←		Cabin meeting		→	
7:00-8:30	Parent meeting*	←		Activity period 4	→	Campers depart‡	
8:30-9:30	Preparation for bed	←		Activity period 4	→		
9:30 PM	Lights out	←		Activity period 4	→		

*Campers with counselors attend period 4 activity.

† Individual tutoring and therapy sessions may be scheduled after this time.

‡ Counselors confer with parents.

The evaluator observes activities throughout the session, including the pre- and postcamp workshops. He is a nonparticipating observer. On occasion, the evaluator will confer directly with a counselor or instructor on matters concerning the health and safety of the children.

Remediation unit

The remediation schedule is the same as that presented in Chapter 5 for the day camp.

During the residential camp, instructors are on duty from 8:00 AM to 2:00 PM daily. The half hour from 8:00 to 8:30 AM is used for planning. Instructors attend a daily staff meeting from 1:00 to 2:00 PM.

The instructor remain with their campers during activity period 1 and lunch, that is, until 1:00 PM. This arrangement permits the counselors to (1) attend staff meetings, (2) confer with their coordinator and other counselors, (3) observe the campers during remediation, and (4) rest.

Recreation-socialization unit

Many recreation-socialization activities described in Chapter 5 for the day camp are applicable in the residential setting. Handi-

Ready to explore the unknown.

Working together.

Sharing a new discovery.

capped campers *who are not integrated* for activities follow a schedule similar to the campers *who are integrated* for activities. However, these nonintegrated children remain with their cabin groups throughout the day.

For integrated campers, various activities are available daily, including archery, golf, fishing, sports, hiking, swimming, and so on. Campers select their activities as a member of a group of 15. However, the group must choose three activities for each period to avoid overloading the available facilities. Generally, each group selects a water and an arts-and-crafts activity.

Evening activities include all-camp songfests, campfires, variety shows, hayrides, cookouts, movies, and the like.

If the campers and their counselors elect to participate in an overnight camp-out or a field trip, the group's regular schedule is canceled. Usually, each group participates in some special activity weekly.

Residential unit

Handicapped children may be integrated into activities with nonhandicapped campers after the remediation period, that is, after 10:30 AM. Residential unit personnel are responsible for integration activities; they must confer with the receiving counselor and monitor the child's program.

The general policy of the camp is: *anything a camper is capable of doing for himself, he does for himself.* To facilitate this philosophy, counselors and instructors are encouraged to apply behavior management techniques compatible with life-space interviewing (Morse, 1959), reality therapy (Glasser, 1965), and behavior modification (Walker and Shea, 1976). These and other behavior change interventions are presented in Chapter 9.

ADVANTAGES AND DISADVANTAGES

The advantages of the residential camp for special populations are:
1. For the moderately to severely handicapped child with social and emotional problems, the therapeutic milieu created at the camp is effective in modifying his difficult-to-change behaviors. Many of these behaviors are resistant to change in the child's home, school, and community environment.
2. For the undiagnosed child, time in the residential camp is devoted to a comprehensive evaluation.
3. For the child behind his peers in academic achievement, the camp is instrumental in facilitating his progress in school subject matter content.
4. For the child requiring short-term residential care, for his benefit or for the benefit of his parents, the camp is a more acceptable alternative than institutionalization or foster care placement. Parents who live with their handicapped child 24 hours a day, 365 days a year, find that the child's placement at camp gives them a much-needed vacation.
5. For the child with affective and/or psychomotor handicaps, the camp is instrumental in helping accelerate his progress in the development of compensatory skills.
6. If properly coordinated, the camp facilitates the delivery of clinical services offered to children by the community agencies, including schools.

The disadvantages of the camp are:
1. For the child with extremely weak ego development, the camp is contraindicated. For this child, the change in environment is too drastic. He becomes frightened and confused, and withdraws.
2. For the child with a poor self-concept, camp can be a frustrating, negative experience unless he is programmed to ensure his success.
3. For the young child of 4 or 5 years of age, the camp is inappropriate. Activities are not designed for this age group. In addition, the child is deprived of his immediate family—especially his mother—for an extended period of time. Of course, in some circumstances this deprivation of family and mother may be the treatment of choice.

THE SPECIAL PURPOSE RESIDENTIAL CAMP*

I hope my mother will let me go. Never been on a horse.

> Marion J.
> *12-year-old student*

Can we really go in a boat, Ms. Woodall?

> Elmer C.
> *10-year-old student*

Do we stay for a whole 2 weeks?

> Frances M.
> *13-year-old student*

Are you going to be with us all the time, teacher? Even at night?

> Jonathan F.
> *8-year-old student*

Man, it was fun. We did all sorts of stuff—even went on a raccoon hunt. Are we gonna go again?

> James B.
> *14-year-old student*

Camp is such a great experience in the summer. It is an even greater one in the winter. It provides a break from the routine of the classroom and a unique experience with nature at an invigorating time of year.

> Beverly Holden
> *College student,*
> *counselor*

My boy really liked camp. He went in the winter and summer and still talks about it.

> Mrs. B.
> *Mother*

The weeks of winter camping gave both the teacher and the students a new perspective of the student-teacher and peer group relationships. There were endless opportunities for getting to know each other that would never be possible in the traditional classroom. We ate together, slept together, played together, and learned together. Most of all, we shared fun and adventure in the great outdoors.

---

*The description of the special purpose residential camp is based on an article published previously: Shea, T. M., Phillips, T. L., and Campbell, A. Outdoor living and learning complement each other. *Teaching Exceptional Children* 4(3), 1972, 108-118.

Not only did a new kind of respect develop, one for the other, but a bond of friendship was kindled among classmates and teachers that existed long beyond the days of camping.

> Jan Holloway
> *Teacher, junior high class*
> *for educable mentally*
> *handicapped*

Educational experiences for children with special problems need not focus only on the classroom. Experiences such as those that are provided at the Laboratory are an important complement to the traditional classroom education of children. Where else can words, books, and pictures be related to life more relevantly than in the study of one's history, health, art, and nature in the out-of-doors? It would seem that experiences relevant to life is what education is all about.

> Dick Smith
> *Director of Special*
> *Education, Carbondale,*
> *Illinois*

The more relaxed and "fun" aspects of camping seem in many cases to make learning easier . . .

This format for learning gives the subject double exposure . . .

The teachers and students who have experienced the winter camping program have found it both an enjoyable and valuable learning situation . . .

> Louis Freitag
> *Program Coordinator,*
> *Little Grassy Outdoor*
> *Laboratory*

PURPOSES AND OBJECTIVES

Special educators share with parents and other professionals the responsibility of preparing exceptional children to live and work in a complex socioeconomic society. In the choice of instructional objectives, particular consideration should be given to interpersonal relationships; environmental awareness; economic independence; community, group, and family responsibilities; and the proper use of leisure time.

One of the most challenging aspects of teaching handicapped children, especially the educable mentally handicapped and the experientially deprived, is the creation and organization of experience units sufficiently stimulating and self-reinforcing to ensure learning. Teachers and administrators strive to provide programs that avoid subject matter content and sequential learning gaps that the child cannot fill independently and that are commensurate with the child's rate of learning by providing opportunities for direct application in the environment of concepts presented in the classroom (Johnson, 1958). The special purpose residential camp model presented here is designed to meet these criteria.

The camp provides handicapped children opportunities to apply abstract concepts presented by the teacher in the classroom by means of traditional instructional methods in a "real" environment. This environmental reinforcement is as near to immediate as is feasible in the camp setting.

In addition to the cognitive learning benefits, the children participating in this camp derive many of the motivational, recreational, self-care, emotional, and social benefits of the residential camp for special populations.

The outdoor environment provides a setting in which several experience units, taught by special education teachers in both local and camp classrooms, are reinforced. Through a combination of classroom instruction and environmental experiences, the children develop greater interest and insight into the subject matter content of the instructional unit. Students develop insight into their abilities and disabilities as they relate in and to an unfamiliar environment.

At camp, classroom groups are involved in a cooperative living experience. For the teachers and children, the program is an experience in adaptability to an environment that, by its nature, makes demands on the individual.

POPULATION

The camp on which this model is based was attended by educable mentally handicapped children. However, the program can be a learning experience of considerable

benefit for other handicapped groups: learning disabled, emotionally disturbed, socially maladjusted, and speech handicapped. Children who are physically handicapped may attend if the physical facilities of the camp permit it. The program can be of value to children from urban areas who are deprived of the opportunity to experience rural and camp life.

The camp is recommended for middle and upper elementary school and junior high school age children. Exceptions should be made on the basis of specific populations and on the availability of physical facilities and personnel. Boys and girls (usually 2 or 3 classroom groups of 15 children each) ages 10 to 15 years attended the camp at the Little Grassy Outdoor Laboratory.

Only total classroom groups are enrolled in the special purpose camp. The groups must include the teacher and the teacher's aide, if one is assigned to the class. This method of enrolling only intact groups reduces the time required to develop group cohesion.

Although the emphasis here is on special education classroom groups, other groups from regular classes in urban communities, training schools, hospitals, and mental health facilities may participate.

ADMINISTRATION

The special education teacher and the camp coordinator are coadministrators of the program. The camp coordinator is responsible for all the group's physical needs, such as personnel, equipment, and materials. He is responsible for all living accommodations, including meals, lodging, health services, and transportation. The teacher is responsible for selecting and teaching the experience units to be presented during the program and for supervising the children and counselors.

Cooperative decision making between the teacher and camp coordinator is desirable and necessary. However, the coordinator is ultimately responsible for all decisions concerning the health and safety of the campers. The teacher is ultimately responsible for all subject matter content and instructional decisions.

Trained counselors are assigned by the coordinator to assist the teacher and the teacher's aide in the supervision and instruction of the campers. Counselors are trained to reinforce the concepts presented during classroom activities throughout the remainder of the day during environmental activities.

Five children are assigned to each counselor. If severely handicapped children attend camp, the camper-to-counselor ratio is 3:1 or less.

Counselors are employees of the camp and are paid for their labor. They are usually advanced undergraduate or graduate students assigned to the camp for academic credit. Students majoring in recreation, physical education, psychology, elementary and secondary education, and special education are excellent counselors.

PHYSICAL FACILITIES, EQUIPMENT, AND MATERIALS

The specific instructional materials and equipment needed for the instructional program depend on the experience units selected by the teacher. Examples of the instructional materials and equipment used in the experience units are presented below under Program description.

PERSONNEL TRAINING PROGRAM

Counselors are trained before the camp session begins in a program similar to the precamp workshop described in Chapter 5.

The teacher and aide receive training on camp policies, procedures, and programs in discussions at camp with the coordinator or his representative.

During a precamp meeting, teachers familiarize the counselors with the characteristics of the children and with the experience units to be utilized. Individual and group behavior management techniques to be used during the camp session are discussed.

PROGRAM DESCRIPTION

The 4-week program consists of 3 phases: a precamp phase (1 week) conducted in the local classroom by the special education teacher and children with assistance from the camp staff; a camp phase (2 weeks) conducted at the camp by the teacher, children, and camp staff; and a postcamp phase (1 week) conducted by the teacher and children in the local classroom.

Precamp phase

Before coming to camp, the teacher selects the unit or units to be presented. Some suggested topics are:

Animal life
Conservation and ecology
Language development
Natural resources
Outdoor use of leisure time
Pioneer life
Safety in the out-of-doors
Self-care
Socialization
Working together

In the local classroom during the precamp phase, the teacher presents slides of the physical facilities in which the class will live and work. It is useful to have a representative of the camp available for this portion of the program to answer questions.

Next, the teacher introduces the basic concepts of the experience unit to the group. For example, the teacher and children may decide that a unit on animal life (beginning with animals in general and then focusing on horses) is appropriate. In the classroom, (Fig. 18) the children learn about animals in general: how they move, breathe, and need food, water, and rest. They learn that animals have coverings of fur or feathers that protect them from heat and cold; they learn that these coats change from season to season.

Camp phase

During the 2 weeks at camp, the campers, teachers, and counselors review the material studied during the precamp phase and continue to explore the topics of the unit or units of study.

The camp phase of the unit includes two primary activities. The first of these is classroom instruction by the teacher, supple-

ANIMAL LIFE

Day	1 and 2	3	4 and 5
Program	Introduction to camp's physical facilities	Introduction to experience unit	Continuation of unit and presentation of basic concepts

I. Concepts presented
  1. Animalness.
  2. Kinds of animals.
  3. Familiar animals.
  4. Differences and similarities among animals.
  5. Classification of animals.
  6. Animal needs.
II. Instructional activities
  1. Have children list familiar animals on the chalkboard, getting clues from around the room, from book covers, and from bulletin boards.
  2. Present and discuss film *Animals are Different and Alike.*
  3. Classify and relist animals on chart paper. Discuss common characteristics of animals in each category to build awareness of similarities and differences. Place pictures of animals on the chart.
  4. Discuss their common needs if animals are to be healthy (water, rest, proper diet, grooming, and so on).
III. Instructional materials and equipment
  1. Bulletin boards with pictures of mammals, fish, birds, reptiles, and amphibians.
  2. A display with stuffed animals, if available.
  3. Library books about animals, particularly horses and other domestic animals.
  4. Film *Animals are Different and Alike* (Cornet).

Fig. 18. Precamp phase of unit (presented in the local school classroom).

mented by film, slides, and other instructional materials. These sessions are scheduled twice daily, morning and afternoon, and are then immediately reinforced by related activities presented in the environment. These environmental activities are directed by the teacher with the assistance of the counselors.

Fig. 19 presents the camp phase of the unit on animal life. This phase of the unit focuses on horses. During activity periods the children may go to the stables, where they observe and then help saddle and bridle the horses before actually riding. They watch as the stableman hitches a team of horses to a wagon for a hayride. After the ride, the stableman takes off the harness. He instructs the group on the reasons for brushing, watering, and feeding the horses. The campers are

then given an opportunity to care for the animals.

By this time, the instructional concepts have been well established through both classroom instruction and actual experiences. However, the concepts presented are reviewed, when the occasion arises, by the counselor throughout the remainder of the day. For example, a counselor taking the campers on a hike may ask questions such as "Who runs faster, a horse or a man?" "Who eats grass and hay, a horse or a man?" "Who feeds himself with a spoon, a person or a horse?" "Whose hair needs daily brushing?" "Who takes a shower, a person or a horse?"

At camp, all activities are potentially meaningful learning experiences. Leisure time is available to the children in the late

ANIMAL LIFE

Day	6	7 and 8	9 and 10	11 and 12	13 and 14	15
Program	Review basic concepts	Breeds of horses	Care of horses	Continuation of care of horses	Uses for horses	Review of previous activities

I. Concepts presented
   1. Differences among horses in size, color, and shape.
   2. Similarities and differences between the parts of horses and humans.
   3. Horses' work.
II. Instructional activities
   1. Have colored pictures of several different breeds of horses. Discuss and compare size, color, and shape of various horses.
   2. Using a large outline of a horse, name and label parts such as the withers, shoulders, fetlock, and frog. Compare parts of the horse to parts of the human body.
   3. Make a list of suggestions offered by the children concerning what horses can be used for.
   4. Show the film *Horse*.
   5. As the discussion progresses, add suggestions of the use of horses to the list made before the film was shown.
III. Experience activity
   1. Visit the stable to actually compare size, color, and shapes of horses. This also affords an opportunity to become familiar with horses and to allay fears.
   2. Look at the teeth, hoofs, coat, and mane. Try to remember all the parts of the horse that were labeled in the classroom.
   3. Note use of horses in camp environment (pleasure, riding, pulling wagons).
   4. Go for a ride on a horse-drawn wagon or sleigh. Listen to the rhythm of the hoofs. Try to duplicate this rhythm through clapping.
   5. Listen to "On the Trail" from the *Grand Canyon Suite* (Grofe).
IV. Instructional materials and equipment
   1. Colored pictures of various breeds of horses.
   2. Large outline of man and horses.
   3. Pictures of horses at work.
   4. Film *Horse* (Encyclopedia Britannica Films, Inc.).
   5. Stable.
   6. Horses.
   7. Equipment for use of horse.

Fig. 19. Camp phase of unit: focus on horses (presented in camp classroom and in environment).

afternoon and evening, and after meals. However, the campers are encouraged to engage in meaningful activities such as quiet games, table games, conversation, and planning discussions.

The typical day at camp is long and filled with planned activities. Campers are awakened at 7:00 AM, at which time they prepare for breakfast. Between breakfast and the beginning of class at 9:00 AM, cabins are swept, beds are made, and personal belongings are stored for the day. Classes are conducted from 9:00 to 11:15 AM (usually 30 minutes in the classroom and the remaining time in the environment).

Before lunch, the children play field sports or participate in arts and crafts or a similar activity. After lunch and a rest period, the

ANIMAL LIFE

Day	16	17, 18 and 19	20
Program	Thank you letters describing activities	Review of experience units' content	Final discussion and evaluation

   I. Concepts to be reviewed (see Fig. 18)
  II. Instructional activities
     1. See Fig. 18.
     2. Construct models (stable, wagon, cabins), draw pictures, make scrapbooks, and write stories.
 III. Instructional materials and equipment
     1. See Fig. 18.
     2. Construction materials such as clay, cardboard, paint, glue, wood, and nails.

Fig. 20. Postcamp phase of unit (presented in local school classroom).

groups attend classes from 2:00 to 3:30 PM. The late afternoon is devoted to a variety of high-interest activities, such as field sports, nature study, fishing, and the like.

Evening meals are followed by movies, skits, songfests, campfires, and other total-group activities. Campers retire to their cabins at 8:30 in the evening to relax and prepare for bed. Lights-out time varies with the age of the group. The evening is for personal discussions, introspection, and much-needed rest.

Saturdays and Sundays (not noted on Fig. 19) are special days. Wake-up time is 8:30 AM. The majority of each day is devoted to small-group activities. On Saturdays, field trips are arranged to points of historical and educational interest and to the local community for shopping. Evenings may be used for television, movies, or table games.

Sunday is devoted to attending church, either at camp or in the community, and to visiting with parents and other family members.

Postcamp phase

The teacher, teacher's aide, and campers have experienced many things at the camp. Each person in the group has a greater appreciation for the other members. All have a variety of common experiences.

In the local school during the week following the camp phase, the class reviews the activities of the precamp and camp phase (Fig. 20). They write thank you notes to their sponsors and counselors.

The teacher and children relate what they have experienced to others in many ways; they write stories, make scrapbooks, draw pictures, display projects, and discuss their activities with parents, teachers, and other children.

ADVANTAGES AND DISADVANTAGES

The advantages of the special purpose residential camp are:
1. It facilitates learning by permitting the the children to apply abstract concepts presented in the classroom, in the environment.
2. It provides opportunities for campers to develop group-living skills and self-care skills under supervision.
3. It provides teachers and aides an opportunity to interact with their children in a nonschool environment. They often discover previously unrecognized strengths and handicaps among their group.

4. For many handicapped children who may never have an opportunity, it is a chance to experience rural living, group living, and camping.

The special purpose residential camp, more than any other model discussed in this volume, provides continuity for the child's school program. It is specifically designed to extend and strengthen the teacher's efforts in the classroom.

The disadvantages of the camp are:

1. If the units and activities are poorly organized and presented, the children will not benefit cognitively.
2. If the public school is not sensitive to the unique learning needs of handicapped children, the very suggestion of the program to school personnel could result in disadvantages to the children and teachers wishing to participate.

The special purpose camp concepts should not be restricted to the setting and population described in this chapter.

Residential facilities and several hundred acres of forest are not available in every community; but woodlands, parks, zoos, and recreation facilities exist in nearly all communities. With minor modifications, this program could be a beneficial day camp learning experience for handicapped children.

REFERENCES

Apter, S. J. Therapeutic camping in the 1970's. Newsletter: Council for Children with Behavioral Disorders, 1975, **12**(3), 3-6.

Cyr, D. Everybody makes the scene. *Arts and Activities*, 1970, **67**(3), 26-28.

Damon, W. Camping therapy for delinquents. *Recreation*, 1959, **52**, 106.

Endres, R. Northern Minnesota therapeutic camp. *Journal of Health, Physical Education, and Recreation*, 1971, **42**(5), 75-76.

Flax, N., and Peters, E. N. Retarded children at camp with normal children. *Children*, 1969, **16**(6), 232-237.

Glasser, W. *Reality therapy.* New York: Harper & Row, Publishers, 1965.

Herr, D. E. Evaluating camp Easter Seal from a camper's perspective. Newsletter; Council for Children with Behavior Disorders, 1975, **12**(2), 8-15.

Higdon, H. Michigan's remarkable summer speech camp. *Today's Health*, 1968, **46**(5), 34-37, 74-75.

Johnson, G. O. The education of mentally handicapped children. In W. M. Cruickshank and G. O. Johnson (Eds.), *Education of exceptional children and youth*, Englewood Cliffs, N.J.: Prentice-Hall, Inc., 1958.

Kokaska, C. A summer camp experience for institutionalized mentally retarded children. *The Training School Bulletin*, 1966, (**62**)(3), 158-162.

Larson, R. The mentally retarded at camp. *Recreation*, 1957, **50**, 66-78.

Lowry, T. P. (Ed.). *Camping therapy.* Springfield, Ill.: Charles C Thomas, Publisher, 1974.

Martin, W. B. Overnight camp aids retardates. *Camping Magazine*, 1972, **44**(7), 20.

Morse, W. C. An interdisciplinary therapeutic camp. *Journal of Social Issues*, 1957, **13**(1), 15-22.

Morse, W. C., and Small, E. Group life-space interviewing in a therapeutic camp. *American Journal of Orthopsychiatry*, 1959, **29**, 27-44.

Rawson, H. E. Research attests to behavior change in programs geared to specialized camping. *Camping Magazine*, 1973, **45**(5), 16-17.

Redl, F. *When we deal with children:* New York: The Free Press, 1966.

Rourke, R. A share of summer fun. *Journal of Health, Physical Education, and Recreation*, 1971, **42**(5), 71-72.

Shea, T. M., and Booth, N. J. Comprehensive service for emotionally handicapped children: an experiment in collaborative programming. Newsletter: Council for Children with Behavioral Disorders, 1968, **5**, 16-22.

Shea, T. M., Ott, M. F., Overturf, E., and Phillips, T. L. The Little Grassy Outdoor Laboratory for emotionally handicapped children. Newsletter: Council for Children with Behavioral Disorders, 1969, **6**(4), 13-19.

Shea, T. M., and Phillips, T. L. Emotionally disturbed in camping experiment. Newsletter: Information Center, Recreation for the Handicapped, 1968, **3**(11), 1, 4.

Shea, T. M., Phillips, T. L., and Campbell, A. Outdoor living and learning complement each other. *Teaching Exceptional Children*, 1972, **4**(3), 108-118.

Smith, J. S. Camping with the mentally retarded. *Recreation*, 1953, **46**(4), 214.

Stoudenmire, J., and Comola, J. Evaluating camp climb-up: a two-week therapeutic camp, *Exceptional Children*, 1973, **39**(7), 573-574.

Wald, M. Camp meeting special needs. *Camping Magazine*, 1974, **46**(6), 24.

Walker, J. E., and Shea, T. M. *Behavior modification: a practical approach for educators*, St. Louis: The C. V. Mosby Co.

CHAPTER 8

The wilderness camp

THE WEEK THE FOREST TURNED BLUE*

Boys beginning to understand boys,
Adults beginning to understand adults,
  Boys beginning to understand adults,
  Adults beginning to understand boys,
All beginning to understand themselves.

We are alone, just our group—15 individuals—9 preadolescent boys and 6 counselors. We hardly know one another, yet we have a week to live in the wilderness, miles from home, family, and friends. We face a 24-mile backpacking trip through an unknown forest.

Who are we?

The Phantom (George). Ten years old. Always here but never here—never really a part of any group; trying, trying desperately to overcome being left out; friendless.

The Sick One (Randy). Twelve years old. A mamma's boy and a hypochondriac—constantly complaining of aches and pains, strains and bruises—but always struggling on, meeting the challenges of the trail.

Muscle Mouth (David). Thirteen years old. Incessantly talking and ordering others; constantly cursing and swearing; attempting to manipulate everyone. The facade slowly falls away; anxiety and fear take its place.

The Soiler (Sean). Twelve years old. Everyday, sometimes twice a day, walks to the creek to wash and change his clothes. Appears unconcerned about his problem, unashamed. No one comments; no one makes fun. A good camper. I don't understand.

The Bug (Kyle). Ten years old. The youngest in the group; always underfoot; always seeking adult companionship; always asking questions, questions, constant questions.

The Camper (Theodore). Thirteen years old. The oldest in the group, a leader. Learns quickly; friend to everyone; willingly helps the less skilled. Has a speech problem. A pleasure to be with.

Mr. Competent (Kirk). Twelve years old. Always wears his blue baseball cap and sunglasses. Learns quickly; quiet and reserved; manifests many of the characteristics of Austria, where he lived for 5 years. I see no problems. The school personnel must be wrong.

M & M (Kevin). Ten years old. The most handicapped in the group. Appears out of contact with reality most of the time but tries, tries very hard. Hiking, camping, and sleeping not a problem. Slowly becoming a part of the group; observing, listening, talking, and then at week's end, a few stories and jokes. The other boys help him. They never poke fun. I am proud of them.

The Regular Boy (Mick). Thirteen years old. A leader. Polite, competent, and interested in

---

*The notes in this section are from my camping log (1973). The impressions of the camp, campers, and counselors are immediates ones that I wrote on the trail.

his environment; somewhat quiet and re-served. Why was he referred? School per-sonnel have made an error.

Big Mac. Twenty years old. Sincere and sensi-tive; always willing, always dependable. The boys respond to him. He responds to them.

Old Boyd. Thirty-nine years old. A good man who carries his load of responsibilities. Helps the younger counselors; makes suggestions; watches for potential mishaps and conflicts. A friend.

Mr. Patience (Dan). Twenty-four years old. Quiet, solid, dependable, humorous. Knows his campers and likes them. A willing referee of conflicts. The boys respond to him.

Ranger Rick (Jon). Twenty-seven years old. A camper's camper; knows the wilderness and likes the boys. They respect his skill. Always forging ahead in the lead; a constant teacher of flowers, trees, animals, camping skills.

The Cook (Paul). Twenty-six years old. Not a camper but a man—a man who cares. Takes care of his boys; loves to cook, clean, and organize. Always willing to referee a conflict, find a solution.

The General (me). Thirty-eight years old. Try-ing to prove that packing can rehabilitate. Often overconcerned, overanxious, and overstructured. Willing but clumsy. At times, too blunt, too direct; but cares and feels.

What happened?

Cursing and bickering. At first, this made the forest turn blue; but on the third day, it stopped.

A few bad dreams, a couple of nightmares, a bit of homesickness. Counselors talked, however, and these became less frequent.

A night of drenching rain. We survived, and we learned.

An evening of magic. Creative minds at work around a campfire; everyone was involved.

The creek. A discovery of never-ending adven-tures.

Cooking. "Me, a cook? My mother won't even let me in the kitchen. OK, but you guys better like these pancakes, if you know what's good for ya."

A backpack. "You mean I gotta carry that thing? I'll do it, but I won't like it. Are you trying to kill me?"

A tent. "Hey, you, help me. I can't get this dumb thing up."

A hike. "How far have we come? Must be 50 miles."

A ride. "If he can ride, why can't I? Just 'cause he's got a blister—he's faking. Well, I'm getting one—you wait."

Grossing out the local populace. "Boy, did you see those people in the cafe look at us? They were really scared. They probably never saw real packers before."

Swearing. "OK, but I'm saying 'strawberry.' It ain't swearing, and you'll know what I mean."

What did we learn?

How to walk and carry a pack.

How to make camp and care for ourselves.

How to pace the expenditure of our energy to complete a task.

How to work together; how to erect a tent, adjust a pack, build a fire, cook a meal.

How to maintain our environment.

How to avoid accidents and illnesses—tics, snakes, leeches, cold, rain, wind.

How nature functions—flowers, plants, trees, animals, fish, insects, water.

Most of all, we learned to live with each other. We learned how to give, how to take, how to be acceptably aggressive, how to with-draw with honor when the time was appropri-ate, how to cope. We learned about others; but most of all, we learned about ourselves.

The wilderness camp for handicapped youth includes three phases: a 1-day hike with training and planning sessions, a 3-day backpacking trip with training and planning sessions, and a 6-day backpacking trip. The camp on which this model is based was conducted during the spring of 1973 at Clark National Forest in Missouri. The group camped on the Berryman Trail, which begins and ends 17 miles west of Potosi.

The program was sponsored by grants from the Department of Special Education and the Graduate School at Southern Illinois Univer-sity at Edwardsville. Many individuals loaned the group a variety of needed equip-ment and materials.

PURPOSES AND OBJECTIVES

The rehabilitation of preadolescent and adolescent emotionally disturbed and so-cially maladjusted youth is the most critical problem confronting the mental health and education professions in the United States today. Thousands and thousands of our young men and women are in chronic difficulty in their schools and communities. Some are totally alienated from society. They have dropped or been forced out before they have had an opportunity to begin building their life.

Few therapeutic services have been developed for this age group. The effectiveness of traditional counseling, recreation, special education, vocational education, and institutional services for them is of questionable value. A cursory review of the recidivism rates among youthful offenders indicates that today's rehabilitation services are, for the most part, not effective. Camping, wilderness camping in particular, has the qualities for being an effective rehabilitation agent.

The basic purposes of the wilderness camp are:

1. To provide a therapeutic milieu in which the camper's concept of himself as an individual person, a member of a group, a learner, and a worker can be modified in a positive direction
2. To serve as an intervention to modify some specific problem behaviors that appear to alienate the camper from others, including peers and adults
3. To provide a milieu in which the camper learns to live with others cooperatively
4. To asist the camper in learning the knowledge and skills needed to live in the wilderness

POPULATION

The wilderness camp group, including counselors, should not exceed 18 persons: 12 youth and 6 adults. The effectiveness of the camp as an agent for rehabilitation is highly dependent on the development of close positive interpersonal relationships between the group members, especially between each camper and his counselor. Groups numbering in excess of 18 reduce the probability that these desired relationships will develop during the trip. However, camping groups may be as small as three persons: two campers and one counselor.

The wilderness program is especially beneficial for youth classified as socially maladjusted and juvenile delinquent. Other handicapped groups, such as the speech handicapped, educable mentally retarded, and slow learners also benefit from the program.

Both boys and girls enjoy the outdoors and should be encouraged to participate in the wilderness camp. However, sexually mixed groups are not recommended, because of the nature of the living conditions.

The camp is suggested for youth who are 11 years of age and older. Younger children may be included when they have physical stamina to hike 5 or 6 miles a day while carrying a 15- to 25-lb backpack.

The young men who participated in the camp on which this model is based were selected from 20 persons referred by local school personnel in Madison County, Ill. These boys were referred as those most in need of therapeutic assistance in their schools. Ages ranged from 10 (almost 11) to 14 years. Before the program began, the members of the group, both campers and counselors, were at best only casual acquaintances.

ADMINISTRATION

The wilderness camp is a group activity. All phases of the program are to be discussed and agreed on by the total group—campers and counselors.

The group is divided into subgroups of one or two counselors and their campers, who plan and organize various facets of the program: the schedule, the menus, food purchases, obtaining equipment and materials, training sessions, transportation, and so on. These subgroups report to the total group.

A camp coordinator is designated to organize the activities of the various subgroups. He is responsible for relations between the camp and parents, school and agency personnel, and interested community groups. He is the public spokesman for the wilderness camp.

Excluding the coordinator, a camper-to-counselor ratio of 2:1 is recommended. This ratio is necessary especially when the individual members of the camp are unknown to each other. If an intact classroom or hospital cottage group is participating in the program, the camper-to-counselor ratio may be increased to 3:1.

Counselors must be trained personnel. They should be competent in working with handicapped youth as a result of either successful training or experience. The counselors involved in the 1973 camp were graduate students and faculty members involved in the education of emotionally disturbed and socially maladjusted children and youth at Southern Illinois University at Edwardsville.

Counselors must either be experienced campers or willing to learn and practice the necessary skills before the program begins. It would be foolhardy to venture into a wilderness area with inexperienced counselors.

PHYSICAL FACILITIES, EQUIPMENT, AND MATERIALS

A wilderness or some type of isolated area is suggested for the backpacking trips. The area selected should be remote from the distractions found in the majority of communities and public camping areas. The effectiveness of the program is enhanced when the group is alone to challenge the natural environment without concern for others. Many of the abundant national, state, and provincial primitive areas available in North America have marked hiking and backpacking trails with sanitary facilities, drinking and washing water, emergency shelters, and emergency aid stations. Readable maps of the trails and access roads are generally available from the local rangers on request.

The Berryman Trail in Clark National Forest, the site of the 3-day and 6-day backpacking trips on which this model is based, is a 24-mile riding and hiking trail looping through a sparsely settled part of south central Missouri.

The trail is constructed for single file traffic through Ozark mountains and timberland. It winds through stands of pine, oak, and bottomland hardwoods, climbing switchback fashion from level bottoms to high ridges. During the trip, the dogwood trees and spring flowers were in bloom. A wide variety of flora and fauna abounds in abandoned farm fields, on rock outcroppings, and in the deep forest. The wildlife habitat improvement program of the United States Forest Service has produced healthy populations of deer and turkey, as well as a broad variety of small animals and birds. There are many springs, creeks, caves, and rock formations along the trail.

Streams, creeks, and watering ponds can be used for wading and fishing. Sanitary facilities, primitive fireplaces, and drinking water are located at some of the developed campsites. Each campsite is accessible by vehicle. A map of the trail is available from the office of the district ranger.

Camp Lakewood, operated by the St. Louis YMCA, was used as a base camp for the backpacking trips. This camp is located about 10 miles from the trail head.

A community park in Wood River, Ill., was the site selected for the 1-day hike. Playing fields, a lake, shelters, fireplaces, and sanitary facilities were available to the group at this park.

A considerable amount of sturdy lightweight equipment is needed for a backpacking trip such as the one presented here. The equipment listed here is the minimum necessary. The needed equipment will vary with individual preferences, the length of trip, the season of the year, and the geographic area selected. Several excellent references on equipment are presented at the end of this chapter.

Listed below is the individual equipment carried by each counselor and camper in the 1973 program as he traveled from campsite to campsite. In addition, each camper and counselor was required to leave one change of clothing at the base camp for the trip home.

Quantity	Item
1 pair	Hiking boots
2 pair	Heavy woolen or cotton socks

1 pair	Tennis shoes or moccasins
2 or 3 pair	Lightweight socks
3 sets	Underclothing (shirts and shorts)
2 pair	Trousers or jeans
2 or 3	Shirts
1	Heavy sweatshirt, sweater, or lightweight jacket
1	Hat or cap with brim
2 each	Towels and washcloths
5	Handkerchiefs
1	Comb
1	Bar of soap in a container
—	Personal medication
1	Pocket knife (optional for campers)
1	Swimming suit
1	Raincoat or poncho
1 each	Plate, cup, knife, fork, and spoon; or a mess kit.
1	Flashlight with fresh batteries
1	Sleeping bag or bed roll
1	Sleeping pad (for those over 35 years of age)
1	Ground cloth
1	Backpack with frame
1	Watch (optional for campers)
1 can	Insect repellent
1 copy	Trail map (optional for campers)
1	Compass (optional for campers)
1	Canteen
1 per 2 persons	Tent, nylon, 2-man with poles, pegs, and guy lines
1	Personal first aid kit, snake bite kit, and water purification tablets
1	Belt
1 pair	Gloves
1 set	Primitive fishing tackle
1 each	Signaling mirror and whistle
—	Camera and film (optional)
1	Nylon cord, 50-foot length
—	Foodstuffs for lunch

Items not available to campers were provided by the camp. No camper was required to purchase special equipment for the trip. The majority of the equipment was rented from an equipment rental store or the St. Louis YMCA, or was borrowed from friends.

Listed below is the group equipment used on the trip. This equipment was transported from campsite to campsite in a vehicle. This was done because of (1) the length of the trip, (2) the lack of experience among the campers in carrying heavy packs, (3) the bulk-

iness of the rented equipment, and (4) the coordinator's desire to have an emergency vehicle available at each campsite.

Quantity	Item
1	First aid kit (including foot powder and moleskin)
3 or 4	Washbasins, plastic
3 or 4	Nylon cord or rope, 50-foot lengths
1	Dining fly with poles, pegs, and guy lines
2	Axes or hatchets
2	Saws
3	Cooking kits with frying pans
1 container	Matches, waterproof
4 or 5	Water bags
—	Water purification tablets
—	Cleaning materials (soap, scouring pads, pot holders, Handiwipes, paper towels, toilet tissue, and litterbags)
—	Equipment repair kits and spare parts
—	Foodstuffs for entire trip excluding daily lunch
2	Shovels

Prepackaged dried foods are available from speciality firms and camping stores. However, food purchased in bulk at the local supermarket, although heavy and bulky, is of excellent quality and less expensive.

Sample menus for backpacking trips of various lengths of time can be found in several of the reference texts listed at the end of this chapter. The specific menus selected will depend, to a great extent, on the personal preferences of the campers and on available funds.

PERSONNEL TRAINING PROGRAM

The wilderness camp training program is a two-part activity of planning, and training. The planning phase is for counselors only. Campers are included in the training phase, which includes the 1-day hike and the two backpacking trips.

Planning phase

Planning for the camp begins several weeks before the actual camping trips. All counselors participate in planning activities.

The group conducts a series of evening sessions to discuss:

1. Processes and procedures for selecting the campers
2. Roles and functions of the counselors and coordinator
3. Decision-making processes to be applied during the program
4. Equipment, materials, and commodities needed and their availability
5. Rules of behavior to be applied during the program
6. Behavior management guidelines and techniques
7. Emergency procedures
8. Potential campsites
9. Dates and the schedule of events
10. Evaluation procedures

The rules developed for the campers in the 1973 program were:

Remain with your counselor and group at all times.

Either participate in a scheduled activity or sit out the activity. No special activities will be scheduled for any individual.

You must care for yourself (personal grooming).

You must care for your equipment. Any equipment left around the camping area will be confiscated for 24 hours.

The behavior management techniques the counselors chose to apply during the program were transactional analysis (Harris, 1969; James and Jongeward, 1971), reality therapy (Glasser, 1965), and life-space interviewing (Redl, 1966).

As a part of their training, the counselors attended an American Red Cross First Aid course offered by a certified instructor in a nearby community.

In an effort to evaluate the project, each counselor agreed to write a daily log. He would record his group's experiences, his perceptions of the campers, and his concerns. One counselor was selected to be the official photographer and was to make a pictorial log of the entire program.

We were fortunate to have among our group of counselors several individuals with unique talents that could be applied during the trips. One counselor was an amateur geologist; another was greatly interested in plants, trees, and flowers; another was an experienced hunter; another was interested in outdoor cooking.

Nearly all of the counselors were experienced campers and comfortable in the wilderness.

It was agreed on by the planning group that all of the plans developed during this phase of the personnel training program were tentative. As the counselors became involved with the campers and elicited their suggestions, the plans would be modified if there was a consensus among the total group.

Training phase

The training phase, as previously stated, is the actual camping program. The discussion of this phase of the personnel training program is incorporated into the program description.

PROGRAM DESCRIPTION

Our rationale for conducting the 1973 camp in three phases of increasing difficulty —a hike and two backpacking trips—was:

1. We could assure ourselves that each camper was in adequate physical condition for the trip.
2. We could include the youth in meaningful planning of the program.
3. We could communicate and reinforce the camp rules.
4. We could assure ourselves that each youth developed at least a minimum number of the needed safety and camping skills.
5. We could obtain, repair, and adjust equipment for each member of the group.
6. We could begin, ahead of time, to develop group cohesiveness.

At the end of each phase, campers and counselors were permitted to withdraw from the program, that is, not return for the remaining activities. However, once an individual committed himself to participate in an activity, he was not permitted to withdraw until the end of that particular phase. Members were not permitted to participate in any

phase of the program unless they had participated in the previous phase. Only one
camper withdrew from the program; he withdrew at the end of the 1-day hike.

The initial phase of the camp is a time for
the counselors and campers to become acquainted. The counselors have an opportunity to test the behavior management and
therapeutic techniques they have selected for
implementation at camp.

In discussions that followed each phase of
the 1973 program, many perceptions were
modified.

The 1-day hike

The objectives of this phase of the wilderness camp are:

1. To assess the campers' and counselors'
   physical stamina to participate in the next
   phase
2. To begin organizing the campers and
   counselors into a group and into subgroups for planning purposes
3. To assess the initial effectiveness of the
   behavior management and therapeutic
   techniques
4. To permit each camper and counselor to
   decide for himself if he wishes to participate in the remaining phases of the camp
5. To communicate and explain to the campers the rules to be followed at camp
6. To develop some basic camping skills
7. To list and discuss the personal equipment
   needed by each member for the 3-day
   backpacking trip
8. To plan the 3-day trip

SCHEDULE OF EVENTS

9:00 AM	Counselors arrive
9:15	Campers arrive
9:15-9:30	Introductions; review day's schedule
9:30-9:45	Orientation to campsite
9:45-10:15	Present and discuss camp rules; review tentative plan for the 3-day backpacking trip
10:15-11:15	2-mile hike
11:15-11:30	Rest and field games
11:30-12:00	Build fires, prepare lunch
12:00-12:30 PM	Lunch; clean up
12:30-1:15	Organize into subgroups; plan for 3-day trip
1:15-1:45	Subgroups report to total group on menus, equip- ment, safety, behavior, schedules, and campsites for 3-day trip
1:45-2:30	2-mile hike
2:30-3:00	Rest and field games
3:00-3:45	Camp skills training session: erecting, taking down, and caring for a tent; packing, carrying, storing, and us- ing a backpack; care of self, clothing, and equip- ment; first aid and safety
3:45-4:00	All-camp meeting (cheers, songs, and farewells)
4:00	Campers' depart
4:00-5:00	Counselors write a log; counselors' meeting; counselors' depart

For the camp skills training session, four
teaching stations are set up at the campsite.
The campers move from station to station
approximately every 12 to 15 minutes. Each
boy is given an opportunity to erect and take
down a two-man tent and to manipulate and
carry a full backpack.

The 3-day backpacking trip

The objectives of this phase of the wilderness camp are:

1. To continue the assessment of the campers' and counselors' physical stamina to
   participate in the final phase of the camping program
2. To continue planning activities for the 6-
   day trip
3. To assess the effectiveness of the modified
   behavior management and therapeutic
   techniques
4. To permit each camper and counselor to
   decide for himself if he wishes to participate in the final phase of the camping
   program
5. To communicate and explain to the group
   the rules of the camp
6. To continue instruction in the needed
   basic camping skills
7. To introduce the areas of nature study
   and survival skills

Packing through the wilderness.

Resting at trail side.

Washing before dinner.

Preparing the campsite.

SCHEDULE OF EVENTS

DAY 1

1:00 PM	Counselors and campers arrive at departure point
1:00-1:30	Camp meeting; discuss schedule of events and the rules of the camp
1:30-2:15	Issue equipment, inventory, personal possessions, and stow equipment in vehicles
2:15-4:45	Travel to camp
4:45-5:00	Explore campsite
5:00-5:45	Set up camp (erect tents, collect firewood, prepare kitchen and dining areas, start fires)
5:45-7:00	Prepare supper, dine, and clean kitchen and dining areas
7:00-8:00	Free time; personal hygiene; prepare tents and equipment for night; discuss day's activities with counselor
8:00-9:30	Campfire (see p. 160)
9:30	Retire to tents

DAY 2

7:00 AM	Rise
7:00-7:45	Personal hygiene; break camp
7:45-8:30	Breakfast; pack and adjust backpacks; stow group equipment in vehicle; clean campsite and dispose of litter
8:30-8:45	Camp meeting; discuss schedule for day and rules for the trail
8:45	Depart on trail for next campsite (approximately 4½ miles); rest at least 10 minutes after each mile walked; explore side trails at leisure but remain with counselor
12:00-12:30 PM	Arrive at campsite; explore campsite; lunch
12:30-12:45	Camp meeting to review schedule for remainder of day
12:45-1:30	Set up camp (kitchen, dining, and tent areas)
1:30-2:00	Free time

2:00-2:30	Camp skills training session (see p. 160)
2:30-3:15	Free time and recreation
3:15-3:45	Camp skills training session (see p. 160)
3:45-5:00	Free time and recreation
5:00-7:00	Prepare supper, dine, and clean kitchen and dining areas; personal hygiene; prepare tents and equipment for night
7:00-8:00	Rest; discuss day's activities with counselor
8:00-9:30	Campfire (see p. 160)
9:30	Retire to tents

DAY 3

7:00 AM	Rise
7:00-7:45	Personal hygiene; break camp
7:45-8:30	Breakfast; repack and adjust backpacks; stow group equipment in vehicle; clean campsite and dispose of litter
8:30-8:45	Camp meeting; discuss schedule for day
8:45	Depart on trail for return walk to original campsite; rest at least 10 minutes after each mile walked, explore side trails at leisure but remain with counselor
12:00-1:00 PM	Arrive at campsite; lunch; rest
1:00-1:30	Stow all equipment in vehicles; clean campsite and dispose of litter
1:30-4:00	Return to original point of departure
4:00-4:30	Inventory and stow all group and personal equipment
4:30	Campers depart
4:30-5:00	Staff meeting
5:00	Counselors depart

The 6-day backpacking trip

The objectives for this final phase of the wilderness camp are a continuation of those applied during the previous two phases.

The schedules for days 1 and 6 of the 6-day trip are similar to those for days 1 and 3 of the 3-day trip.

The end of a long day: good friends, good food.

During the 1973 camp, the one major exception to the final day's schedule presented for the model was a stop at YMCA Camp Lakewood to clean up before going home. The campers and counselors rested, showered, and changed their clothing before departing for home.

SCHEDULE OF EVENTS

DAYS 2 TO 5

7:00 AM	Rise
7:00-7:45	Personal hygiene; break camp
7:45-8:30	Breakfast; repack and adjust backpacks; stow group equipment in vehicle; clean campsite and dispose of litter
8:45	Depart for next campsite (distances range from 4½ to 6½ miles between campsites)
12:00-12:30 PM	Arrive at new campsite; explore campsite; lunch
12:30-12:45	Camp meeting
12:45-1:30	Set up camp
1:30-2:00	Free time
2:00-2:30	Camp skills training session (see p. 160)
2:30-3:15	Free time and recreation
3:15-3:45	Camp skills training session
3:45-5:00	Free time and recreation
5:00-7:00	Prepare supper, dine, and clean kitchen and dining areas; personal hygiene; prepare tents and equipment for night
7:00-8:00	Rest; discuss day's activities with counselor
8:00-9:30	Campfire (see p. 160)
9:30	Retire to tents

During the 1973 camp, each camper's day was filled with a variety of interesting activities; yet an attempt was made to allow the campers sufficient free time to develop personal relationships with their peers and counselors and to explore their environment as they chose. During this program no one ever asked or heard the question so often heard at home and in school: "What should I do now?"

Campers and counselors looked forward to the evening campfires. These were comfortable times after a busy day. Much of the time we just sat and talked around the blazing fire. On other occasions, we conducted activities such as the following:

Story telling
Singing
Talent shows
Magic shows
Snacks (popcorn, hotdogs, some-mores, and so on)
Tall tale telling
Jokes

The group also looked forward to the camp skills training sessions conducted each day. Among the topics presented in these sessions were:

Care, proper use, and repair of the tent; the backpack; and the saw, ax, and hatchet (Fletcher, 1974; Thomas, 1974); and the cook stove (Barker, 1975)
Care and proper use of personal equipment: boots, knife, mess kit, poncho, and personal medication (Fletcher, 1974; Thomas, 1974)
Compass and map reading (Boy Scouts of America, 1948, 1967)
Fire building (Barker, 1975)
Latrine construction and care (Boy Scouts of America, 1967)
Water purification (Boy Scouts of America, 1967)
Cooking in the wilderness (Barker, 1975)
Proper methods for walking and climbing (Fletcher, 1974)
First aid and safety skills (Bleything, 1971)
Survival skills (Burt, Dawson, and Heyl, 1963; Olsen, 1973)
Campsite maintenance and nature study (Boy Scouts of America, 1948, 1967; Bleything, 1971, 1972; Fletcher, 1974; Olsen, 1973; Thomas, 1974)
Edible plants
Poisonous plants
Animal life

Dangerous and/or poisonous animals (including snakes and insects)
Identifying trees, flowers, and plants

Although camp skills training sessions were scheduled daily, the majority of our learning took place naturally as campers and counselors traveled over the trail. The scheduled sessions became a time to rest, summarize, review, and discuss those things experienced on the trail.

Work assignments were learning activities. Each subgroup of counselors and campers was assigned specific responsibilities each day. The work assignments were rotated among the subgroups on a preestablished, fixed schedule. This schedule was used to eliminate potential confusion and bickering.

The principal tasks were:

Gathering firewood
Maintaining the campsite
Building and maintaining the campfire
Cooking meals
Washing and storing the cooking equipment
Loading and unloading the equipment vehicle

On occasion, special tasks were assigned as the need arose.

ADVANTAGES AND DISADVANTAGES

The wilderness camp has many advantages when compared with the other models discussed in this volume:

1. The camp is an opportunity for each camper (and counselor) to grow in self-esteem, self-worth, self-discipline, and pride in himself and his accomplishments (Hughes and Dudley, 1973).

2. The camp program encourages and permits the appropriate expression of aggression in a controlled environment. Counselors are trained to accept and channel this aggression into productive activities.

3. In the wilderness, the camper must learn to trust and depend on others, both campers and counselors, for his comfort and safety. Conversely, he learns that others perceive him as trustworthy and dependable.

4. Although the wilderness is a challenging environment, it is a fair environment.

All the campers enter the program on an equal footing—unskilled as campers. Consequently it is *safe* to make mistakes and to ask for help without fear of derogation.

5. The program provides acceptable adult identification models after whom the camper may model his behavior.
6. The wilderness camp provides temporary removal from a contaminating environment to a controlled environment. This removal permits the camper to discover and try new ways (for him) of interacting with others (Hobbs and Shelton, 1972).
7. Wilderness camping is a great adventure to which young men and women in their teens and preteens naturally respond. They love the challenge and mystery of the unknown.

The camp has a few disadvantages that are not characteristic of the other models discussed in this text:

1. It is expensive. The cost of food, equipment, and transportation are sometimes prohibitive.
2. It is frequently difficult to find counselors who can devote the needed time to planning and carrying out the complete program.
3. Because of the restriction imposed on the program by money and staff, the camp session is frequently too brief to obtain the desired behavioral changes among the group. The camper is then returned to his contaminated environment without the skills needed to change or tolerate it.

REFERENCES

Angier, B. *Home in your pack.* New York: MacMillan, Inc., 1972.

Barker, H. *The one-burner gourmet.* Chicago: Greatlakes Living Press, 1975.

Bleything, D. *Poisonous plants in the wilderness.* Beaverton, Ore.: Life Support Technology, Inc., 1971.

Bleything, D. *Primitive medical aid in the wilderness.* Beaverton, Ore.: Life Support Technology, Inc., 1971.

Bleything, D. *Edible plants in the wilderness* (Vols. 1 and 2). Beaverton, Ore.: Life Support Technology, Inc., 1972.

Blume, R., and Blume, D. E. Camping with inner-city kids. *Today's Education,* 1971, **60**(3), 32-33.

Boy Scouts of America. *Handbook for boys.* New Brunswick, N.J.: Boy Scouts of America, 1948.

Boy Scouts of America. *Fieldbook.* New Brunswick, N.J.: Boy Scouts of America, 1967.

Bridge, R. *America's backpacking book.* New York: Charles Scribner's Sons, 1973.

Burt, C. P., Dawson, R. L., and Heyl, F. *Wilderness survival manual.* Beaverton, Ore.: Life Support Technology, Inc., 1969.

Fletcher, C. *The complete walker* (2nd ed.). New York: Alfred A. Knopf, Inc., 1974.

Glasser, W. *Realty therapy.* New York: Harper & Row, Publishers, 1965.

Harris, T. A. *I'm OK—You're OK.* New York: Harper & Row, Publishers, 1969.

Hobbs, T. R., and Shelton, G. C. Therapeutic camping for emotionally disturbed adolescents. *Hospital and Community Psychiatry,* 1972, **23**, 298-301.

Hughes, A. H., and Dudley, H. K. An old idea for a new problem: camping as a treatment for the emotionally disturbed in our state hospitals. *Adolescence,* 1973, **8**(29), 43-50.

James, M., and Jongeward, D. *Born to win: transactional analysis with Gestalt experiments.* Reading, Mass.: Addison-Wesley Publishing Co., Inc., New York: 1971.

Langer, R. W. *The joy of camping.* New York: Saturday Review Press, 1973.

Larson, M. Campout in a crater. *Instructor,* 1972, **82**(4), 52.

Lowry, T. P. *Camping therapy.* Springfield, Ill.: Charles C Thomas, Publisher, 1974.

Morse, W. C., and Small, E. R. The life-space interview: group life-space interviewing in a therapeutic camp. *American Journal of Orthopsychiatry,* 1959, **29**, 27-44.

O'Donnell, J. Snow trek. *Parks and Recreation,* 1973, **8**(4), 5-51, 55.

Olsen, L. D. *Outdoor survival skills.* Provo, Utah: Brigham Young University Press, 1973.

Redl, F. The life-space interview: strategy and techniques. In *When we deal with children.* New York: The Free Press, 1966.

Smallman, R. E. *The golden guide to camping.* New York: Western Publishing Co., Inc., 1965.

Sullivan, G. *The backpacker's handbook.* New York: Grosset & Dunlap, Inc., 1972.

Thomas, D. *Roughing it easy.* Provo, Utah: Brigham Young University Press, 1974.

BEHAVIOR MANAGEMENT AND ADMINISTRATION

In Chapters 9 and 10 two important camp problems are discussed: behavior management; and camp programming, planning, and administration.

A variety of behavior management techniques for application in a camp setting are reviewed in Chapter 9. These techniques range from those derived from psychodynamic theories to those based on learning and behavioral theories. A camp behavior management philosophy and the importance of the counselor and instructor in behavior management are discussed. In addition, behavior modification, medical, psychody-namic, milieu (environmental), and group intervention techniques are presented for the reader's study. At the conclusion of Chapter 9, several unique behavior management problems are discussed.

Chapter 10 is a camp planner's and administrator's guide. A broad variety of planning, programming, and administrative concerns are presented and discussed. The chapter is primarily designed to alert administrators to potential and actual problems that arise at camp. Attention to these concerns will increase the probability of an effective and efficient program.

CHAPTER 9

Behavior management

Without doubt, the vast majority of a camp staff's meeting and discussion time is devoted to considerations of behavior management:

How can we control this individual's behavior?

How can we control this group's behavior?

Should we reward this behavior? If so, how?

Should we ignore this behavior? If so, how?

Should we punish this behavior? If so, how?

How can we instruct when they are doing so and so?

Will this technique work? Is it helpful? Is it harmful?

Meeting after meeting is devoted to discussions of these and other behavior management questions and concerns.

For our purposes in this chapter, behavior management techniques may be defined as all those actions (and inactions) staff members engage in to enhance the probability that a camper or group of campers will develop effective behaviors that are personally self-fulfilling and productive for the child and that are socially acceptable.

Behavior management is a complex issue that cannot be approached from a simplistic theoretical point of view. It is an issue that must be broadly studied and objectively applied with equal emphasis focused on all relevant variables: the child or group of children, the specific behavior under consideration, the setting in which the behavior occurs, and the individual counselor or instructor applying the management technique. This statement recognizes that a management technique that successfully changes a behavior of a specific child or group under one set of conditions when applied by a specific counselor may be ineffective under another set of conditions when applied with a different child or group by a different counselor.

The approach to behavior management presented here is eclectic; techniques described have been derived from learning, psychodynamic, ecological or environmental, and biophysical theories and have been applied effectively in the camping programs presented in Section Two.

Consideration is given to (1) some behavior management guidelines, (2) the counselor/instructor, (3) the environment as a therapeutic tool, (4) the group and grouping, (5) counseling techniques, (6) some adjunctive therapeutic techniques, (7) behavior modification techniques, and (8) medical intervention.

ρ, regardless of its
ganizational pattern,
, guidelines to govern
pplication of behavior
ues. As a staff, we must
issues such as: "Why does
"Why are the children en-
are the realistic behavior
ptions at this camp?" and
ected of the campers?" Such
e important but frequently for-
n we become involved in the day-
rk with all its rewards, frustrations,
ppointments.

lation and time. Frequently, we for-
at our camp is populated by exceptional
ren—children who are enrolled in camp
ause of their limitations and problems.
ten, we approach our task of helping them
s if their handicaps did not exist.

It is not unusual to have a counselor or instructor arrive at the director's cabin during
the first week of camp completely frustrated
because an unacceptable behavior in a
camper is not changing in the desired direction with the desired immediacy. The same
frustration exists among counselors concerned with academic and nonacademic skill
training.

Perhaps we are too impatient and too
easily frustrated as a result of living most of
our life among the nonhandicapped population and in a society that is conditioned to
instant change, instant solutions to problems,
and little or no frustration.

At a camp for the handicapped, we must
be patient and adjust to slow, time-consum-
ing progress. This is a camp. The miracles
are few in number and always difficult to observe. The children have certain habitual
ways of acting and reacting in their environment. These are ways of coping that the children have established over a span of several
years. As coping or defense mechanisms,
they have been more or less successful for
the child. He cannot (and should not be
forced to) relinquish them immediately and
begin using "new" (and from our point of

view more acceptable, more productive)
ways of coping.

To change behavior takes time and energy.
We must be patient, focusing on the progress
the camper makes during the camp session
rather than on *our desired* end product.

Options available. Rotman (1973) suggests
that the camp director and his staff have
three options available to them in relation to
the behavior problems of children in the
camp setting; they can tolerate, treat, or
terminate the offending child. Although
these options may be available to the director
and staff of a camp for nonhandicapped
children, two of them are not available
to personnel of the camp for exceptional
children.

As professionals with training and experience in the education of exceptional children,
we cannot simply tolerate a child's unacceptable behavior and meet our responsibilities
to the child. Although we may purposely
choose to ignore certain behaviors as a behavior management technique, we cannot
overlook and/or endure a behavior because
to do so is less fatiguing and frustrating for us.
To *tolerate* an emotionally handicapped
child's deviant behavior is to avoid responsibility toward a child who is enrolled at the
special camp as a result of the very behavior
we are tolerating. In the special camp, such
actions are a disservice to the child.

With very few exceptions, the termination
of a camper is not an option available to us as
members of a special camp staff. To *terminate*
a child is to give up on him and thus further
limit his opportunities for rehabilitation. If
our application and selection processes are
adequate, terminating a child for behavior
problems should not occur. The only possible
exception to this position occurs when a
child's manifest behavior differs radically
from the behavior we anticipated and when
he is in danger of physically harming himself
or others.

To *treat* the handicapped child is the special camp's reason for existence. Treatment
by a trained, competent staff in a camp setting is the only acceptable purpose for enrolling a child in a special camp. Treatment is

the only option available to us if we sincerely wish to meet our responsibilities to the child.

Discipline. Self-discipline is the desired result of the behavior management interventions presented in this chapter. This self-discipline, or process of achieving self-control over personal behavior in a variety of circumstances with a variety of persons, is not instantaneous. Self-control is developed by all human beings over a long period of time (years) and includes a number of developmental phases. During the process of attaining self-control, the child naturally progresses and regresses as he and his environment changes. He may appear perfectly self-disciplined one day and not the next day. Progress—maturing, growing up, and so on —is often measured by the slowly increasing lengths of time between the occurrences of the child's unacceptable behaviors.

The word *discipline* is derived from the word *disciple* (or follower of a master's teachings). This concept contains the idea of something learned from a teacher whose example an individual personally desires to model. Indeed, the best discipline comes out of the respect and understanding of one human be-

ing for another. Discipline should be
ative and voluntary, not imposed from
by an authority figure (Chetkow, 1964

Harsh, punitive, and negative discip
techniques are avoided at the special
Most exceptional children have a poor o
torted self-image as a result of their fail
and of being negatively disciplined for m
years. These children have psychologic
isolated themselves from the effects of neg
tive discipline.

At the special camp, discipline is benign
and positive.

Fun. An important objective for each child attending camp is that *he have fun*. His program must be enjoyable and rewarding, or it will not meet his normal childhood needs: to seek out and explore the new, the different, the unknown, and the exciting.

Even though the staff has academic and nonacademic remedial objectives for a child, these remedial tasks cannot be so consuming of the child's time and energy that camp becomes drudgery for him.

Camp is a positive experience; it offers the child a variety of opportunities to learn new skills and participate in new activities.

Conversation with a friend.

nt and administration

ent **167**

ooper-
above

inary
mp.
dis-
res
ny
ly

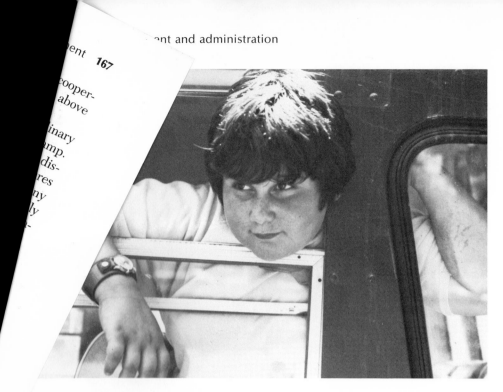

eeing new places.

Empathy, not sympathy. Exceptional children do not need sympathy. Inappropriate sympathy clouds the problems the staff person is attempting to help the child overcome. It places the counselor or instructor in an emotional condition that prohibits objective analysis. When a counselor becomes deeply emotionally involved with a child's problem, he frequently functions in a nonhelpful way. He reacts with his emotions rather than with his intellect.

Although relationships based on sympathy are avoided in the special camp, empathy is a recommended and necessary quality for all staff personnel. The counselor must be able to understand how the child feels. He must be able to perceive the child's world from the child's point of view. This capacity is frequently referred to as "taking the position of the other" or "being in the other guy's shoes."

Having empathy for a child will enable the counselor to provide the child with the direction, guidance, and support he needs, when it is needed.

Staff expectations for campers. Many years ago, we were told by our grandparents or parents, "As the twig is bent, so grows the tree." For decades, educators did not heed this simple message. However, during the last decade, researchers have confirmed what grandma took for granted: our expectations of the exceptional child have a significant effect on his performance.

This self-fulfilling prophecy means that, to a significant extent, if we believe a child is and will continue to be incompetent, then he will be incompetent. If we are convinced that a child won't learn to read, behave, compute, socialize, speak, and so on, then the probability that he will not learn these skills is significantly increased.

Conversely, if we believe that the exceptional child can learn to read, behave, compute, socialize, and speak, then the probability that he will respond to our expectations of him and learn these skills is increased.

As members of a special camp staff, we must have high, but realistic, expectations of the campers. The camp is an environment developed around a "can do" attitude. Children are told repeatedly throughout the day, "You can do it," "I know you can do it," "You did it!" "Great," "Super," "Beautiful."

Free to learn and grow.

Obviously, this "can do" attitude is meaningless unless the camp program is designed to ensure that the child receives the needed emotional support and skill training required to attain our expectations of him.

Facilitation, not domination. A general policy at the special camp is to allow and encourage the exceptional child to grow and learn as much as possible without adult assistance. Anything (within limits) that a child can do for himself, he should do. Counselors and instructors should facilitate, not dominate, the child's efforts. They are available to demonstrate, assist, and provide encouragement and support for the camper. Children need freedom to explore, investigate, and try without adult interference if they are to grow. Frequently, they will succeed. Occasionally, they will fail.

Although constant failure is not recommended, failure is a part of every person's life. We cannot and should not shelter the child from all failure. This is unrealistic because the camper must return to home and school after the camp session and will not be sheltered from failure.

In camp, the child is allowed to confront the logical consequences of his actions and behavior (Dreikurs and Grey, 1968). The camp counselor must help the child learn to cope appropriately with both success and failure.

Freedom and democracy. Complete freedom for many children becomes total boredom. The child is usually attending camp to develop productive skills and activities to use during his leisure time. The staff is responsible for planning the activity program either for the children or with the children. To do otherwise would be irresponsible and a disservice to the child and his sponsors.

Democracy without structure, discipline, program, or predictability becomes anarchy. Campers are learners. They are not adults skilled in the principles and practices of democracy. They are to be allowed to learn and apply these principles at camp under the guidance of the staff. Democratic leadership provides the children with the structure, discipline, and guidance that they need until they are able to assume responsibility for their actions. The staff must provide this leadership.

THE COUNSELOR/INSTRUCTOR

The counselor/instructor is the most important element in the life-space of a child attending a camp for the exceptional. No other element has greater potential therapeutic impact on a camper than does the interpersonal relationship existing between the counselor/instructor and the child.

Special camps can be (and have been) operated successfully under very adverse conditions—lacking adequate facilities, materials and equipment, funds, sufficient numbers of personnel, transportation, and so on. However, no camp can be successful without counselors and instructors who can relate positively and productively with children.

The authentic counselor

The authentic counselor must be an authentic person—a real person. It is difficult by means of employment applications and personal interviews to select authentic counselors. However, there are several personal characteristics that the interviewer seeks in those applying for a position as a counselor or instructor:

Self insight: The counselor must know why he wishes to work with exceptional persons. He must have an understanding of why he engages in the activities that make up his life.

Self-acceptance and realistic self-confidence: The counselor must accept himself as he is but continue to aspire. He must be realis-

tically confident in himself and in his ability to be a counselor but not so overconfident (having an "I can do anything" attitude) as to be considered foolish. He must not be afraid to honestly and forthrightly state his practical strengths and weaknesses.

Love and acceptance of children: The counselor must love and be able to demonstrate his love for children. He must understand that love and compliance are not identical. Sometimes love is demonstrated to a child by discipline. The counselor accepts the child as a worthwhile human being, even though he must reject the child's deviant behavior. Finally, the counselor must be capable of accepting children who are different from himself—whether they are tall, short, male, female, black, white, yellow, rotund, slim, deformed, intelligent, retarded, conforming, or deviant.

An understanding of the behavior of children: The counselor must be able to understand behavior and empathize with the child as previously discussed. He must constantly seek insight and understanding into the child.

Curiosity and a willingness to learn: The counselor must have a bit of the child in his adult person. Like the child, he must be curious about the world and enthusiastically explore it.

Patience with himself and children: The counselor should recognize that he is imperfect. He must also recognize this quality in others. He must recognize that learning is a slow, complex process for both himself and his campers. However, with all his patience, he must continually strive to attain his goals and help the campers attain their goals.

Flexibility: The counselor must be flexible. He is frequently confronted by boredom and resistance from his campers. For the sake of the children, he must know when to change activities to attain a broader objective.

Humor: The counselor without a well-developed sense of humor will not survive at a camp for exceptional children. Mistakes

Exploring the unknown with a friend.

and funny incidents occur daily. The counselor who cannot laugh will certainly cry. The counselor must be able to laugh *at himself and with the children*. He can never laugh *at the children*.

The interviewer of potential camp counselors seeks a balance of these personal characteristics in the candidate for employment. It is of little benefit to the children to have a counselor who is very skilled and knowledgeable in a specific activity but who does not understand and accept himself or the children.

Counselor skills

The counselor is a leader. He must have a variety of specific skills to successfully lead children in the camp setting. He must:

1. Establish routines in the daily life of his group.
2. Set and enforce behavior limits. The counselor must accomplish this task without becoming emotionally involved.
3. Not permit emotionally charged situations to get out of control. The counselor must intrude himself into the conflict and cause it to stop.
4. Be consistent. Children are confused by counselors who condone this particular deviation today but will not condone the same deviation tomorrow.
5. Personally investigate a situation before acting rather than acting on second- or third-person information and rumors. The counselor must confer with *all* persons involved in the incident.
6. Ignore certain behaviors. Many behaviors manifested by exceptional children are normal and age-appropriate; others are simply not important enough to respond to. The counselor must be selective in responding to and ignoring behaviors.
7. Communicate verbally and nonverbally with children. The counselor must talk *with* children, not *to* children. He must learn that many of the things in this world he considers to be universal knowledge are mysteries to his campers. The counselor must be tuned-in to the children and their actions.
8. Learn to avoid confrontation when it is therapeutically appropriate. Yet the counselor must confront situations when

necessary for the benefit of the camper or group.

9. Learn to change program activities for therapeutic purposes. Some counselors are so personally committed to "their thing" that they fail to recognize disinterest and resistance among their campers.

10. Work independently and as a team member but communicate with his peers and supervisors. The counselor must be accountable for his actions and inactions.

11. Make a direct appeal to a camper or group when their actions are confusing and discomforting. Many times a direct appeal to the humanness and common sense of a child will solve a problem as quickly and as effectively as a lengthy discussion.

12. Provide each camper with security. The counselor must communicate to the child, who is in a new and strange environment at camp, that he will be protected by the counselor from physical and psychological harm.

The counselor seldom arrives at camp with these specific skills. They are learned through experience with the help of a competent supervisor, from fellow counselors, and in preservice and inservice training sessions.

THE ENVIRONMENT (MILIEU)

As important as the counselor is the impact of the environment in which the camper lives during the camp session. A staff objective for each child attending camp is the development of an environment, or milieu, to facilitate the child's rehabilitation.

Milieu is defined here as a clinical concept. It implies the total environment that a child lives in, the whole culture that surrounds him—in other words, everything that is done to, with, for, or by a child in the place where he finds himself (Long, Morse, and Newman, 1965).

According to Redl (1959), a milieu is not "good" or "bad" for a child in itself; its effects on the child are dependent on its interaction with the child's needs. Redl further indicates that no single aspect of the environment is more important than any other aspect of the environment. The importance of the various discrete aspects of the environment is dependent on the needs of the child or group living in that environment.

Since it is not possible, a priori, to design with certitude a therapeutic milieu for a child, milieu therapy is a continuous process conducted throughout the child's residence in camp. The staff must be constantly alert to the impact of the milieu on the camper and adjust it when feasible to facilitate the child's rehabilitation. Such environmental manipulations are difficult, requiring counselors who are observant and sensitive to the needs of individual campers and groups of campers.

Redl (1959) has identified several critical factors in the milieu; these factors are presented here as questions that staff members should ask themselves about the camp environment and its impact on the camper:

Social structures: What is the role of the counselor? Of the supervisor? Of the director? Of the instructor? Of the children? Are the staff members parent surrogates? Are they surrogate brothers and sisters? Are they friends? Are they democratic leaders? Are they authority figures? Who is in charge here? Counselors? Campers? The director? No one? Is there communications between counselors and campers? Between campers and counselors? Between supervisors and counselors? Between campers and campers?

Value systems: What is being consciously and unconsciously communicated among the members of the camp? Sympathy? Empathy? High expectations? Low expectations? Like? Dislike? Acceptance? Rejection? (We are concerned here with the communcations of campers as well as those of staff personnel.)

Routines, rituals, and regulations: Are camp routines, rituals, and behavioral regulations or limits facilitating or frustrating the therapeutic goals of the program?

Impact of the group process: What is the impact of the group process on individual campers and on cliques of campers within the group? Are individual group members cast in the role of a leader? In the role of a follower? In the role of scapegoat? In the role of a mascot or pet? In the role of an isolate? Can the child at his present stage of development function effectively in a group setting?

Impact of the individual's psychopathological characteristics: What is the effect, on self and others, of the individual camper's behavior? Does it result in aggression? In withdrawal? In respect? In fear?

Staff attitudes and feelings: What is the impact of staff members' attitudes and feelings on their personal behavior? On the campers? Is the impact positive? Is it negative? Is it productive? Is it destructive?

Overt behavior: Regardless of their intentions, what are campers and counselors *really* doing to each other? What is their overt behavior? Is their relationship helpful? Is it harmful? Is it supportive? Is it personal? Is it impersonal? Is it vindictive?

Activities and performances: Is the activity program, including its structure, designed to facilitate rehabilitation? Is it productive? Is it busywork? Is it tedious? Is it frustrating? Is it boring? Is it wasteful? Is it destructive?

Space, equipment, time, and props: Are the space, equipment, time, and props available in the milieu adequate to conduct the activities in the program?

Effect of the outside milieu: What is the effect on the camper of visits, therapy sessions, and so on by persons from outside the camp?

Effect of the nonimmediate milieu: Are the camp administrative, housekeeping, clerical, and maintenance staffs affecting the camper? Is the effect positive? Is it negative?

Limits and enforcement: Are the behavioral limits within which the camper must function established? Are these limits realistic? Are they enforced? How?

Program responsiveness: Is the total milieu adequately monitored to ensure recognition of nontherapeutic elements? Is the structure of the milieu sufficiently flexible and responsive to the needs of the campers to permit and encourage modification to reduce or neutralize nontherapeutic elements?

The therapeutic milieu at camp must be continuously monitored, discussed, and modified for the benefit of the child. The counselor has the primary role in this process of adjusting the milieu in response to the needs of the campers. He assumes this role naturally because of his close continuous relationship with the children.

THE GROUP

A number of highly potent behavior management techniques are closely associated with the individual cabin or activity group. The specific intervention techniques to be used with groups are discussed under Counseling techniques (pp. 175-178) and Behavior modification techniques (pp. 178-190). However, if behavior management within the group is a significant part of a camp's overall behavior management program, two important topics must be considered before specific interventions are discussed: group composition and group processes.

Group composition

Grouping children on the basis of clinical records and preadmission data is an important and difficult task (Morse and Wineman, 1957). All staff personnel are involved in the grouping process.

The variables to be considered with group campers are age; sex; interests; handicapping conditions; personality characteristics (nonpathological); the degree, intensity, and kind of pathological condition; and group experiences and skills. Staff personnel consider these variables, and others, in relation to the individual persons composing the group and in relation to the total group. They seek to avoid extremes in group composition while attempting to form an "average" or "balanced" group. In this situation, the counselors are perceived as cabin or activity group members.

Avoiding extremes in group composition includes:
1. Not placing children of greatly different ages and interests in the same group.

2. Not placing a child in a group lacking like-sex peers.
3. Not placing a child with a severely handicapping condition in a group of children having mildly handicapping conditions if the placement prohibits the mildly handicapped from engaging in important activities. However, if adequately trained personnel are available to assist the severely handicapped child, this potential limitation can be circumvented.
4. Not placing children with potentially conflicting personality characteristics and pathological conditions in the same group. Some conflicts and disturbances within any camp are anticipated and desirable because of the characteristics of the population. However, an effort is made to minimize these conflicts to a manageable level by grouping.
5. Not placing children who are unskilled in group processes in a group composed of campers with considerable skill and experience. This hazard can be avoided if the counselors are skilled in group processes and management.
6. Not placing children in a group when the child is neither ready nor willing to participate in group activities. We are referring here to the severely emotionally handicapped child lacking the skills needed for meaningful group participation. Often, these children remain in a group but do not become "true" members of it. It is desirable to place such children in special groups to learn the needed skills.

Grouping is a difficult process. Mistakes are made in placements. A wise staff allows itself an opportunity to evaluate and regroup, as necessary, after the initial week of the camp session. If the suggestions presented above are followed, the need for regrouping is minimal.

Cabin or activity groups

Cabin or activity groups as self-governing, problem-solving groups (Loughmiller, 1965) are especially beneficial to campers between the ages of 10 and 16 or 17 years.

The general purpose of such a group is to expose campers to a wide range of successful interpersonal experiences and as a result encourage their participation, responsibility, and cooperation (Rickard, Serum, and Wilson, 1971). The campers and their counselors are responsible for their daily activity schedules within predetermined limits. The group finds itself in a situation in which majority rule prevails. Each camper is responsible for his personal behavior and for the behavior of the group (Rickard and Lattal, 1969).

Limits on the group's behavior and activities are usually imposed by the camp administration rather than by the counselor, who is a member of the group. However, the group may impose additional limits on itself.

The limits imposed by the camp administration are generally few in number and are usually concerned with dining and work schedules, attendance at all-camp functions, transportation, health, safety, and the like. These limits must be imposed by the camp director if he is to meet his responsibilities to the campers, counselors, and parents.

Any social cosmos requires certain routines (Morse and Wineman, 1957). Without routines, limits, or prescribed ways of behaving, anarchy would result and the group might disintegrate.

The group, as a group, decides (1) the limits to be set on social interaction, (2) how extreme behaviors are to be managed, (3) how activities and schedules are to be planned and executed, (4) who is to be responsible for the various phases of daily living, and (5) how problems and conflicts are to be solved.

The problem-solving process becomes a part of the group's daily life at camp. When conflicts and problems prohibiting the group from attaining its immediate goal occur, problem solving begins immediately. During problem solving, the group attempts to develop alternative solutions to the problem confronting them. They have two major tasks: (1) identifying and clarifying their problem and (2) discussing and deciding on one or more solutions to the problem. These solutions can be imposed either immediately or in similar future situations (Rickard, Serum, and Wilson, 1971).

At the University of Michigan Fresh Air Camp, Morse and Small (1959) identified several recurring group problems: (1) aggressive peer behaviors, including hitting, fighting, stealing, scapegoating, swearing, teasing, and bickering; (2) disorganized behavior as a result of high excitement levels; (3) sex play and talk, (4) resistance to the program; (5) improper living habits; and (6) hostility toward counselors. Other problems that may arise within the group are leadership-follower conflicts, planning and scheduling problems, and individual and subgroup task responsibilities. These and other problems are discussed during problem-solving sessions.

Morse and Wineman (1957) recommend the application of group life-space interview (LSI) techniques in the camp setting on a regular and emergency basis. These interviews focus on a number of critical group-process issues in addition to specific problems and conflicts. Among these issues are:

Existing social realities that inhibit group desires

Existing defense mechanisms that the group unconsciously applies to protect itself from others outside the group

Techniques for application by the members to admit mistakes, misdeeds, and asocial behaviors

Ways to use the group as a setting in which emotion and frustration may be expressed, and the limits on such ventilation

Strengthening of the group's and individual member's self-image, especially after conflicts and frustrations

Identification, clarification, and finding of mutually acceptable solutions to common problems

The counselor's role is very significant if group behavior management techniques are to be productively applied at the special camp. The counselor must be a model of give-and-take democratic leadership. He must willingly allow the group to make decisions, implement programs, and realize the consequences of its actions. The counselor must allow the group to succeed, and he must allow it to fail.

Although the counselor allows the logical consequences of the group's efforts to occur, he protects the group from constant failure and the individual members from physical and psychological harm.

COUNSELING TECHNIQUES

In this section two counseling techniques for application with individuals and groups at the camp for handicapped children are described. The first technique, LSI (see above), has been successfully implemented at the University of Michigan Fresh Air Camp (Morse and Wineman, 1957). The second technique, reality therapy (RT), has been applied successfully in several settings: schools, mental health centers, hospitals, and detention centers (Glasser, 1965, 1969). Both techniques have great potential for use in the camping programs described in Section Two.

Life-space interview

Redl (1959) recommends the LSI as an integral part of the milieu therapy technique discussed previously in this chapter.

The LSI is a *here* and *now* intervention built around the camper's *direct life experience*. It is conducted by a counselor or instructor who is perceived by the camper as an important part of the camper's life-space. This interviewer has definite role and power influence in the child's daily life (Redl, 1959, Reinert, 1976). The LSI is used to structure an incident in the camper's life so that he can solve the problem confronting him. The interviewer's role is facilitative in this problem-solving situation.

According to Redl (1959), the LSI may be applied by the counselor for either of two purposes: clinical exploitation of life events or emotional first aid on the spot.

In the first situation, clinical exploitation of life events, the counselor uses an actual behavioral incident to explore with the camper one of his (the camper's) habitual behavioral characteristics. This is primarily an effort by the interviewer to use an incident to attain a long-range therapeutic goal previously established for the child by the staff. When the LSI is applied for this purpose, the counselor is assisting the child in increasing his awareness of his (1) distorted perception of existing realities, (2) pathological behaviors, (3) hidden social and moral values, and (4) reaction to the behaviors and pressures of his group. In addition, the counselor uses this interview to discuss with the camper more productive and acceptable ways of solving problems. This particular application of the LSI is *not* recommended for use in the special camp with a staff lacking in training and experience in the LSI.

The LSI is also used to provide the camper with emotional first aid on the spot in times of stress. The LSI for this purpose may be applied in the camp by a staff with minimal training or experience.

The purpose of the LSI in this situation is to help the child over a rough spot in the road in order to continue an activity. The interview is applied to (1) reduce the child's frustration level; (2) support him in emotionally charged situations; (3) restore strained child-counselor communications; (4) reinforce existing behavioral and social limits and realities; (5) assist the camper in his efforts to find solutions to the everyday problems of living at camp and to emotionally-charged incidents such as fights, arguments, and the like.

As with any counseling technique, the application of the LSI is dependent on a variety of variables: the clinical purpose or goal, the specific setting, the training and experience of the staff, and especially the child—his particular pathological condition and the phase of his rehabilitation process.

The use of LSI techniques at a camp is a clinical decision involving all staff personnel. If this technique is adopted for application, it should be used consistently by all staff under the supervision of trained and experienced personnel.

Morse (1971) has outlined a series of steps that occur during the LSI. The steps are not a formal series, and on occasion some are omitted or reordered.

Generally, the LSI begins with a specific behavioral incident in the child's or group's life-space. The interviewer encourages those involved in the incident to state their personal perception of it. At this time, the counselor determines if this is an isolated occurrence or a significant part of a recurring central issue.

The counselor *listens* to the individuals involved in the incident as they reconstruct it. The counselor accepts these feelings without moralizing or attacking.

Although the counselor accepts the camper's perception of the incident, he may suggest alternative perceptions of it for the camper's consideration.

The interview process then moves into the resolution phase. This phase should be nonjudgmental. Many problems are resolved at this point in the interview process, and it is terminated.

However, if the problem is not resolved, the counselor may present his view of the incident in relation to the situation in which the individuals involved find themselves. Finally, the camper and counselor attempt to develop a plan to deal with the present problem and/or similar problems in the future.

Brenner (1969) makes several suggestions concerning counselor behaviors during the interview. Among his suggestions are:

Be polite to the child. If you cannot control your emotions, do not begin the interview.

Sit or kneel so that you have eye contact with the child.

If you are unsure of the history of the incident, investigate. Do not confront a child on the basis of rumors.

Ask sufficient questions to obtain a knowledgeable grasp of the situation. Do not probe areas of unconscious motivation; limit the use of "why" questions.

Listen to the camper and try to understand his perception of the incident.

Encourage the child to ask questions, and respond to his questions appropriately.

If the child is suffering from considerable shame and/or guilt as a result of the incident, attempt to reduce and minimize it.

Facilitate the child's attempts to say what he wishes to say if he is having difficulties.

Work with the child or group to develop a mutually acceptable plan.

Reality therapy

In his 1965 and 1969 publications, William Glasser presents a unique perspective of mental health and mental illness. His thesis departs from the Freudian and Neo-Freudian theory that mental health is a state of "contentment" and mental illness, a state of "discontent." From Glasser's point of view, mental health is the ability to function "competently" in society.

The person in need of psychiatric assistance is unable to fulfill his essential psychological needs. The objective of RT is to lead the individual toward competent functioning in reality. It is designed to help him grapple successfully with the tangible and intangible aspects of the real world and as a result fulfill his needs.

Glasser (1965) suggests that we have two basic psychological needs: to love and be loved, and to feel that we are worthwhile to ourselves and to others. For an individual to be seen as worthwhile to himself and to others, he must maintain a satisfactory standard of behavior.

If he does not maintain the necessary standard of behavior, he suffers pain or discomfort. This pain or discomfort is mental illness or a lack of responsible involvement with significant others.

If the mentally ill person wishes to return to a state of mental health, that is, responsible and competent functioning in reality, he needs a person or persons whom *he genuinely cares about and who he feels genuinely cares about him.*

In RT, the process of therapy and the process of teaching are identical. The therapist's or counselor's objective is to teach the mentally ill person responsible behavior. Responsibility is the ability to fulfill personal needs and to do so in a way that does not deprive others of the ability to fulfill their personal needs.

Learning to be a responsible person, according to Glasser, is not a natural process. The individual is taught to be responsible through involvement with responsible persons via love and discipline. Most individuals learn to be responsible from loving parents and from significant others, such as teachers or guardians.

RT, then, is the process of guiding (teaching) the irresponsible person to face existing reality, function responsibly, and as a result fulfill his needs. This process includes:

Involvement with an acceptable counselor who is perceived as caring about him. This involvement must be sufficient for the individual to face existing reality and begin to perceive his behavior as irresponsible.

A counselor who is accepting of him and maintains involvement with him, but who rejects his irresponsible behavior.

The learning of more responsible ways of fulfilling his needs in reality. This learning process is a cooperative activity that at various times includes direct instruction, discussions, conversations, and planning sessions relative to any facet of the individual's present life.

RT assumes that the counselor or therapist is similar to the authentic counselor described in a previous section of this chapter.

In the camp for the handicapped, the goal of RT is to guide individuals and groups toward more responsible behavior. This goal is accomplished by means of the RT interview. Some guidelines for counselors engaging in the RT interview are:

Be personal. Show that you are a friend who cares and who is interested in the child.

Focus on present behavior, not ancient history. Accept the camper's feelings but do not probe into unconscious motivation. Ask "what," "how," and "who" questions—not "why" questions.

Do not preach or make value judgments on the individual's behavior.

Help the camper formulate a practical plan to increase his responsible behavior. Planning is a cooperative effort.

Encourage the camper to overtly commit himself to the mutually agreeable plan.

Do not accept excuses for irresponsible behavior. If a plan cannot be implemented or fails, develop another.

Do not punish the camper for irresponsible behavior. Allow the camper to suffer the logical consequences of his behavior unless such consequences would be unreasonably harmful.

Provide the child support and security.

The implementation of RT techniques in the camp for the handicapped is a total staff decision. If this approach to behavior management is adopted by the staff, provision for training should be made and the techniques applied with consistency.

USE OF EXPRESSIVE ARTS IN BEHAVIOR MANAGEMENT

In Chapter 4 the expressive arts are presented as media to facilitate the exceptional child's cognitive and psychomotor learning abilities. In this chapter, the expressive arts are presented as a potential behavior management technique. As a behavior management technique, the expressive arts are used to facilitate the management of behavior and to prevent behavior problems. In addition, the arts can be instrumental in enhancing the staff's understanding of the camper's feelings and emotions.

The term *expressive arts* refers to those activities that permit and encourage the camper to express his feelings, emotions, and creative urges with minimal restriction. The expressive arts that can be utilized to fulfill these purposes are:

Role play and dramatics
Puppetry
Two-dimensional arts (coloring, drawing, sketching, and painting with fingerpaints, tempera paints, watercolors, and so on)
Three-dimensional arts (sand, clay, plastic, and plaster sculpturing, crafts projects, collages, and so on)
Music (making music and listening to music)
Creative movement and dance
Creative story telling
Creative writing
Free-play activities with and without specific play materials and equipment

All human beings, including children, have feelings and emotions that they express in many ways, both physically and verbally.

Frequently, children (and some adults) unconsciously express their feelings and emotions in unacceptable ways. This results in conflict with others and consequently has a negative impact on the child's self-concept.

The expressive arts can be used by the child as a legitimate and acceptable mode for expressing his positive and negative feelings and emotions. When expressed through these media, the child's feelings do not generally interfere with others in his environment. Consequently, these feelings do not become a behavior management concern.

As adults, we frequently reduce personal stress and frustration by such means as conversations or discussions with trusted friends; games; avocations, hobbies, or projects; and trips or vacations. For the child who is generally less capable in verbal communications and less able to control his lifestyle, the expressive arts are media he may select to reduce his frustrations and thus minimize the effect of stress in his life.

If the arts are to be used effectively as a behavior management technique, the child must be provided opportunities to express himself freely and with some consistency. Although some limitations and structure relative to time, place, and media are desirable, the child's activities should not be prescribed. He should be permitted and encouraged *to do what he selects*, not what the counselor or instructor wants him to do.

The counselor can grow in understanding of his campers and their handicaps if he observes them during expressive art activities and discusses their products (drawing, painting, stories, and so on) with them.

BEHAVIOR MODIFICATION TECHNIQUES *

"What you do is influenced by what follows what you do" (Sarason, Glaser, and Fargo, 1972). This statement is an apt description of the basic theory underlying the behavior management techniques presented in this

---

*This section is an overview of Walker, J. E., and Shea, T. M.: *Behavior modification: a practical approach for educators*, St. Louis: The C. V. Mosby Co., 1976.

section. The consequences and probable consequences of behavior more than any other factor determine the behavior we exhibit. If the results of a behavior are rewarding for us, the behavior is repeated; if the results are not rewarding, the behavior is not repeated.

In the last decade, there has been a dramatic increase in the use of behavior modification interventions in various settings (home, school, camp, office, factory, military service, and playground) with many individuals and groups (old, young, rich, poor, male, female, normal, and maladjusted) for various purposes (to maintain appropriate behavior, to decrease inappropriate behavior, and to increase appropriate behavior). Behavior modification has been used to correct many handicapping conditions (psychoses, autism, neuroses, marital conflicts, alcoholism, narcotic addiction, learning problems, speech problems, and others).

The behavior modification practitioner perceives behavior problems as learning problems. Either the behaviorally handicapped person has not learned the appropriate behavior necessary to work his environment successfully or he has learned inappropriate, nonproductive behavior.

The behaviorist is concerned with *what* an individual or group does, not *why* the individual or group manifests a behavior. The etiology of behavior exists outside of the individual, that is in the environment. To modify behavior, the therapist manipulates the environmental responses or consequences of the behavior to be modified.

Principles of reinforcement

The learning of both appropriate and inappropriate behavior is dependent on the lawful application of the principles of reinforcement (the principles of learning). Applicable to all the techniques described here, the principles of reinforcement are:

1. Reinforcement must be dependent on the manifestation of the appropriate behavior.
2. Appropriate behavior must be reinforced immediately.
3. During the initial stages of the behavior change process the desired behavior should be reinforced each time it is exhibited.
4. When the newly acquired behavior reaches a satisfactory frequency level, it should be reinforced intermittently.
5. Social reinforcers must always be applied with tangible reinforcers.

These principles must be applied by the practitioner with precision and consistency if the behavior modification intervention is to be effective.

Steps in the behavior change process

There are several steps in the behavior change process, including (1) selecting the target behavior; (2) collecting and recording baseline data; (3) identifying appropriate reinforcers; and (4) implementing the specific intervention, and collecting and recording intervention data. These steps are applied in *all* behavior change programs.

Selecting the target behavior. The initial step in the behavior change process is the identification of a target behavior (the behavior to be changed or modified). In most human situations it is not difficult to select one or more behaviors that are unacceptable or inappropriate to some individuals under some circumstances. The practitioner is cautioned against the arbitrary and capricious selection of a target behavior. Decisions leading to the choice of a target behavior are governed by the following considerations, at a minimum: (1) the overall number of behaviors potentially needing modification, (2) the frequency of the behavior, (3) the duration of the behavior, (4) the intensity of the behavior, and (5) the kind or type of behavior.

Beginning behavior therapists should limit themselves to the modification of one or two individual or group behaviors at any given point in time. Attempting to change several behaviors simultaneously requires considerable skill in developing and managing complex interventions. If this is not done with precision and consistency, it frequently results in confusion, discouragement, and failure for both the child and the practitioner.

The frequency, duration, intensity, and

kind of behavior being changed has a significant bearing on (1) whether a behavior modification intervention is appropriate or even necessary, (2) the characteristics of the intervention to be applied, (3) the probable course of the behavior change process, and (4) the probable result of the intervention. More specifically: some behaviors respond to behavior modification interventions efficiently, whereas other behaviors do not respond; some behaviors should be changed for the child's welfare, whereas other behaviors are innocuous and need not be changed. The counselor must use common sense and good judgment when selecting a target behavior. As a responsible person, he cannot change a behavior simply for the sake of changing it; nor can he change a behavior so that a child will conform simply for the sake of conformity. This would be irresponsible.

Finally, during the process of selecting a target behavior, the practitioner must determine if the behavior is observable and quantifiable.

Collecting and recording baseline data. Information collected before implementation of the behavior change intervention is referred to as baseline data. Baseline data provide the foundation on which the behavior modification process is established. It is used to determine the effectiveness of the intervention during the process of change.

To obtain meaningful and useful baseline data, the practitioner engages in two activities. First, he counts the frequency of the behavior during a predetermined period of time. Usually, he uses a time-sampling observation technique on a daily basis for 1 week. Next, the practitioner charts the baseline data to prepare a visual display of the enumerated behavior in graphic form (Fig. 21).

These two processes, counting and charting, are of paramount importance to the behavior change process. When the practitioner knows the number of occurrences and/or the average duration of the occurrences of a behavior in a temporal framework, he can select an efficient reward schedule before implementing the intervention. Equally important is the application of baseline data for evaluative purposes. By comparing baseline data to data collected during the intervention, the practitioner can determine the effectiveness of the reward schedule and/or the reinforcer. Judgments can be made regarding the responsiveness of the target behavior to the intervention; that is, is the behavior increasing, decreasing, or being maintained as expected?

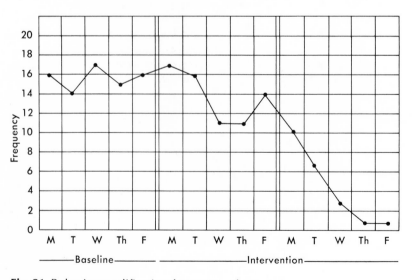

Fig. 21. Behavior modification frequency chart.

Identifying appropriate reinforcers. A behavior modification intervention is *only* as effective as its reinforcer (reward). Regardless of the intervention applied in any behavior change program, if the exhibition of the desired behavior is not rewarded with a reinforcer acceptable to the individual exhibiting the behavior, then the probability of his continuing to exhibit the behavior is reduced.

A reinforcer must be rewarding to the individual being rewarded. The *only* true test of the effectiveness of a *specific* reinforcer for a *specific* child is implementation (try it). The two most effective means for selecting reinforcers for an individual are to observe the individual and note the rewards he selects for himself when given a choice and to ask the individual what he would like to have or do for a reward. The following are potential reinforcers, tangible and social, for application in the camp for the handicapped:

Consumable food reinforcers
Fruit (apples, peaches, grapes, raisins)
Vegetables (carrots, celery, radishes)
Cookies
Candy (gumdrops, fruit drops)
Ice cream
Juice, fruit drinks
Soda
Milk
Gum
Cake, brownies, cupcakes
Potato chips, popcorn
Cereal
Reinforcing activities for use with food reinforcers
Distributing reinforcers
Cleaning area after distributing rewards
Popping popcorn
Scooping ice cream
Preparing snacks
Token reinforcers
Checks and points on cards and charts
Happy faces and stars
Tags, certificates, metals, feathers
Poker chips, trading stamps, counselor-made tokens
Play money
Game activity reinforcers
Table games (checkers, dominoes, Tip-it)
Blocks, Lincoln Logs, Leggo

Toys (trucks, cars, dolls)
Friend and circle games
Educational games (word, number)
Puzzles
Guessing games
Reinforcing activities
Working on self-selected projects
Singing, dancing
Coloring, painting, drawing
Going on field trips, camp-outs, hikes
Having barbecues, cookouts
Helping counselor, instructor, cook, peer
Having free time
Social reinforcers
Verbal praise
"Show and tell"
Work and project displays
Skill demonstrations
Clapping and cheering by others
Smiles or winks
Hugs, handshakes, or pats on the back

The ultimate goal of behavior modification is to encourage the child to respond appropriately to the normal social reinforcers society offers him. Consequently, social reinforcers (a pat, a smile, a kind word) are *always* presented with tangible reinforcers (food, games, toys, tokens).

Implementing a specific intervention, and collecting and recording intervention data. Intervention data provide information collected on the effects of the intervention during the implementation phase of the change process. Equally important as baseline data, this information is a yardstick for comparing baseline behavior to new behavior. By comparing these two sets of data, the practitioner can determine the changes that have occurred as a result of intervention. These data are counted and charted as discussed in the baseline phase (Fig. 21).

Methods for increasing behavior

Behavior modification practitioners have developed several techniques for increasing the frequency of target behaviors. Among these are (1) shaping, (2) modeling, (3) contingency contracting, and (4) the token economy. Each of these techniques is applicable by a counselor or instructor in the camp for the handicapped.

Shaping. Shaping is the reinforcement of successive approximations of behaviors leading to the desired behavior. Shaping is primarily applied to establish behaviors that have not been previously manifested in the camper's behavioral repertoire.

Shaping is accomplished by the *consistent, systematic, immediate* reinforcement of approximations of the desired behavior. Just as the sculptor shapes and molds an object of art from clay, the behavior modification practitioner shapes and molds a "new" behavior from an undifferentiated behavioral response (Neisworth, Deno, and Jenkins 1969).

EXAMPLE: Russell had great difficulty throwing the ball accurately during softball games. He released the ball from his hand early, and he did not keep his eyes on the person to whom he was throwing the ball. As a result of this handicap, he was frequently derogated by his peers and was always selected last for the team. This was very frustrating for Russell, and he frequently became physically aggressive during the games.

Mr. Milt, his counselor, wished to reduce Russell's aggressiveness on the ball diamond and increase his throwing skills. To accomplish these objectives, the counselor established a shaping intervention. Russell was exempted from softball, and a throwing accuracy program was designed for him.

During these exercises, Russell practiced throwing various-size balls at various-size targets at various distances. He began with an 18-inch playground ball, which he threw at a 3-foot target located 6-feet away. He was verbally reinforced each time he hit the target. The counselor demonstrated various throwing techniques and presented the boy's reinforcer.

Each time Russell performed with 90% accuracy with a specific-size ball or target, or at a specific distance, one of these components was changed: the ball or target was reduced in size, or the throwing distance was increased. Russell was never rewarded for a session performance less accurate than his previous performance. After several weeks of daily 15-minute practice sessions, Russell ventured onto the softball diamond to try his new skills. Although he was not the best thrower on the team, his performance was acceptable to himself and his peers.

Shaping is like climbing a ladder: one rung at a time with a foot firmly on the previous rung.

Modeling. Modeling is the provision of an individual or group behavior after which a camper is to pattern his behavior. During the modeling intervention, the camper is systematically encouraged to imitate or copy the behavior of his model.

According to Clarizio and Yelon (1967), exposure to a model may have three possible effects:

1. *Modeling effect:* The child may acquire behavior from a model that was not previously a part of his behavioral repertoire.
2. *Inhibitory or disinhibitory effect:* The child may inhibit unacceptable behavior that his model is punished for or otherwise discouraged from exhibiting.
3. *Eliciting effect:* A behavior that approximates the model's behavior may be elicited from a child. This need not necessarily be a "new" behavior. These behavioral approximations are reinforced.

Practitioners applying modeling techniques should consider the following questions:

Is the child cognitively and developmentally capable of imitating a model?

Will the child be rewarded for imitating the model?

Is the model worthy of imitation in the child's perception?

Is the model an acceptable model within the social context in which the child functions?

EXAMPLE: Mr. Don, a counselor, was responsible for a group of three boys and two girls at Camp Kibo. The campers' names were Mary, Shirley, John, James, and Charles. Of the group, Charles was the most uncooperative. He was constantly walking off during activities and exhibiting feelings of indignation about the actions of Mr. Don and the other members of the cabin group. His behavior occurred throughout the day.

During the initial days of the camping session, Mr. Don gave Charles considerable attention for this unacceptable behavior. As a result, the frequency of the behavior increased. Mr. Don punished, nagged, and otherwise attempted to reduce the behavior. Concurrently, Mr. Don was ignoring the cooperativeness of the other members of the group.

Finally, in an effort to improve the situation, the counselor implemented a modeling intervention. He ignored Charles' uncooperativeness and positively reinforced the cooperative behavior of the other campers. Charles realized that he would not receive attention for unacceptable behavior and that others in the group were receiving attention for their cooperative behavior. During the intervention, the counselor immediately reinforced Charles's cooperative behavior each time it occurred.

The frequency of cooperativeness by Charles gradually increased.

Contingency contracting. A contract is an agreement, written or verbal, between two or more parties, individuals or groups; this agreement stipulates the responsibilities of the parties as they are concerned with a specific item or activity. Contingency contracting in behavior modification is well defined by Becker (1969) in his statement "Arrange the conditions so that the child gets to do something he wants to do following something you want him to do."

We are all parties to verbal and written contracts in daily life: marriage; divorce; bank loans; deferred payment plans; water and disposal services; and a variety of verbal agreements with husbands, wives, sons, daughters, peers, and so on.

In behavior modification, contingency contracting is based on the Premack principle: "A behavior that has a high rate of occurrence can be used to increase a behavior with a low rate of occurrence" (Premack, 1965).

CONTRACT

Date_____

This is an agreement between _____ and
                                    (camper's name)

_____ . The contract begins on _____
        (counselor's name)   (date)

and ends on _____ . This contract will be reviewed on
                      (date)

_____ .
        (date)

The terms of the agreement are:

Camper will _____

_____

_____ .

Counselor will _____

_____

_____ .

If the camper fulfills his part of the contract, he will receive the agreed-on reward from the counselor. However, if the camper fails to fulfill his part of the contract, the rewards will be withheld.

Camper's signature _____

Counselor's signature _____

Fig. 22. Sample contingency contract.

The simplest contracts can be articulated as *X-Y* statements; that is, *if you do X, then you can do or get Y:*

"If you eat your spinach, then you can have some ice cream."

"If you clean your cabin, then you can play volleyball."

"If you do your reading assignment, then you can join the group on the beach."

More complex contracts are frequently written. An example of a written contract is presented in Fig. 22.

The following ten basic rules for writing a contract (Homme, Csanyi, Gonzales, and Rechs, 1968) also apply to verbal contracts:

1. The contract payoff (reward) should be immediate in accordance with the terms of the contract.
2. Initially, contracts should call for and reward approximations of the target behavior.
3. The contract should provide for frequent rewards in small amounts.
4. Contracts should call for and reward accomplishments rather than just obedience.
5. The performance should be rewarded only after it occurs.
6. The contract must be fair to all concerned parties.
7. The terms of the contract must be clear to all concerned parties.
8. The contract must be honest.
9. The contract must be positive.
10. Contracting, as an intervention, must be used systematically.

In addition, contracts must be *freely* negotiated and agreed to by both the camper and the counselor, and they must include a date for review and renegotiation (Walker and Shea 1976).

Token economy. The token economy is perhaps the most versatile and widely used of the behavior modification interventions. It is a system of exchange that provides immediate feedback cues for appropriate behavior. These cues, or tokens, are later exchanged for backup reinforcers.

Many children are not able to function appropriately if they must wait an extended time for their rewards. In addition, some children have not developed to a level at which social rewards are satisfactory reinforcers for them. Other children are so anxious about their behavior that they cannot function without immediate feedback. The token economy has proved to be an effective behavior change intervention for all of these children.

Tokens are usually valueless to the campers when originally introduced to them. However, their value becomes apparent as the campers learn that their tokens can be exchanged or traded for backup reinforcers: tangible rewards and activities.

There are ten basic rules to be applied in the establishment of a token economy in the camp:

1. Select the target behavior or behaviors (see Steps in the behavior change process, pp. 179-181).
2. Clarify and discuss the target behaviors with the camper and/or group. It is a well-known fact that an emphasis on "what you can do" is more palatable to children than an emphasis on "what you cannot do." Many unsuccessful behavior modification practitioners have determined their own failure by introducing a program as follows: "Now, you people are going to stop this noise and fooling around. I have this new . . . [and so on]." The campers are immediately challenged; they prepare to defeat the counselor and defend their personal integrity.
3. Select an appropriate token. Some tokens can be lost, stolen, or counterfeited. Others are noisy and difficult to handle. It is suggested that tokens be made of soft, flexible materials, such as paper or vinyl, or that they be simple pen or pencil markings. Among the useful tokens are checkmarks on a point card, stars, smiling faces, conservation and trading stamps, counselor-made tokens, or play money. An example of a point card that the child carries with him is presented in Fig. 23. As the camper accumulates points, they are marked on the card by his counselor or instructor.

Camper's name_____   Date_____

	Activity periods							
	1	**2**	**3**	**4**	**5**	**6**	**7**	**8**
Monday								
Tuesday								
Wednesday								
Thursday								
Friday								

Fig. 23. Point card.

Monday	
Tuesday	
Wednesday	
Thursday	
Friday	
Total	

The camper presents the card for the exchange.

4. Establish backup reinforcers. The token economy simply will not work if the tangible and activities rewards the campers are working for are not available. It is suggested that a camp store be established where the child may publicly ex- change his token for a reward of his choice. The store can be stocked with many of the rewards presented on p. 181, including certificates admitting the camper to activities. The store should be in a specific location and always open at the appropriate time.

5. Develop a reward menu and post it in

the cabin, classroom, or dining hall. The campers should be permitted to thoroughly discuss the items on the menu. They are encouraged to make their selections from these items. They are not permitted to debate the cost of the various rewards after the cost has been established. Of course, the cost of rewards must be reasonable and attainable. An example reward menu is presented in Table 3.

6. Implement the token economy. The counselor should introduce the token economy on a limited basis, initially. A complex, sophisticated system during the initial exposure would confuse and frustrate the campers. The counselor must explain the program with clarity and precision. He should be patient and respond to all the campers' questions. It is better to delay implementation than add to the existing confusion and frustration.

7. Provide immediate reinforcement for acceptable performance. The campers will lose interest if the process for obtaining the token is more effort than the backup reward is desirable. Many token economies fail because the counselor neglects to dispense the tokens at the appropriate time.

8. Gradually change from continuous to intermittent presentations of the tokens.

9. Provide time to exchange tokens for backup rewards. Lunch, recess, or highly desirable activity time should not be used for this exchange.

10. Revise the menu of available backup reinforcers frequently. Children become bored with the same old rewards.

The properly managed token economy works very effectively at camp for two primary reasons: the camper is competing only with himself, and the reward menu provides sufficient variety to prevent boredom.

Methods for decreasing behavior

Behavior modification practitioners have developed several interventions for decreasing the frequency of unacceptable or inappropriate target behaviors. Applicable to both individual and group behavior in the camp for the handicapped, these techniques include (1) extinction, (2) time-out, (3) punishment, (4) reinforcement of incompatible behaviors, and (5) desensitization.

Extinction. The discontinuation or withholding of the reinforcer of a target behavior that has previously reinforced that particular behavior is called extinction.

EXAMPLE: Tommy was constantly attempting to obtain Mr. Kevin's attention during cabin group planning sessions by jumping up and down, frantically waving his hand, and whispering in a loud, hoarse voice, "Mr. Kevin, Mr. Kevin, me, me, I know." Mr. Kevin noted that

Table 3. Reward menu

Reward	Time	Cost*
Free time	20 minutes	40 points
Watching television	60 minutes	90 points
Attending a movie	—	120 points
Extra arts-and-crafts period	—	80 points
Extra swimming period	—	80 points
Sleeping late	30 minutes	50 points
Extra dessert	—	30 points
Soda	—	30 points
Candy	—	10 to 40 points
Item from camp store	—	10 to 500 points
Overnight camp-out	1 night	600 points

*Cost in points will vary according to the particular system designed for implementation. The cost of the various items must be within the attainable limit for the campers.

if he called on Tommy when he engaged in these antics, the boy would say a few words, sit down, and begin jumping, waving, and whispering again. The counselor decided he was reinforcing Tommy's inappropriate behavior by calling on him.

For an intervention, Mr. Kevin selected extinction. He would completely ignore Tommy's antics. However, he would attend to and reinforce the boy's appropriate attention-getting behavior. The intervention was implemented and applied consistently during planning sessions for the next 2 weeks. Tommy's inappropriate behavior decreased.

To be effective, extinction must be applied consistently and the practitioner must persist.

Time-out. Time-out is the removal of a camper from an apparently reinforcing setting to a presumed nonreinforcing setting for a specified and limited period of time.

EXAMPLE: Benji in Mr. Keith's group was constantly disrupting arts-and-crafts lessons. He openly criticized the instructor, made jokes about his peer's projects, and destroyed the completed projects of others. His behavior was unacceptable to his peers, instructor, and counselor. A time-out intervention was selected to decrease these behaviors.

Baseline data was collected for three sessions, and the unacceptable behavior was specified. Benji was told by the instructor exactly the behaviors he would be timed-out for exhibiting. Benji was to be timed-out for 4 minutes for each occurrence of the target behaviors.

After several weeks a decrease in the behavior was observable.

The effectiveness of time-out is contingent on several factors: (1) the characteristics of the camper, (2) the consistency with which the intervention is applied, (3) the characteristics of the time-out area, (4) the camper's understanding of the rules of behavior and for time-out, (5) the duration of the time-out period, and (6) the evaluation of the intervention.

The counselor must know the camper's characteristic reactions to isolation or time-out. For the acting-out, aggressive, group-oriented child, time-out may be an effective intervention. Such campers usually want very much to be "with their group" and "involved in the activity program." For them, time-out is not reinforcing. However, for the withdrawn, passive, solitary child who is prone to daydreaming, time-out may be reinforcing. These children may be quite content to engage in "their own little world" while in time-out.

If time-out is to be used as an intervention, it must be applied with consistency over a predetermined period of time. Frequently, counselors are inconsistent in their application of this technique; as a result, the camper becomes confused and the target behavior is unwittingly rewarded.

Care must be taken in the selection of a time-out area. Areas that appear to be nonreinforcing but in effect are very reinforcing to children should be avoided. Such areas include busy pathways, corridors, doorsteps, offices, and other high-traffic areas. The time-out area should offer minimal visual and aural stimulation. It should not be located near activity areas. In camp, the time-out area may be an empty cabin, a little-used pathway, or a clearing in the woods. Frequently, it is adequate to have a child sit on the ground with his back to the activity from which he was removed.

The camper must know the behaviors that are inappropriate and the consequences for exhibiting those behaviors. The rules of behavior should be verbally communicated and posted in the cabin or dining hall. These rules should be reviewed frequently and applied fairly.

Time-out loses its effectiveness if a child is required to remain in time-out for lengthy periods of time. Four or 5 minutes should be the maximum duration of time-out. Under extraordinary conditions, the period may be longer but should never exceed 10 minutes. The camper must be supervised during time-out by the counselor or aide.

This intervention also includes the reinforcement of acceptable behavior and approximations of the acceptable behavior. When the camper is not in time-out and is performing acceptably, the counselor rewards the acceptable behavior.

For evaluative purposes, the counselor maintains a log with the following entries: (1) the time the camper begins his time-out, (2) the time the camper ends his time-out, (3) unusual incidents occurring during time-out, (4) the activity taking place immediately before the behavior precipitating time-out, and (5) the activity immediately following the time-out period.

This technique does not include lecturing, reprimanding, and/or scolding the child before, during, or after the time-out period. All explanations are brief and concise.

Punishment. Punishment is the most misunderstood and emotionally explosive of the behavior modification techniques.

Punishment is imposed on a child to decrease or eliminate inappropriate behavior. In general, punishment is defined as the presentation of an aversive stimulus as a consequence of the exhibition of a target behavior.

Punishment can be either physical or psychological. The punisher, if he chooses, may impose physical (a paddling or spanking) or psychological (derogatory statements) punishment to eliminate a behavior.

The short-term or immediate effectiveness of punishment is difficult to dispute. Punishment is without doubt effective for attaining immediate results.

Clarizio and Yelon (1967) offer several logical reasons for avoiding the use of punishment:

It does not eliminate but merely suppresses the target behavior.

It does not provide a model for the acceptable behavior to be exhibited by the child.

Aggression by a punisher presents the child with an undesirable model.

The emotional results of punishment may be fear, tension, stress, or withdrawal.

The child's resulting frustrations may result in further deviations.

In addition to the above, punishment may result in physical harm to the child.

Punishment in the perception of the punished child is often associated with the punisher rather than with the behavior. As a result, the child's reaction to punishment may be dislike and avoidance of the punisher rather than an effort to change his behavior. Counselors and instructors in the therapeutic camp who acknowledge that they are models for their campers will avoid assuming the role of punisher.

Among the punishments commonly used in our society are:

Deprivation of activities
Withholding of snacks and desserts
Time-out (especially when ineffectively applied)
Paddlings, spankings, slaps, and the like
Scoldings and reprimands (especially in public)
Being made to stand in a corner or being sent to bed
Being made to wear symbols of unacceptability, such as signs and dunce caps
Sarcasm, derogatory comments, cursing

There are a variety of behavior management interventions presented in this chapter that are as effective or more effective than punishment. Punishment is of little or no value in the special camp and is *not* recommended. However, if punishment is used, the punisher must adhere to the following guidelines:

1. Specify and communicate the punishable behavior to the camper by means of "rules of behavior," which are posted in a cabin or dining hall and discussed frequently.
2. Provide models of acceptable behavior that the camper can imitate.
3. Punish the child immediately after he exhibits the punishable behavior.
4. Do not apply punishment whimsically; be consistent.
5. Use punishment systematically and fairly (what is punishable for Peter is punishable for Paul).
6. Punishment should be imposed on the child impersonally; do not lose emotional control and become angry.

I am irrevocably opposed to the use of corporal punishment—whether it be paddling, slapping, spanking, or using a cattle prod or an electric wand by a professional or paraprofessional—regardless of the behavior exhibited by the child. I am also opposed to psychological punishments, which, at the least, erode the already fragile self-concept of the child. There are simply more humane ways to manage behavior.

Reinforcement of incompatible behaviors. At times it is necessary and desirable to decrease the frequency of a target behavior by systematically reinforcing a behavior that is in opposition to, or incompatible with, the target behavior. This is the process of reinforcing incompatible behaviors.

For instance, a counselor has two campers in his cabin group who are constantly arguing with each other. After analysis of the situation, it is proposed that the behavior would probably decrease if one of the camper's beds were relocated on the opposite side of the cabin. By this means, the campers are separated; the opportunities for disagreements are reduced, and the behavior decreases.

The effectiveness of this technique is heavily dependent on the selection of the pairs of incompatible behaviors. For example:

1. A child cannot be seated and standing at the same time. Rather than attending to his standing and jumping about (the target behavior), the counselor would reward sitting. He would ignore standing.
2. A child cannot be talking and silent at the same time. If the counselor wished to reduce talking using this intervention, he would reward silence and ignore talking.
3. A child cannot be on task (attending to a project) and off task at the same time. Using this technique, the counselor would reward the camper's on-task behavior and ignore his off-task behavior.

This technique is applicable to a wide variety of behaviors exhibited by children in the camp setting. If applied with consistency over a predetermined period of time, it can be very effective.

Desensitization. Desensitization is the process of systematically attenuating a specific learned fear in an individual. This therapeutic technique was developed, in large part, by Wolpe in the 1950s and 1960s. The technique has been used with many individuals with phobias, fears, and anxieties related to public speaking, school attendance, partic-

ipation in group settings, water, animals, flying, test taking, and the like.

The process of systematic desensitization involves three phases or steps (Wolpe and Lazarus, 1966):

1. Training the subject in deep muscle relaxation
2. Construction of an anxiety-evoking hierarchy of stimuli
3. Counterposing relaxation and the anxiety-evoking stimuli

These three phases are interdependent. Although the camp counselor should not attempt systematic desensitization on the basis of the information provided here, he can apply the underlying principles of this technique in the camp setting when confronted by fearful, anxious, and phobic children.

A potent intervention, desensitization may be applied by the counselor or instructor under the following conditions:

1. The practitioner must have a positive interpersonal relationship with the child. The phobic child must "trust" the counselor and feel free to express his fears in the presence of the counselor.
2. The counselor must construct an anxiety-evoking stimulus hierarchy (a hierarchy of stimuli on a continuum from the least to the most anxiety-evoking stimulus surrounding the specific fear).
3. The counselor must be willing (and have adequate time) to accompany the camper as he progresses through the hierarchy from the least to the most anxiety-evoking stimulus.

The practitioner must recognize that the desensitization process is time consuming. He must be consistent and patient in the application of the technique. It is often necessary to repeat some of the specific anxiety-evoking situations several times until their effect on the child is eliminated.

EXAMPLE: Kurt, an 8-year-old camper, was afraid of water. Swimming lessons are a normal part of the camp activity program. Although swimming is not mandatory, it is encouraged. At the first suggestion of swimming or going to the pool, Kurt would have a temper tantrum of considerable magnitude.

It was the opinion of the staff that Kurt should overcome his irrational fear. Systematic desensitization was selected as an appropriate intervention technique.

The following stimulus hierarchy was constructed and applied:

1. Swimming was announced to the group and discussed with Kurt's peers. Kurt did not attend swimming lessons but watched his peers get on the bus and depart for swimming. (This is a very happy and exciting time at camp.) This step was repeated twice.
2. Kurt rode the bus to the pool and waited outside the building.
3. Kurt rode the bus to the pool and waited in the lobby outside the locker room.
4. Kurt entered the locker room, put on his trunks, and remained in the locker room during the lesson. This step was repeated twice.
5. Kurt, in trunks, observed the lesson from the pool observation room.
6. Kurt observed the lesson from the poolside (approximately 10 feet from the water).
7. Kurt observed the lesson while standing at the edge of the pool. This step was repeated four times.
8. Kurt observed the lesson while sitting on the edge of the pool with his feet in the water.
9. Kurt stood in the pool with his hands on the edge of the pool. This step was repeated twice.
10. Kurt walked in the shallow end of the pool with his hand on the side of the pool.

Throughout this process, Kurt was accompanied by his counselor, who provided positive reinforcement. As a result of desensitization, Kurt began swimming lessons within 3 weeks. After 3 years, it was noted that the fear did not return. Kurt is an excellent swimmer.

MEDICAL INTERVENTIONS

Although the prescribing and administering of medication is not within the province of counselors and instructors, they do need a general knowledge of the types and effects of various symptom-control medications administered to exceptional children. This information can be communicated by a camp physician or nurse during in-service training.

Either a camp physician or nurse is responsible for administering *all* medication. The counselor and instructor are responsible for escorting the camper to the health clinic for his medication at the appropriate time. Under very unusual circumstances, a camp coordinator or his delegated assistant may be given permission by a camper's *parents and physician* to administer medication under stringent supervision.

Procedures for obtaining permission to administer, administering, and safeguarding medications should be established at the camp. These procedures should be clearly communicated to all staff personnel.

The primary role of the instructor and counselor in all medical interventions is to provide current and objective feedback relative to the observable effects of the medication on the camper's behavior. The majority of present-day symptom-control medications are experimental substances whose effect on a particular child cannot be predicted with exactitude. Thus, meaningful feedback to the prescribing physician assists the physician in his efforts to adjust the type of medication, the quantity, and the schedule for administering it to respond to the individual child's needs most effectively. Because the counselor and instructor are trained observers and are with the child throughout each day, they are in an excellent position to observe the effects of the medication and report, through the appropriate channels, to the physician.

SPECIAL CONCERNS

At camp, some issues will arise that will be of special concern to the director and his staff.

Loss of privileges. The loss of a privilege is frequently used as a behavior management intervention at camp. Although effective for modifying short-term behavior, this punishment must be used with caution. The privileges lost must be in proportion to the child's misdeed. Campers should be deprived, as punishment, of small, relatively unimportant privileges rather than of their most desirable activities.

For example, a child should not be deprived of swimming lessons for a week or of an overnight campout for not finishing his lunch or making up his bunk. This would not only be unjust, it might discourage him from involvement in any activities.

The deprivation must fit the infraction of the rules.

Runaways. At every camp there is usually one child who copes with his frustration by running away. Whether the camp is in the wilderness, suburbs, or in the city, the runaway causes great concern among staff and children.

A plan for dealing with runaways should be developed and communicated to all staff and campers at the beginning of the session. This plan should contain options for the counselors to implement.

For example, option 1 might be that the counselor would follow the camper, if possible, and keep him in sight until he was ready to return to camp. However, this technique might encourage the child to repeat this behavior to attain the counselor's individual attention. Option 2 might be that the counselor would find and return the child to camp. The behavior could then be discussed and the appropriate intervention imposed.

A punishment should not be imposed for the first offense unless the counselor is certain that the camper understood the rules concerning running away. A punishment should never be imposed if the child found himself lost or simply strayed away from his group.

Anytime a child is missing from camp, the camp coordinator should be notified immediately. Depending on the available options, he may choose to organize a search party or notify the forest ranger, or the state or the local police for assistance.

The rules governing running away should be discussed with the campers during orientation sessions and briefly reviewed after each offense. This review should be conducted in a manner that will minimize embarrassment for recent offenders.

Water activities. Accidents on the beach, at the pool, or in the lake create the most emotionally explosive problem at camp. The

rules for behavior in, on, and around the water must be very clearly communicated to the campers and the staff.

Whenever a child deviates from the rules, the staff is to react *immediately*. When a rule is broken, there are *no* warnings, *no* second chances. The child will sit out the remainder of the activity period.

All water-related activities are to be supervised by trained and qualified water safety personnel.

Physical aggression. Children who are so physically aggressive that they endanger themselves and others must be restrained. Physical punishment for aggressiveness, however, is avoided at all cost. Physical punishment confirms the child's belief that "might is right."

The aggressive child should be quickly escorted from the activity area by a counselor and taken to a quiet, private location until he regains his control. The counselor should remain with him. After the camper has regained self-control, his behavior should be discussed with him. He should then be instructed to return to his group. Life-space interviewing and time-out are effective interventions for aggression.

In cases of extreme physical aggression, the camper must be physically restrained to prevent injuries. At such a time, the counselor should minimize his verbalizations. When a child has lost self-control he is not in the mood for talk.

Toilet training. There are usually some toilet-training problems at camp. The child is always aware of his problem; thus, telling him about it or discussing it is usually a waste of effort. If a counselor wishes to be helpful to the child he will keep his knowledge of the child's problem from other campers and plan a program with the child to help the child overcome his problem.

Some planning aids for counselors of campers with this problem are:
Do not embarrass the camper.
Suggest that the camper not drink liquids after the evening meal.
Adjust the camper's schedule so that he is not overtired when he retires.

Tell the camper to awaken you at night and escort him to the restroom.

Tell the camper that you will awaken him when you retire, during the night, and/or early in the morning and escort him to the restroom.

When an accident occurs, help the child. Be sure he has clean, dry clothing and bedding. Show him where he can wash and dry his clothing and bedding.

Protect the child from harassment by his peers and others.

If the problem persists, notify the coordinator, nurse, or physician.

Toilet training should be put in proper perspective. It is one of the thousands of behaviors a camper emits each day. It should not be allowed to ruin his entire life. Almost always, he is totally *incapable* of controlling this behavior without help.

Nightmares, fears, and homesickness. As adults, we often forget the reality of our childhood nightmares, fears, and homesickness. We forget the terror in our hearts when we awoke from a "bad" dream, had a "bad" experience with a feared animal or bug, or realized we were a "million" miles from home and mother. Our childhood concerns were not "baby stuff" to us; they were real, and they hurt.

The counselor must manage these problems. He must be helpful and kind to the frightened camper. The counselor can (1) sit with the child, holding him, if necessary; (2) calm him down by talking quietly to him; and (3) talk about tomorrow and the fun to be enjoyed.

There is nothing wrong with tucking a small child into his bunk for the night or giving him a hug, a kiss, or a pat on the back.

Housekeeping duties. Housekeeping duties consume a great deal of time and cause many hassles among campers unless properly scheduled.

Work should be distributed equally among all group members. A specific time schedule should be used daily. Tasks should be rotated among the campers. Each child should be responsible for his belongings and living area.

The counselor should not assume that a child knows how to do a task. He should demonstrate the tasks and help the campers.

CONCLUSIONS

The effectiveness of the various behavior management interventions reviewed in this chapter varies with the particular child, counselor, behavior, and milieu involved in the behavior change process. Some techniques have immediate positive effects on target behaviors; others take effect more slowly, almost imperceptibly, but do have a positive impact on behaviors.

Counselors and instructors are cautioned not to expect miracles—immediate changes in behaviors that have been effective for the child for several years. The art of managing behavior is difficult work; it requires patience, consistency, and persistence. The practitioner must be alert to small changes in behavior and be rewarded by these if he is to successfully help children.

A counselor must be willing and capable of committing himself, totally, to helping children. Those individuals unable to do so should not be employed as counselors or instructors. Their inadequate efforts may be harmful to themselves and the children.

The authentic counselor will "hurt" a little. He will become frustrated and discouraged when those things to which he is personally committed do not work exactly as planned. However, his concern is normal and emotionally healthy—a measure of his commitment to the special child.

According to Morse (1947) "Camp is too often looked at as a "cure-all." Camps for exceptional children are not "cure-alls," but they can and do have a significant impact on the child's life when properly staffed and administered.

Several behavior management interventions have been reviewed in this chapter. The proper implementation of these techniques in the camp for the handicapped require further study. Readers wishing to expand their knowledge of behavior management are referred to the references listed here.

REFERENCES

Becker, W. C. Introduction. In L. Homme and others (Eds.), *How to use contingency contracting in the classroom*. Champaign, Ill.: Research Press, 1969.

Berg, B. R. Combining group and casework treatment in a camp setting. *Social Work*, 1969, **5**(1), 56-62.

Brenner, M. B. Life-space interviewing in the school setting. In H. Dupont (Ed.), *Educating emotionally disturbed children*. New York: Holt, Rinehart and Winston, Inc., 1969.

Bryen, D. N. Teacher strategies in managing classroom behavior. In D. D. Hammill and N. R. Bartel (Eds.), *Teaching children with learning and behavior problems*. Boston: Allyn & Bacon, Inc., 1975.

Chetkow, B. H. Discipline problems in camp. *Recreation*, 1964, **57**(3), 136-137.

Clarizio, H. F., and Yelon, S. L. Learning theory approaches to classroom management: rationale and intervention techniques. *Journal of Special Education*, 1967, **1**, 267-274.

Dreikurs, R., and Grey, L. *Logical consequences: a new approach to discipline*, New York: Hawthorn Books, Inc., 1968.

Glasser, W. *Mental health or mental illness?* New York: Harper & Row, Publishers, 1960.

Glasser, W. *Reality therapy: a new approach to psychiatry*. New York: Harper & Row, Publishers, 1965.

Glasser, W. *Schools without failure*. New York: Harper & Row, Publishers, 1969.

Hammill, D. D., and Bartel, N. R. *Teaching children with learning and behavior problems*. Boston: Allyn & Bacon, Inc., 1975.

Harris, T. A. *I'm OK—you're OK: a practical guide to transactional analysis*. New York: Harper & Row, Publishers, 1969.

Homme, L., Csanyi, A. P., Gonzales, M. A., and Rechs, J. R. *How to use contingency contracting in the classroom*. Champaign, Ill.: Research Press, 1969.

James, M., and Jongeward, D. *Born to win: transactional analysis with Gestalt experiments*. Reading, Mass.: Addison-Wesley Publishing Co., 1971.

Lewin, K. *A dynamic theory of personality*. New York: McGraw-Hill Book Co., 1935.

Long, N. J., Morse, W. C., and Newman, R. G. Milieu therapy. In N. J. Long, W. C. Morse, and R. G. Newman (Eds.), *Conflict in the classroom: the education of emotionally disturbed children*. Belmont, Calif.: Wadsworth Publishing Co. Inc., 1965.

Loughmiller, C. *Wilderness road*. University of Texas: The Hogg Foundation for Mental Health, 1965.

McNeil, E. B. The perception of change in aggressive children. *Children*, 1963, **10**(1), 17-22.

Morse, W. C. From the University of Michigan Fresh Air Camp: some problems of therapeutic camping. *Nervous Child*, 1947, **6**, 211-224.

Morse, W. C. Training teachers in life-space interviewing. In H. Dupont (Ed.), *Educating emotionally disturbed children*. New York: Holt, Rinehart, and Winston, Inc., 1969.

Morse, W. C. Worksheet on life-space interviewing for teachers. In N. J. Long, W. C. Morse, and R. G. Newman (Eds.), *Conflict in the classroom: the education of children with problems* (2nd ed.). Belmont, Calif.: Wadsworth Publishing Co. Inc., 1971.

Morse, W. C., and Small, E. R. Group life-space interviewing in a therapeutic camp. *American Journal of Orthopsychiatry*, 1959, **29**, 27-44.

Morse, W. C., and Wineman, D. Group interviewing in a camp for disturbed boys. *Journal of Social Issues*, 1957, **13**(1), 23-31.

Morse, W. C., and Wineman, D. The therapeutic use of social isolation in a camp for ego-disturbed boys. *Journal of Social Issues*, 1957, **13**(1), 32-39.

Neisworth, J. T., Deno, S. L., and Jenkins, J. R. *Student motivation and classroom management: a behavioristic approach*. Newark, Del.: Behavior Technics, Inc., 1969.

Newman, R. G. *Psychological consultation in the schools*. New York: Basic Books, Inc., Publishers, 1967.

Premack, D. Reinforcement theory. In D. Levine (Ed.), *Nebraska symposium on motivation: 1965*. Lincoln: University of Nebraska Press, 1965.

Redl, F. The concept of the life-space interview. *American Journal of Orthopsychiatry*, 1959, **29**, 1-18.

Redl, F. The concept of therapeutic milieu. *American Journal of Orthopsychiatry*, 1959, **29**, 721-734.

Reinert, H. R. *Children in conflict: educational strategies for the emotionally disturbed and behaviorally disordered*. St. Louis: The C. V. Mosby Co., 1976.

Rickard, H. C., and Lattal, K. A. Group problem-solving in a therapeutic summer camp: an illustration. *Adolescence*, 1969, **4**(15), 319-332.

Rickard, H. C., Serum, C. S., and Wilson, W. Developing problem-solving attitudes in emotionally disturbed children. *Adolescence*, 1971, **6**(24), 451-456.

Rotman, C. B. The problem camper to tolerate, treat, or terminate. *Camping Magazine*, 1973, **46**(1), 16-17, 24.

Sarason, I. G., Glaser, E. M., and Fargo, G. A. *Reinforcing productive classroom behavior*. New York: Behavioral Publications, Inc., 1972.

Shea, T. M., Whiteside, W. R., Beetner, E. G., and Lindsey, D. *Life-space interview: reality rub-in*. Edwardsville: Special Education Department, Southern Illinois University, 1975.

Walker, J. E., and Shea, T. M. *Behavior modification: a practical approach for educators*. St. Louis: The C. V. Mosby Co., 1976.

Wineman, D. The life-space interview. *Social Work*, 1959, **29**, 3-17.

Wolpe, J. The systematic desensitization treatment of neuroses. *Journal of Nervous and Mental Diseases*, 1961, **132**, 189-203.

Wolpe, J., and Lazarus, A. *Behavior therapy techniques*. New York: Pergamon Press, Inc., 1966.

Young, R. A., Miller, L., and Verven, N. Treatment techniques in a therapeutic camp. *American Journal of Orthopsychiatry*, 1951, **21**, 819-826.

CHAPTER 10

Planning, programming, and administration of the special camp

In this final chapter, a wide variety of practical problems confronting camp planners, programmers, and administrators are reviewed. The focus, in large part, is on administrative tasks: personnel, facilities, equipment, transportation, and the like. A few general comments are offered on the topics of planning and programming, which are discussed extensively in Sections One and Two.

The suggestions presented here are the result of my personal experiences as planner, programmer, and administrator of the model camps presented in Section Two.

The material is not intended to provide the reader "hard and fast" solutions to his administrative problems. Rather, it is designed to alert the camp administrator to the multitude of tasks he must confront. The material may serve as a nearly comprehensive listing of the tasks to be accomplished before, during, and after the camp session. Proper attention to these potential problem areas will increase the effectiveness and efficiency of the camp for handicapped children.

PLANNING

The importance of detailed planning cannot be overestimated. Comprehensive plans for all camp activities from precamp publicity and application procedures to final reports and postcamp follow-up surveys should be developed and communicated to appropriate persons. Those to be made aware of the plans for the session include campers and their parents; school, church, and community agency personnel; and others in a position to give logistic and financial support to the program. All camp personnel, including counselors, instructors, and other members of the staff, should be alerted to the plans.

The management team—the coordinator and his appropriate assistant coordinators—are involved in all phases of the planning process. *All* personnel involved in a particular facet of the program should assist in the planning of that particular activity: personnel assigned to the remediation unit should plan the remediation program: personnel assigned to the residential care unit should plan the residential care program; and so on.

It is desirable to include noncamp persons on a broadly representative advisory, planning, and/or development committee. Committee members should be representative of the community-at-large and of the population served by the camp. The membership should include parents of exceptional and nonexceptional children, parent group representatives, school and community agency personnel, and representatives of contributing clubs and service organizations. It should be clearly explained to the committee members that their function is advisory. Their suggestions and recommendations will be considered by the administration and implemented if feasible.

The advice and consent of a representative citizen's committee is extremely important to the success of the camp, especially during its initial years of operation. The members of this committee can, and do, mold community attitudes toward the camp, the campers, and the staff.

It is strongly recommended that the camp administrator ensure sufficient time for detailed planning. Often, it is necessary to begin planning and organizing the camp 6 to 8 months in advance of implementation.

The success or failure of a camp is determined before the arrival of the campers. Many potentially superior programs have failed because sufficient time was not available to the staff for necessary planning.

PROGRAMMING

Programming is equal to planning in importance for the operation of an effective and efficient camp for the handicapped. Every hour of each day the child is enrolled in camp should be carefully planned. This includes his free time, rest periods, meals, bedtime, and so on. Although a child may not be actively involved at a particular time, it is necessary that a minimal plan be developed for all time periods. This plan need only include the location and duration of the activity and the staff person responsible for supervision.

A well-planned program reduces the probability of camper boredom, disruption, and anxiety. The camper and the responsible staff person will know *who* is to be *where* for *what* purpose, for *how* long, and with *whom*.

Programming—the development of hourly, daily, and weekly plans—should involve the staff members responsible for the activity. Although the coordinator and his assistants are responsible for coordination of all plans to ensure a well-balanced program, they must delegate detailed programming responsibilities to appropriate specialists: instructors and counselors. These specialists are supervised by the coordinator and his assistants, and they are held responsible for the activities they conduct.

It is strongly recommended that the initial days or week of the camp session be very structured. This initial structure reduces potential camper boredom and disruption. Structure also reduces the probable increase in camper anxiety due to the unfamiliarity of his situation.

Programming suggestions

Orientation. All camp personnel attend the orientation sessions. At these sessions, all phases of the program are reviewed in detail. The staff is encouraged to analyze and question any phase of the program and make suggestions for change.

It is important, during orientation, to alert each staff member to the role and functions of *all* other staff members. He must be made aware of the importance of his special role and functions within the total program.

Although verbal communications are necessary and desirable at these sessions, it is useful to distribute written material to the staff. This material, perhaps in the form of a handbook or packet, can be reviewed at the session and referred to throughout the camp session at the convenience of the individual staff member.

Included in the handbook or packet are:
A complete description of the program
Copies of all brochures and news releases
Copies of all calendars and schedules
Copies of all forms and applications
Examples of teaching prescriptions, lesson plans, and final reports
Copies of all rules and regulations

In-service and preservice training. Training sessions are scheduled before and during the camp program and are attended by all camp personnel, including the administrators.

At these sessions, all facets of the program

are presented and the entire staff is encouraged to analyze and discuss them. Personnel are free to suggest modifications in the program. These modifications should be implemented by the administration if feasible.

The in-service and preservice training coordinator must make every effort to encourage the members of the camp staff to discuss their problems and concerns during training sessions.

Staffing sessions. A staffing session is conducted for each child applying for admission to camp before the program begins. During the precamp staffing session, the responsible personnel plan the camper's program for the session.

During the program, one or more review staffing sessions are held for each child. During the review sessions, the child's program is evaluated and modified as deemed necessary by the staff.

Finally, the child's program is thoroughly reviewed at the end of camp. At this session, personnel prepare a final report for distribution to the appropriate referring persons.

Supervision and evaluation. Supervision and evaluation are an integral part of the camp program. They are ongoing daily affairs. Supervision and evaluation are never conducted sporadically by a coordinator or assistant coordinator who suddenly swoops from the sky to do his "thing" on some poor unsuspecting counselor or instructor. Such tactics are destructive and harmful.

The supervisor must allot sufficient time in his daily schedule to visit and observe each staff member. He should not devote his supervisory hours to administrative details. During the supervisory visit, the supervisor observes, reviews daily plans, and spends a *brief* time visiting with the staff members and campers. The effective supervisor learns the unique working characteristics of the counselors or instructors, the individual campers, and the cabin or activity groups he is supervising.

Supervision and evaluation discussions are conducted during daily staff meetings. At this time, the related activities and problems of various individuals and groups can be discussed and individual counselors and instructors can be singled out for praise and recognition.

Caution is taken in staff meetings never to embarrass a counselor or instructor about his personal performance or the performance of his campers.

If a specific person is employed as a camp supervisor or evaluator, the role and functions of this individual must be clearly explained to the entire staff. They should be encouraged to discuss and modify the evaluator's functions to meet their needs, if feasible.

Occasionally, there are one or two individuals on the staff who are ineffective and/or destructive. These problem persons must be confronted and the difficulty resolved. Confrontation is difficult for all concerned—supervisors and staff members—but occasionally it is unavoidable. When a staff member must be confronted, it should be done in private and in the presence of the responsible supervisor. The offending person should be encouraged to respond to the charges and defend his position.

The individual is given a specific period of time to improve his performance. If he chooses not to change or cannot change and is potentially detrimental to the welfare of the children, he is discharged immediately. As in all decisions we make, our prime responsibility is to the handicapped children enrolled in the camp.

Program changes. If the camp is to be a dynamic and innovative program, modifications must be made during each session. Our recognition of the variability among campers, staff, and groups indicates that a static program is potentially ineffective in meeting the needs of all persons involved in the camp.

Although program flexibility is desired, program changes cannot be whimsical or arbitrary. All changes that affect more than a single individual must be discussed and agreed to by all concerned individuals. Only after all the pertinent individuals are informed is the program modification implemented.

Forms, schedules, and plans. Many forms,

schedules, calendars, and plans are presented in Section Two. They can be helpful aids in programming efforts, or we can become a slave to these very aids that were designed to help us.

The coordinator should be careful to select and utilize *only* those aids that are needed to effectively operate his specific camp. All of the forms presented in the text are subject to modification to meet specific needs in a specific camp setting.

The aids described in Section Two are listed here with their location in the text for easy reference:

Application form (Appendix A)
Educational assessment form (Appendix A)
Physician's assessment form (Appendix A)
Family information form (Appendix A)
Assessment synthesizer (Chapter 3, Fig. 3)
Weekly plan for the day camp (Chapter 5, Fig. 7)
Daily record for the day camp (Chapter 5, Fig. 8)
Activity plan for the day camp (Chapter 5, Fig. 9)
Behavior intervention plan (Chapter 5, Fig. 10)
Weekly schedule for the day camp (Chapter 5, Fig. 11)
Calendar of events for the day camp (Chapter 5)
Activity schedule for the evening camp (Chapter 6, Fig. 12)
Camp activity plan for the evening camp (Chapter 6, Fig. 13)
Weekly schedule for the 3-hour preschool day camp (Chapter 6, Fig. 14)
Weekly schedule for the 5-hour preschool day camp (Chapter 6, Fig. 15)
Weekly schedule for the residential camp for special populations (Chapter 7, Fig. 17)

Rainy days. It is inevitable in most geographic areas that 1 or 2 days of each camp session will be rainy. The wise camp coordinator prepares his staff for these potentially disruptive days.

Two or more rainy day schedules are prepared by the staff before the beginning of each camp session. Special activities are reserved for these days. The staff is encouraged not to implement these or very similar activities on nonrainy days. The rainy day plans, including the needed materials and equipment, are stored for the inevitable day.

Among the activities reserved for rainy days are:

Educational and entertaining movies
Cooking and baking special snacks
Learning new songs
Marshmallow and weiner roasts
New table and card games
New arts-and-crafts projects

If rain results in the cancellation of a special event (field trip, hike, and so on), it is a great disappointment to the campers. If this occurs, the special event should be rescheduled, if possible, on the next sunny day. The majority of the children will accept this program change without difficulty.

Special events. A variety of special events are suggested in Chapters 5 through 8. These events should be exactly what the phase implies—special. They are unique activities in the life of the camper—new experiences, new happenings.

Special events are planned well in advance and are integrated into the child's program as a logical part of his course of study. For example, it is of greater educational value for a child to visit the Cahokia Mounds as part of a unit of study on American Indian culture than to visit them because it is Friday, the day reserved for special events.

Special events are of educational value only when the campers are properly prepared for the event and are given ample opportunities to discuss their experiences after they occur. These programs are designed to involve campers in activities—not simply to entertain them. If the activity is a carnival, field day, picnic, camp-out, puppet show, and so on, the children must be actively involved in its planning and implementation.

Parent programs. Parents of exceptional children, as are all parents, are anxious and concerned when *their* child prepares to go to camp. For them, the camp and its staff are unknown. It is difficult for the parents of an exceptional child to watch their young one climb aboard the camp bus and disappear from their life for 2 or more weeks. The parents' anxiety and concern for the welfare of the child is real, and the camp staff has a responsibility to help the parents recognize that much of their concern is unfounded.

In an effort to assist the parents, and as a

In costume for carnival day.

result the camper and the camp, several programs are available for implementation by the staff: (1) parent orientation programs, (2) parent group discussions (3) individual parent-staff conferences, and (4) systematic home-camp child communications.

If possible, the *parent orientation program* is conducted at the camp. When this is impossible, photographic slides of the camp may be viewed by the parents in a convenient facility.

During orientation, the parents may (1) tour the camp facilities, (2) listen to an explanation of the camp program, (3) review daily and weekly schedules, (4) meet the camp staff who will work with their child, and (5) be informed of all health and safety contingencies available at camp.

It is desirable to conduct orientation meetings at a facility in which parents and staff can relax, talk informally, and perhaps share a meal. If the campers are present at these sessions, they can share in the discussion with their parents. Finally, during the orientation program, parents have an opportunity to meet and talk with other parents and children.

If a camp is situated in the local community, *parent group discussions* can be held on a weekly or biweekly schedule. At these sessions, the parents discuss their problems and concerns about their child relative to both the camp and noncamp settings. Time is also devoted to instruction in behavior management techniques. The implementation of this approach to parent orientation is dependent on the availability of a qualified discussion leader to work with the group on a regular basis.

Individual parent-staff conferences are

helpful to both parents and staff. These are structured, child-centered conferences, usually conducted by a counselor or instructor. The purpose of the conference is to inform the parent about his child's progress at camp.

The conference may be viewed as a verbal report card, during which the appropriate staff member discusses with the parent the camper's:

1. *Social behavior:* Self-control, affect, group participation skills, use of social amenities, and so on
2. *Communications skills:* Modes of communication, listening skills, language development and skills, and so on
3. *Basic knowledge:* General and specific information; problem-solving skills; skills in reading, spelling, writing, arithmetic, and so on
4. *Special knowledge:* Knowledge of art, music, drama, arts and crafts, and so on
5. *Sensory motor skill and development:* Gross and fine motor skill, physical abilities, sport skills, perceptual and perceptual-motor skill, body usage, and so on
6. *Self-care and practical skills:* Use of work and play, completion of chores, meeting of responsibilities, helpfulness to others, personal hygiene and grooming, and so on

Individual parent-staff conferences are preplanned by the counselor or instructor. The conferences are brief, approximately ½ to 1 hour in duration, and focus on the child's, not the parents' or counselor's personal problems. The staff member conferring with the parent uses "plain English" devoid of all professional jargon.

During the camp session, arrangements are made for systematic parent-camper communications. These communications, scheduled regularly, may be either by mail or telephone.

In the event of illness or injury to a camper, the parents are notified immediately by the coordinator or his representative.

As a general rule, all communications from the camp staff to the parents concerning their child should be *positive*. Parents of handicapped children do not need negative feedback on their children. They are usually very aware of the child's limitations; these need not be reinforced by the camp staff.

Of course, staff communications to the parents must be honest. I am not suggesting that camp personnel lie to parents or distort the truth. Neither am I suggesting that counselors build with the parents false hopes for the child. However, the tone of communications does make a great deal of difference to a parent who is trying to help his child. In discussions with parents, it is better to say: "John recognizes 10 of his letters," *than* "John still doesn't recognize 16 of his letters"; *or* "Joan has made progress during the last 2 weeks; she has been dry 4 mornings each week," *than* "Joan still has a problem; she wet her bunk 3 nights last week."

Adjunct service personnel. Camps coordinating their services with community agencies must arrange camp programs and schedules to facilitate the delivery of community services with a minimum of inconvenience to all concerned persons. Cooperating agencies may offer the camp a variety of services, such as individual and group therapy sessions, special instructional services, program consultation and evaluation, and so on. These services are desirable and useful; however, they cannot interfere with the on-going program.

A consistent schedule for the delivery of such services must be arranged between the coordinator and agency personnel. All concerned (campers, camp staff, and adjunct personnel) are expected to abide by this schedule.

Special sessions should not be scheduled to conflict with the high-interest activities of the campers. This may be perceived as punishment by the child, and he will resist the offered services.

Consultants function at the camp as consultants, not as administrators or immediate agents of change. They are not permitted to change the program directly. Their recommendations are communicated to the coordinator and discussed with the staff before implementation. To do otherwise would be confusing and demoralizing for the staff.

ADMINISTRATION

Where to have a camp. It is not advisable during the present economic inflation in North America to construct a camp facility. Construction costs are very high and result in the assessing of a high fee to campers. This high fee places attending camp out of financial reach of many parents. Consequently, the camp is unable to serve the exceptional children in greatest need of a camping program.

There are two ways to approach the problem of obtaining an acceptable camp site: renting a camp or borrowing a camp.

Many state and national youth-serving organizations, such as the Boy Scouts, Girl Scouts, 4-H Clubs, and church-affiliated groups, have camp facilities that are unoccupied the majority of the year. These organizations will usually loan their facilities for a special camp. If a fee is charged, it will be minimal.

Many state and national park and recreation facilities have excellent camping facilities for rent at a minimal fee. Frequently, these camps include cooking, dining, and sanitary facilities, as well as cabins and lodges. Normally, the fee is approximately $1.00 per day per person.

Tent camping and backpacking are usually free. There are hundreds of camp sites available for tent camping in national, state, regional, and local parks and recreation areas. These are available at little or no charge in most locations.

Day camps can be operated nearly anywhere that 5 or 10 acres of land are available for use by children. The only requirements are accessibility to sanitary facilities, drinking water, shade trees, and a shelter for rainy days. The day camp can be located at a city or county park or at a private or public school playground.

Those who serve handicapped children must make an effort to locate the most inexpensive, safe, serviceable, accessible camp site available in their community.

It is not necessary to construct or purchase a modern physical plant. Campers and counselors are innovative and creative people; they will rearrange and reconstruct the environment to respond to their personal and program needs and desires with little difficulty.

Food, drink, and snacks. Food is a large item in any camp budget. If possible, all foodstuffs and beverages are purchased at wholesale prices and in large quantities. Of course, this type of purchasing necessitates that the camp coordinator plan consumption carefully to avoid waste, and have proper storage and refrigeration facilities available.

At a day camp, the campers and staff can carry their bag lunch each day at no cost to the camp. The camp provides beverages— soda, milk, and juice—and snack foods— cookies, cupcakes, and the like. These items can be purchased at local supermarkets at a substantial discount or at cost when purchased in quantities. Milk and juice can be delivered or purchased daily.

Often, the members of community service organizations volunteer to serve the camp as food finders. These individuals contact local markets and fast-food outlets to ascertain the best possible price for the camp. Occasionally, they are so enterprising that they find themselves with an excess of food. Many times, local outlets for national fast-food restaurants meet their community responsibilities by contributing food and services to community projects such as a camp for the handicapped.

Those planning a residential camp or a backpacking trip are advised to seek the services of a qualified dietitian for help in planning a well-balanced diet for campers and staff. The dietitian can develop menus, provide instructions for food preparation, and calculate the quantities of foodstuffs to be purchased. Frequently, the dietitians employed in schools and other community agencies are pleased to provide this service free of charge.

Persons interested in organizing backpacking trips are referred to the excellent menus found in references at the end of Chapter 8. Backpackers are encouraged to investigate the purchase of dehydrated foods. These are more expensive than nondehydrated foods but are lightweight and not bulky.

Materials and equipment. The materials and equipment needed to implement the program described in this text vary with the camp model selected, the children to be served, the staff available to provide regular and specialized services, the physical facilities, and many other factors.

After a thorough reading of Chapters 5 through 8, the reader should have an excellent grasp of the materials and equipment needed to implement each particular model. This information is not reviewed here; rather, a few general comments related to obtaining materials and equipment are presented.

The camp should purchase all expendable materials from a few sources at wholesale prices. It pays to shop and compare the prices of items at two or more outlets. There is often significant variability in the price of a specific item among dealers.

Before a substantial sum of money is expended on equipment and materials, bids should be requested from several companies. All items should be evaluated for durability and usability before they are purchased. It is prudent to investigate warranties and service contracts applying to each item. Occasionally, we find equipment that lacks a warranty and cannot be repaired because it is a self-contained, sealed unit.

Backpackers and tent campers can rent equipment at a reasonable cost from many large sporting goods stores and rental outlets. They have available such items as tents, stoves, backpacks, sleeping bags, and so on. Other sources for renting or borrowing equipment are the regional council headquarters of the Boy Scouts, Girl Scouts, and the YMCA. These organizations have, in some areas, a substantial inventory of equipment that is not in use by their members throughout the year.

Expendable instructional materials, such as paper, pencils, brushes, and paints, can be purchased in quantities from school supply stores. These stores also sell educational and entertaining table games, and sports and physical education equipment.

In every community, there are many sources of free and inexpensive materials. These sources should be explored and exploited by the staff and volunteers from local service groups. We have obtained useful equipment and materials from restaurants, hardware stores, lumber yards, junkyards, nurseries, variety stores, printers, lithographers, supermarkets, bargain stores, and others.

If a camp includes a remedial program, the staff may request the child to bring his schoolbooks and other instructional materials to camp. Many schools are pleased to loan books and workbooks to camp for their children's use. This material is not only free, it is helpful to the child, camp staff, and school staff because it is material that the child is familiar with and must master for school.

It is not necessarily desirable to have all the equipment and material to be used at camp new and modern. Often, the children can construct, with staff assistance, the equipment needed for activities. Children are innovative and creative and should be given opportunities to demonstrate their abilities to construct safe, durable equipment.

Perhaps more important than the quantity of equipment and material for use at camp is their availability and accessibility. All nonexpendable items should be located in a central equipment room or cabin. This room is to be supervised by a librarian or equipment person at specific times each day. Equipment room personnel distribute all materials and equipment. A staff member may borrow a nonexpendable item for a specific period of time. Each item is signed out and checked for completeness before and after the loan period.

Expendable materials are also distributed from the equipment room. This system for distributing materials and equipment greatly reduces loss and misplacement. It also facilitates inventory and ordering.

Insurance. Health and accident insurance is purchased for all campers and staff personnel. This coverage is necessary to protect and, in case of mishaps, provide for individuals involved in the camp. It is also purchased to protect the camp and the individuals responsible for its administration.

The cost of insurance coverage for camping programs varies among the companies issuing the required type of policy. Although some improvements have been made in the last decade, the language used in insurance policies remains complex and technical. It is confusing, if not unintelligible, to the average purchaser.

The camp coordinator is urged to contact several insurance companies to compare costs and coverage. The local independent insurance agent is an expert in this field and can be of valuable assistance.

The cost of insurance coverage can be charged directly to the parents of the camper or included as a part of the camp fee. Costs to camp personnel may be deducted from their salary. Insurance coverage should not be optional for children or staff.

Public relations. A well thought-out public relations program is an important part of the camp. The camp must project an excellent image to the community if it is to attract the appropriate children and a superior staff. There are several methods of putting the camp before the public: (1) news releases, (2) feature articles, (3) brochures, and (4) presentations to interested community groups. It would be wise for the public relations person to employ as many of these as feasible.

Routine *news releases* can be written and distributed to the local and regional news media before, during, and after the camp session. These releases focus on the who, what, where, when, why, and how of the camp. They are brief and concise; if possible, they mention individuals and groups from the communities served by the particular news media. Newspapers, and radio and television stations are usually interested in presenting items of local and regional significance.

News releases announce such items as population served, communities served, groups and clubs interested in the camp, application dates, camping dates, staff members employed or volunteering, committee membership, special events, and so on.

Feature articles about the camp are occasionally of interest to local newspapers and television stations. These features focus on unique or innovative aspects of the camp. It is helpful to have a brief sketch of the featured item and the camp program prepared before the media is contacted. The media will then assign their personnel to complete the feature article. After the sketch has been prepared, the newspaper or television station is contacted by telephone or mail to ascertain their interest in the camp.

The camp *brochure* is one of the most useful public relations tools available to the camp. The brochure is controlled by camp personnel from its design to its distribution. The camp should print several hundred brochures for distribution within the geographic area it serves.

The brochure is distributed via individual mailings and in quantities through selected community agencies and groups, such as public health, mental health, and social welfare departments; the Lions Club; the chamber of commerce; the Kiwanis Club; schools; churches; and parent groups.

The brochure answers all of the reader's questions by presenting a brief, concise verbal picture of the camp. The contents of a typical camp brochure include:

Camp name, address, and telephone number
Name and title of coordinator, assistant coordinators, and other key staff members and committee members
Purposes and objectives of the camp
Brief description of the program: groups, schedules, activities, events, and the like
Personnel and their qualifications
Admission procedures
Population: exceptionalities, age, sex, socioeconomic considerations, scholarships, fees, number of campers at various ages, and so on
Dates and hours, including holidays
Location of facilities and a map
Transportation
Meals and sleeping accommodations
Religious services
Special clothing and labeling
Camp rules

Day and night emergency telephone numbers

An invitation to visit, write, and/or telephone

Camp personnel can make *presentations* at the meetings of community service clubs. The material presented at these meetings generally parallels the content of the brochure. Photographic slides and arts-and-craft work completed by the campers are used to supplement the presentation. The speech should be brief, and time should be reserved for a question-and-answer period.

The children, their parents, and the camp staff must be protected from embarrassment in all public relations activities.

Volunteers. In the majority of camps for the handicapped, volunteer help is necessary if the program is to be operated effectively. Volunteers are essential in a camp that individually programs each child's activities.

Volunteers, as well as counselors and instructors, are recruited from colleges, universities, and high school student bodies and faculties. Volunteers can be recruited from youth and adult community service organizations and church groups. There are many talented and creative individuals residing in every community who would be pleased to contribute their time and energy to a camp for the handicapped.

Recruiting is conducted by means of news releases, announcements mailed to interested organizations and agencies, and word of mouth. It is not surprising for a camp coordinator to receive several dozen telephone calls before the opening of camp from individuals volunteering their services. This is especially true if the camp has been in operation for a few years and has a superior public relations program.

In recent years, many camp coordinators have avoided employing or accepting the services of junior and senior high school students. In my opinion, this is not a wise decision. In each of the camps described in this text, junior and senior high school students have functioned as counselors, aides, and observers. These teenagers have contributed greatly to the camps as a result of their creativity, enthusiasm, energy, and willingness to learn, work, and respond to supervision. When properly trained and supervised, these young adults make excellent models for the campers to emulate.

All volunteers are interviewed by the coordinator or his assigned assistant before they are accepted into the camp. They are interviewed to determine, if possible, their motivation for volunteering services, their special talents and skills that can contribute to the program, and their availability to serve.

When a volunteer is accepted, he is assigned specific duties and responsibilities on a specific time schedule and is held responsible by his supervisor for completing these assignments. Any volunteer unwilling or unable to accept and respond to supervision is not permitted to remain in the camp's service.

Contributions and gifts. Camp cannot be operated successfully without gifts and contributions. There should be no embarrassment involved in either seeking or accepting help from those willing, and in many cases anxious, to contribute money and goods to the camp.

There are a variety of productive methods for soliciting funds:

Mail solicitations: A letter requesting assistance from selected individuals and groups is usually very productive of funds. Many clubs, fraternities, and sororities are committed to contributing funds to worthy causes such as a camp for handicapped children. Timing is important, however, when soliciting from these organizations. Many groups complete their annual budgets and commit their funds before the beginning of the calendar year. Consequently, letters of solicitation are usually mailed in the fall of the previous year. An early request will allow the group to allocate funds for the camp during their budget development activities.

Person-to-person solicitations: Staff members and volunteers can conduct telephone or personal contact campaigns to obtain funds from individuals, service clubs, and businesses in the community.

Project solicitations: Some community groups

who are unable to contribute funds are willing to sponsor fund-raising events in behalf of the camp. These events can be dances, tag days, selling of small items— bags of peanuts, candy bars, and the like —fish fries and barbecues, car washes, and so on. Not only are these activities productive of funds, they are excellent ways to increase community interest and involvement in the camp.

Speeches: Funds can be solicited during speeches and other public relations presentations before community service organizations.

Business solicitations: Some national fast-food restaurants have procedures for helping groups who wish to raise money for worthy causes. For example, one company issues food certificates, which groups sell to contributors. The certificates sell for $1.00 each. The purchaser may buy $1.00 worth of food at the restaurant with the certificate. The certificate is redeemable on a specific day at a specific outlet. The group selling the certificate receives 50¢ for each redeemed certificate and $1.00 for each sold, but unredeemed, certificate. Other companies have methods of helping their communities. These should be investigated and, if possible, exploited.

Grants: Many public and private agencies, foundations, and communities have funds available for community projects. Although the competition for these funds is great, the coordinator is well advised to apply for them.

Many persons of means will contribute to the camp simply because they prefer to assist projects of worth within their community. Caution should be used when soliciting individuals. They should not be cajoled or embarrassed. Parents should not be solicited except under very unusual circumstances.

A personal, signed letter of acknowledgment and thanks should be mailed to every individual and group who contributes money and goods to the camp. During the camp session, the children can write a letter of thanks to contributors. Another excellent technique for keeping contributors interested in the camp is to mail them an end-of-session report. This brief summary of activities may be under the heading "This is what your help did for the children at Camp _____."

Visitors. Visitors are welcome to visit the camp. Parents, contributors, and public and private agency and school personnel are encouraged to tour the facilities, observe the activities, and meet the campers and staff.

Visitors should not interfere with the normal operation of the camp. They should be requested to make a definite appointment so that a staff member can be assigned to guide their tour and explain the program.

Visitors should not be scheduled during the first week of camp. Both staff and campers are anxious and excited during the initial week of the session. Visitors may unwittingly disrupt the program.

Although the camp coordinator may be too busy to conduct the tour, he should *always* greet each visitor and spend some time discussing the program with them.

Fees. Charges to the parents and sponsors of children who attend a camp for the handicapped should be minimal. In these inflationary times, parents must commit their available money for their child's basic needs, medical care, and education. They cannot afford to pay unreasonable camp fees regardless of the quality of the program or the needs of the child.

The following procedures may be used to support the program while minimizing application and camping fees:

Conduct fund-raising campaigns. There is a direct relationship between the amount of money obtained during these campaigns and the fee to be assessed parents and sponsors.

Contact local school districts to ascertain if they have funds for special and summer school programs for exceptional children. Some states allocate funds to local school districts that can be used for camping programs with remedial units.

Contact local and state welfare, education, developmental disabilities, and mental health departments. These agencies frequently have funds available for services to some of the children applying for admission to camp.

Recruit volunteers to fill all staff positions except those that must be filled by specialized personnel if the camp is to function effectively. Salaries are the most costly item in the camp budget.

Camp costs and expenditures are based on a break-even budget. At the maximum, only $300 or $400 is reserved for unanticipated expenditures. The camp budget is planned in advance and adhered to by all responsible personnel. The coordinator is advised to explain and discuss the budget with the entire camp staff. A staff that understands the budgeting restrictions usually adheres to them.

A small fee ($5.00 or $10.00) accompanies all applications submitted to the camp. The application fee is not refundable. This fee is a commitment by a parent or sponsor that the child will attend camp if accepted. Assessing the fee tends to drastically reduce the number of children who do not attend camp after applying.

Some handicapped children, regardless of the efforts of their parents and sponsors, simply do not have the money needed to attend camp. Often, these are the very children who are in the greatest need of the services offered by the camp. Consequently, some campers—approximately 10% to 15%—attend camp without paying. The overall budget and fee scheduled must be adjusted to compensate for this necessary loss of revenue.

Fees can be assessed to parents and sponsors on a variable fee schedule: the parent pays according to his ability to pay. The variable schedule enables the camp to charge substantial, yet reasonable, fees to those parents who can afford to pay and minimal fees to those who cannot afford to pay.

Letters of acceptance. A pleasant, fact-filled letter of acceptance should be sent to the parent or sponsor immediately after the child is accepted into the camping program. This letter should be addressed to a specific individual or family. The letter of acceptance should be signed by the camp coordinator, personally, and should include:

An announcement of acceptance
Camp dates
A discussion of transportation arrangements
A statement of fees to be assessed and when they are due

Attached to the letter is a camp brochure, all forms to be completed by the parents or sponsors, and a stamped, self-addressed envelope.

Sample letters of acceptance sent to parents and agency personnel are presented in Appendix D.

Permission and release forms. Several permission and legal release forms designed for use in the camps described in Chapters 5 through 8 of this text are presented in Appendix D:

General permission form
Parent permission-agreement form
Wilderness camp permission form
Alternate wilderness camp permission form
Drug (medication) administration permission form

The legal value or worth of these and similar forms is very debatable. Some authorities believe that in a court of law these forms would be useless; others believe the signed forms release the camp and its staff from responsibility, at least financial liability, in certain accident and injury cases. Those concerned with this potential problem area should consult an attorney familiar with the laws in their state.

At a minimum, the forms demonstrate to parents and guardians the camp's recognition of potential hazards and problems, and the camp's concern for their child or ward. The forms also demonstrate the staff's awareness of the parents' and guardians' authority to make final decisions concerning their child's activities.

The signing of the forms should be witnessed by individuals who are neither relatives of the camper nor members of the camp staff.

Medical care. There are few camps for the handicapped that can afford a full-time medical doctor on the staff, even if such a person were available for employment. Usually, in the camp environment, there is no single individual who can provide all of the possible routine and emergency medical services required. Consequently, the coordinator and staff must develop a plan to overcome their inability to provide this service. Medical care plans include a consideration of first aid services, policies and procedures for administering medication, and emergency care.

It is recommended that a registered nurse be employed either full-time or part-time, if a physician is not available, to supervise the camp's medical care service. If a nurse is not available, a qualified paramedic can be employed.

Key staff personnel—coordinator and assistant coordinators—and selected instructors and counselors should complete, at a minimum, a Red Cross basic first aid course. One or more of these individuals should be available to provide care at all times.

A clean, private, well-lighted and ventilated room or cabin should be used as a camp health center. This facility is furnished with a desk or table, chairs, a cot or bed, and storage cabinets with locks. A telephone for emergency use is necessary. A refrigerator should be available. The storage cabinets should contain basic first aid equipment and materials. It is wise to consult an office of the Red Cross, a local medical center, or a physician for a listing of the appropriate materials and equipment.

Physician's assessment forms (see Appendix A) are on file for each camper in the health center. These forms are studies by the medical supervisor, and their pertinent content is communicated to the appropriate staff members.

All medication must be properly labeled and stored in locked cabinets in the health center. Medication is *only* administered under the directive of the prescribing physician. Drug (medication) administration permission forms (see Appendix D), properly signed by the camper's parents and physician, are on file in the health center for each camper receiving medication.

A medication schedule is prepared by the individual responsible for the health center. This schedule is posted, and copies are distributed to all counselors and instructors. The counselor and instructor are to escort the camper to the health center for medication in accordance with the schedule.

Sick call is scheduled, at a minimum, twice daily (after breakfast and lunch) at the health center. All children complaining or appearing ill are escorted to sick call by a counselor or instructor. If qualified personnel are on the staff, the campers' needs are administered to at the health center. If qualified medical professionals are not available at the camp, arrangements for professional health care and emergency services are made before the session begins. An agreement for service can be made with an individual physician, a local or regional health care center, or a hospital. This agreement should include arrangements for emergency services and transportation.

Backpackers and tent campers are advised to contact the forest ranger responsible for the geographic area in which they will be camping before entering the wilderness. They can discuss with the ranger the availability of emergency services, including systems of communications and emergency transportation. The group should leave their camping schedule with the ranger. This schedule should include exact times, dates, and locations.

Providing superior medical care and emergency services for campers and staff is an important function of the camp coordinator. It cannot be left to chance. All such services should be planned well in advance of the opening day of camp.

Transportation. Some large camps own and operate vehicles to transport campers and staff members. These vehicles must be properly maintained and insured. Drivers must have the appropriate license to operate the vehicle in the state in which the camp is located.

The majority of camps for the handicapped rely on private companies to transport campers and staff members. When a contract is written with a private transportation company, the camp coordinator is responsible for discussing, with a company representative, not only costs and services but also insurance coverage for passengers and driver qualifications.

As a policy, it is recommended that privately owned vehicles *not* be used to transport children on camp activities. If no alternative to the privately owned vehicle is available to the camp, then the coordinator must be certain that the vehicle is properly insured and that the driver has an appropriate, valid license. The required insurance coverage should be discussed with a qualified insurance representative. An independent insurance agent is most helpful in this matter; he is familiar with the insurance laws in the geographic area in which the camp is located.

Regardless of the specific vehicle used by the camp, strict rules of behavior must be enforced in the vehicle. These include:

Remain seated while the vehicle is in motion.

Use seat belts if available.

Do not throw *any objects* in or out of the vehicle.

Do not put any part of the body out of the windows of the vehicle at any time. This includes hands, arms, heads, hair, shoulders, trunks, legs, feet, and so on.

No shouting or screaming is permissible. Conversation and group singing is permissible.

Do not talk to or otherwise distract the driver.

Obey the driver's and/or bus supervisor's orders, immediately.

A head count or roll call of campers and staff is taken whenever a vehicle is loaded or reloaded on a trip. All passengers must be accounted for before the vehicle departs.

Emergency procedures. The safety and security of the campers and staff is a major responsibility of the camp administration. In large part, this responsibility is met by the counselors and instructors who are with the child throughout his camping day. However, a few safety procedures are suggested:

Fire drills should be conducted several times during each camp session to familiarize campers and staff with fire exits, emergency procedures, and safety zones.

All combustible materials should be properly stored. Such materials should not be available to campers or staff members without authorization from the coordinator. This rule applies also to poisonous materials and dangerous equipment.

Weekly fire and safety inspections should be conducted by the coordinator or an assistant coordinator. During this inspection, all improperly stored potentially hazardous materials and equipment are confiscated. The inspector should note all potential hazards, such as broken steps, windows, doors, cots, water faucets, electrical outlets, lights, boats, paddles, and sport equipment. These items must be repaired immediately.

Counselors and instructors should know the location and use of safety equipment: fire bell or alarm, hoses, fire extinguishers, emergency telephone, and so on.

A centrally located telephone should be available in a lighted area at all times for emergency use. Emergency numbers should be affixed to the telephone. Included on this list of emergency numbers are the rescue squad, the nearest hospital, a doctor's office, the fire department, police departments (local, county, and state), and the ranger station.

Emergency information cards. It is inevitable that one or more emergencies will occur during a camp session. When the emergency occurs, it is necessary to have readily available the information needed to respond appropriately and immediately. If the needed information must be hunted in files, file folders, desk drawers, and other inconvenient locations, precious time is lost. To avoid this potential problem, a small (3 × 5 inch) file box, labeled and painted a distinctive color, is located next to the emergency telephone discussed in the previous section. The emergency information cards contained in this box for each camper and member of the staff include the following information:

Camper's or staff person's name, address, and telephone number

Parents' or spouse's name, address, and home and business telephone numbers

Name and telephone number of a relative, neighbor, or friend who can either locate the parents or spouse at any time during the 24-hour day or act in their behalf during an emergency

Physician's name, address, and office and emergency telephone numbers

Name, address, and telephone number of the hospital of choice

A brief statement of unusual physical conditions and health problems (allergies, seizures, and so on)

An example of an emergency information card is presented in Appendix D.

Attendance. Attendance is taken one or more times daily at camp. In the residential camp, it is best to take attendance twice each day, in the morning (after breakfast) and in the evening (before lights-out). In the day camp, a check-in station is set up in a convenient location, preferably near the bus stop, parking lot, or main lodge. As soon as a camper arrives in the morning, he is requested to check in with the staff person in charge of attendance.

During the first day or two of a camp session, all campers and staff personnel wear temporary name tags. These facilitate taking attendance and enable staff personnel and children to address one another by name. One of the first arts-and-crafts projects of the camp session is making permanent name tags. Not only do the campers and staff members enjoy this project, the tags are useful for the remainder of the session for identification and attendance purposes.

No-shows (children who are absent) are a potential problem at the day camp. Occasionally, campers are sick, miss their bus, get off the bus at the wrong stop, or skip camp. When a child does not arrive at camp in the morning, the parents are immediately notified by telephone. A call should be made to the parents every day that a child is absent. It is recommended that one staff member be assigned attendance responsibilities for the entire camp session. This will eliminate confusion over who is responsible, when, and for how long.

After attendance procedures (check-in and

telephone calls) are completed, a roster of absent campers is prepared and distributed to all staff members. The roster includes the child's name, his group, and the reason for his absence.

Emergency procedures are initiated when a camper cannot be located within a reasonable time.

Follow-up procedures. The camp for the handicapped does not abruptly discontinue its relationship with parents, referring agency personnel, and school personnel at the end of the camp session.

After camp, it is recommended that the coordinator and assistant coordinators (1) write a letter to the parents, guardian, and/or sponsor of each camper; (2) prepare a final report on each child for distribution with the end-of-camp letter; and (3) conduct a survey by mail, telephone, or a home or school visit to ascertain the camper's perceptions of his camp experiences.

The end-of-camp letter must be positive and friendly. Brief and simply worded, it is devoid of technical jargon. The letter focuses on a few of the highlights of the child's experiences at camp. It expresses the pleasure the staff derived from serving the child and his parents during the session. It concludes with a note of thanks for the parents' help during the camp session and an offer to provide further assistance in the future. The letter is signed by the coordinator and the child's counselors and instructors, if possible.

An example of an end-of-camp letter is presented in Appendix D.

The final report of the child's progress during the camp session is usually attached to the end-of-camp letter. The purpose, tone, and format of the final report should be similar to the parent-staff conference, discussed on p. 199.

If a camp follow-up survey is conducted, it is brief and straightforward. Lengthy, complex opinionnaires are frequently unanswered. To ascertain a camper's, parent's, or teacher's impressions of the camp, it is best to ask those individuals directly, in a face-to-face conversation. If this is impossible, a follow-up survey may be conducted by mail or telephone.

A few recommended questions for the follow-up survey are:

What did you like most at camp?

What did you like least at camp?

If you could change one thing at camp, what would it be?

What one thing would you most dislike seeing changed at camp?

Name one activity you wish you could have participated in *more* frequently at camp.

Name one activity you wish you could have participated in *less* frequently at camp.

Who were your best friends at camp?

Would you return to camp for another session?

If the follow-up survey is to be conducted by means of home or school visits, an appointment is made in advance.

REFERENCES

Anderson, C. Give youth a volunteering chance: Saturday morning recreation program for handicapped children. *Parks and Recreation*, 1971, **6**(10), 44-45.

Endres. D. Scrounging at camp confidence. *Journal of Health, Physical Education, and Recreation*, 1972, **43**(6), 72-73.

Ford, P. M. Two modern challenges for every camp director. *Camping Magazine*, 1969, **41**(7), 18-19.

Kingsley, R., and Hartig, C. Measuring counselors' needs aids success predictions in camps for the handicapped. *Camping Magazine*, 1969, **41**(7), 20.

Kronick, D. Making exceptional children a part of the summer camp scene. *Journal of Health, Physical Education, and Recreation*, 1969, **40**(5), 57-58.

Kronick, D. You can make exceptional children part of your regular summer camp. *Camping Magazine*, 1972, **44**(2), 14, 16.

Lainoff, H. M. EMR campers gain from regular camp. *Camping Magazine*, 1969, **41**(2), 24-25.

Maisel, L. How five camps found a way to stretch their camps' responsibility to include those who wouldn't otherwise ever get to camp. *Camping Magazine*, 1971, **43**(3), 8-10.

Moore, A. H. Include *all* children. *Recreation*, 1962, **55**(8), 404-406.

President's Council on Youth Opportunity. *Camping opportunities for disadvantaged youth, a planning and coordinating guide*. Washington, D.C.: U.S. Department of Health, Education, and Welfare, Children's Bureau. 1971.

Recreation Center for the Handicapped, Inc. *Camp Manual 1974*. San Francisco: the Center, 1974.

Richards, C. V. *Good camping for children and youth of low-income families*. Washington, D.C.: U.S. Department of Health, Education, and Welfare, Children's Bureau, 1968.

Robinson, F. M. Pioneering legislation provides recreation for the handicapped. *Recreation*, 1963, **56**(9), 403-410.

Saunders, R., and Schact, H. A camp for exceptional children. *Recreation*, 1959, **52**, 102-103.

Schreiber, M. Community recreation resources for the mentally retarded. *Training School Bulletin*, 1965, **62**, 33-51.

Staver, N., McGinnis, M., and Young, R. A. Intake policies and procedures in a therapeutic camp. *American Journal of Orthopsychiatry*, 1955, **25**, 148-161.

Thompson, M. Widen your doors: how to organize a community recreation program for the handicapped. *Recreation*, 1964, **57**(1), 27-28.

APPENDIXES

Application and preadmission forms

APPLICATION FORM

Camp Kibo
Remediation and Recreation Program
Special Education Department

PLEASE TYPE OR PRINT

1. Child's name _____
   Sex _____ Age _____ Birth date _____

2. Parent's name _____
   Home address _____ Home phone _____
   Business address _____ Business phone _____ Emergency phone _____

3. If the child is attending an educational program in the community, complete the following:
   Teacher's name _____ Grade _____
   Name of school, preschool, or day care center _____
   Address _____
   Phone _____ School district _____
   May we contact the school for information? Yes ____ No ____ (Check one.)

4. Is the child being provided service in any of the following programs? (Check those applicable.)
   _____ Special education program
   _____ Regular class in a private or public school
   _____ Day care or preschool center
   _____ Mental health or social service agency

Continued.

APPLICATION FORM—cont'd

Name of contact person in agency checked (Use reverse side for additional agencies.)

_____

Name of agency _____

Address _____ phone _____

May we contact these persons or agencies for information? Yes ____ No ____ (Check one.)

5. Please state the reason for requesting the child's admission to Camp Kibo. _____

_____

_____

_____

_____

6. Does the child present behavioral problems? (Please specify.)

_____

_____

_____

_____

7. Does the child have difficulty learning in school? (Please specify.)

_____

_____

_____

_____

8. Does the child have a physical disability or handicap? (Please specify.)

_____

_____

_____

_____

9. If the child is being referred to camp by someone other than his parent, complete the following.

Name of referring person _____

Title _____ Relationship _____

Address _____ Phone _____

10. Child's physician _____

Address _____ Phone _____

Date of last physical examination _____

(If the child has not had a physical examination within the past 6 months, he must be examined before the beginning of camp. Please have the results of the last examination forwarded to this office by the child's physician.) May we contact the child's physician for information? Yes ____ No ____ (Check one.)

FORWARD COMPLETED FORM TO: DIRECTOR, CAMP KIBO

EDUCATIONAL ASSESSMENT FORM

1. Identifying data
   Child's name _____
   Parent's name _____
   Address _____ Phone _____
   Sex _____ Age _____ Birth date _____
   Name and title of person(s) completing form _____
   _____

2. Statement of the problem
   What is the child's difficulty? (Cite specific examples.) _____
   _____
   _____
   _____

   When was the problem first noticed? _____
   _____

   Did it develop gradually? _____
   _____

   Is the problem the same or worse since onset? _____
   _____

   Is the problem behavior consistent (recurring in response to the same conditions)? _____
   _____

   Does the child realize that he has a problem? _____
   What are the child's feeling concerning the problem? (Does he verbalize or try to explain it?) _____
   _____
   _____

3. School data
   Name of school _____ Grade _____
   Psychological test data (including subtest scores and total scores) _____
   _____
   _____

   Achievement test scores _____
   _____

   Attendance record this school year: Days present _____ Days absent _____
   Age when child entered school _____
   Average grades: This year ____ Last year ____ Two years ago ____ Three years ago ____
   Special disability areas _____
   Attitude toward school _____
   Aspirations _____
   Size of present classroom group _____
4. Work habits
   Attention span (approximate number of minutes) _____
   Ability to finish a task _____

Continued.

EDUCATIONAL ASSESSMENT FORM—cont'd

4. Work habits—cont'd

Ability to follow simple directions _____

Neatness of work _____

Handling of materials and equipment _____

5. Educational information

Readiness	Yes	No
Holds pencil or crayon	☐	☐
Can color within lines	☐	☐
Can cut on line	☐	☐
Can identify shapes	☐	☐
Can reproduce shapes	☐	☐
Can trace over a dotted line	☐	☐
Can copy work from chalkboard to paper	☐	☐
Can run	☐	☐
Can skip, jump, hop	☐	☐
Can manage stairs	☐	☐
Can throw and catch a ball	☐	☐
Can tell when things are the same	☐	☐
Can tell when things are different	☐	☐

Comments* _____

Language	Yes	No
Can express self clearly	☐	☐
Will express wants and needs verbally	☐	☐
Has eye contact when talking	☐	☐
Speaks in sentences	☐	☐
Listens to directions	☐	☐
Can follow directions	☐	☐
Understands words	☐	☐

Comments _____

_____

Reading	Yes	No
Can recognize and write name	☐	☐
Can recognize and write alphabet	☐	☐
Can write on lines	☐	☐
Can listen to a story and answer questions about it	☐	☐
Can tell what happened in a story	☐	☐
Can tell a story in sequence	☐	☐
Can tell when words begin the same	☐	☐
Can tell when words begin differently	☐	☐
Has basic sight vocabulary	☐	☐

(Approximate level _____)

_____

*If more space is needed, use reverse side.

EDUCATIONAL ASSESSMENT FORM—cont'd

Can read with assistance	☐	☐
Can read alone	☐	☐
Can work independently in a workbook	☐	☐
Can work in groups	☐	☐
Can use context clues and punctuation	☐	☐
Can analyze words phonetically	☐	☐

Comments _____

Spelling	*Yes*	*No*
Can spell	☐	☐

(Approximate level _____)

Comments _____

Mathematics	*Yes*	*No*
Can rote count to 10, 25, 100	☐	☐
(Circle one)		
Can recognize numerals	☐	☐
Can write numerals to 10, 25, 100	☐	☐
(Circle one)		
Can add	☐	☐
Can subtract	☐	☐
Can multiply	☐	☐
Can divide	☐	☐
Can solve problems	☐	☐
Can count money	☐	☐
Can tell time by the hours	☐	☐
Can tell time by the minutes	☐	☐
Can measure in feet, inches, fractions	☐	☐

Comments _____

Motor control	*Yes*	*No*
Can balance self	☐	☐
Has rhythm	☐	☐
Is coordinated	☐	☐
Has difficulty in chewing or swallowing	☐	☐
Has difficulty in grasping objects	☐	☐
Can roll in a controlled manner	☐	☐
Can sit erect without support	☐	☐
Can crawl	☐	☐
Can run without a change of pace	☐	☐
Can locate parts of the body	☐	☐

Comments _____

Continued.

Sensory-motor control	*Yes*	*No*
Can move in an integrated manner around	☐	☐
and through objects in the spatial environment	☐	☐
Has good reaction speed	☐	☐
Can discriminate tactilely	☐	☐
Has awareness of time	☐	☐

Comments _____

_____

Perceptual-motor skills	*Yes*	*No*
Hearing (discrimination and reception)		
Can understand spoken words	☐	☐
Asks for statements to be repeated	☐	☐
Responds meaningfully and vocally to auditory stimuli	☐	☐
Retains and recalls auditory information	☐	☐
Recalls auditory information in correct sequence	☐	☐

Vision (discrimination and reception)	*Yes*	*No*
Can follow objects with coordinated eye movements	☐	☐
Can differentiate forms and objects	☐	☐
Can discriminate figure from ground	☐	☐
Can recall previous visual experiences	☐	☐
Can reproduce (motorwise) previous visual experiences	☐	☐
Has fine muscle coordination	☐	☐
Can discern movement in space and manipulate three- dimensional materials	☐	☐
Can learn motor skills from repetitive experiences	☐	☐
Has tendency to turn head to get a clear focus	☐	☐
Squints	☐	☐
Has inflammation of the eyeballs or lids	☐	☐
Has watery eyes	☐	☐

Comments _____

_____

_____

Speech	*Yes*	*No*
Talks an adequate amount	☐	☐
Uses single-word utterances	☐	☐
Has inaccurate articulation	☐	☐

Comments _____

_____

6. Adjustment and emotional behavior	*Yes*	*No*
Is responsive to people	☐	☐
Is primarily responsive to objects	☐	☐
Is sensitive to vibrations	☐	☐
Is alert to movements in the environment	☐	☐

Comments _____

_____

EDUCATIONAL ASSESSMENT FORM—cont'd

Does the child manifest any of these behaviors?	Yes	No	Approximate frequency
Is nervous	☐	☐	_____
Is shy	☐	☐	_____
Is rude	☐	☐	_____
Shows off	☐	☐	_____
Disobeys	☐	☐	_____
Whines/cries	☐	☐	_____
Has temper tantrums	☐	☐	_____
Breaks things	☐	☐	_____
Fights	☐	☐	_____
Is selfish	☐	☐	_____
Has nightmares	☐	☐	_____
Manifests sleeplessness	☐	☐	_____
Walks in sleep	☐	☐	_____
Wets bed	☐	☐	_____
Hurts self on purpose	☐	☐	_____
Hurts others	☐	☐	_____
Is overactive	☐	☐	_____
Daydreams	☐	☐	_____
Is jealous	☐	☐	_____
Tells lies	☐	☐	_____
Steals	☐	☐	_____
Runs away	☐	☐	_____
Set fires	☐	☐	_____
Is difficult to toilet train	☐	☐	_____
Sucks thumb	☐	☐	_____
Bites nails	☐	☐	_____
Has speech defect	☐	☐	_____
Manifests attachment to parents	☐	☐	_____

Comments _____

_____

Child's sexual behavior (including knowledge, attitudes, traumas, masturbation, and so on) _____

_____

7. Social development

How does this child compare with his group? _____

Describe his group _____

What is his role in the group? _____

_____

How does he get along with:

Persons of his own age out of school _____

Adults out of school _____

_____

Continued.

EDUCATIONAL ASSESSMENT FORM—cont'd

7. Social development—cont'd

Other children in school _____

Adults in school _____

Does he have friends? _____ Comments _____

_____

Child's hobbies, special interests _____

_____

Child's recreational activities _____

What kind of books, TV programs, and movies does the child like? _____

_____

Does the child like pets? _____

Is the child courteous? _____

Does the child show interest in others? _____

Does the child have respect for property? _____

Seeking a future with help and guidance.

PHYSICIAN'S ASSESSMENT FORM

1. Prenatal

   Were there any accidents or unusual conditions during the mother's pregnancy? _____
   _____

   Was the pregnancy full-term? _____

   Was the delivery normal? _____

   Were there any birth injuries? _____

   Comments _____
   _____

2. Postnatal

   Did the child have convulsions? _____

   Did the child have difficulty in sucking or chewing? _____

   Were there any feeding problems? _____

   Comments _____
   _____

3. Early development

   Indicate the approximate *age* at which the following occurred:

   Teeth erupted _____   Had control of bowels _____

   Held head erect _____   Had control of bladder _____

   Stood _____   Fed self _____

   Walked _____   Dressed self _____

   Talked _____

   Comments _____
   _____

4. Medical history

   If the child had any of the following, please provide the information requested.

	Age	Severity		Age	Severity
Measles	___	_____	Influenza	___	_____
Mumps	___	_____	Tuberculosis	___	_____
Whooping cough	___	_____	Appendicitis	___	_____
Scarlet fever	___	_____	Convulsions	___	_____
Chicken pox	___	_____	Polio	___	_____
Pneumonia	___	_____	Allergies	___	_____
Tonsillitis	___	_____	Unusual colds	___	_____
Ear diseases	___	_____	Stomach upsets	___	_____
Hay fever	___	_____	Epilepsy	___	_____
Asthma	___	_____	High fever	___	_____

   Were there any permanent effects from these diseases? _____

   Does the child have any physical handicaps, disabilities, or injuries? _____
   _____

   Has the child had any major surgery or injuries? _____

5. Physical condition

   Is the child left- or right-handed? _____

   Does the child have normal muscular strength? _____

   Can the child work or play for a reasonable time without tiring? _____

   Is the child taking any medications? _____

   Please specify. _____

FAMILY INFORMATION FORM

Name	Age	Does the person live in the home?		Vocation	Level of education	Outstanding personality traits	Physical and emotional health
		Yes	No				
Father							
Mother							
Stepparents							
Guardians							
Siblings							
Grandparents							
Boarders							
Friends							
Others							

Attitude of the family toward the child _____

Attitude of the child toward the family _____

General tone of the family _____

Child's role in the home _____

Is the child disciplined? _____

Who does the disciplining? _____

What methods of discipline are used? _____

How does the child react to punishment? _____

Economic level of the family _____

What language(s) are spoken in the home? _____

What is the general social, economic, and cultural condition of the child's neighborhood? _____

What responsibilities does the child have at home? _____

APPENDIX B

Additional readings

Arnheim, D. D., and Sinclair, W. A. *The clumsy child: a program of motor therapy.* St. Louis: The C. V. Mosby Co., 1975.

Bain, M. F. Day camps serve handicapped and non-handicapped. *Camping,* 1975, **47**(6), 5-7.

Benson, K. R., Frankson, C. E., and Buttery, T. *Arts and crafts for home, school, and community.* St. Louis: The C. V. Mosby Co., 1975.

Blumin, S. S. A summer program for children who need additional education experience. *Journal of Health, Physical Education, and Recreation,* 1972, **43**(5), 78-79.

Cole, W. Three summers: experiments in temporary residential care of retardates. *Training School Bulletin,* 1970, **67**(2), 137-140.

Cormany, R. B. Outdoor education for the retarded child. *Education and training of the mentally retarded,* 1974, **9**(2), 66-69.

Ferguson, R. Totem beads help motivate handicapped campers. *Camping Magazine,* 1972, **44**(1), 18.

Handicapped camper survey. *Camping Magazine,* 1968, **40**(4), 31-33.

Herr, D. Camp counseling with emotionally disturbed adolescence. *Exceptional Children,* 1976, **41**(5), 331-332.

Information Services Division, Department of National Health and Welfare (Ottawa, Canada). Developing skills for the retarded child. *Recreation,* 1954, **67**(10), 599-600.

Krisshef, C. Recreation: the plus factor. *Recreation* **53:** 10, 1960, 470, 493.

Lainoff, H. An EMR camper steps up to "staff." *Camping Magazine,* 1968, **40**(7), 23.

Lynch, W. Canoeing for recreation and rehabilitation. *Parks and Recreation,* 1972, **7**(7), 20-21.

Park, D. Therapeutic programs: a community responsibility. *Parks and Recreation,* 1970, **5**(7), 25-26, 66.

Purvis, J., and Samet, S. (eds.). *Music in developmental therapy: a curriculum guide.* Baltimore, Md.: University Park Press, 1976.

Sengstock, W., and Stein, J. Recreation for the mentally retarded: a summary of major activities. *Exceptional Children,* 1967, **33**, 491-497.

Shellhaas, M. Sociometric status of institutionalized retarded children and nonretarded community children. *American Journal of Mental Deficiency,* 1969, **73**, 804-808.

Shnid, C., and Volkman, A. Music and movement involve the whole child. *Teaching Exceptional Children,* 1975, **7**, 141-145.

Summertime—camp time? *Exceptional Parent,* 1972, **1**(5), 36-39.

Thompson, M. Adapting games for the handicapped. *Recreation,* 1963, **56**, 136-137.

Thompson, M. National survey of community recreation services to the mentally retarded and physically handicapped. *Recreation,* 1965, **58**, 191-192.

Tremonti, J. B., and Reingruber, M. Programs for handicapped: Kankakee State Hospital Summer Camping Program. *Journal of Health, Physical Education, and Recreation,* 1972, **43**(5), 77-78.

Van Krevelen, A. *Children in groups: psychology and the summer camp.* Monterey, Calif.: Brooks/Cole Publishing Co., 1972.

Winsor, M. T. *Arts and crafts for special education.* Belmont, Calif.: Fearon Publishers, 1972.

Camp and recreation information resources

This appendix is a resource list of public and private agencies, organizations, societies, and corporations from which information relative to camps, camping, and recreation programs for special populations may be obtained at little or no cost. This resource list is the result of a questionnaire survey that I conducted in 1974.

In addition to the groups listed, interested parents and professionals may obtain information and assistance from various state and local service organizations and agencies, such as:

State departments of mental health and local mental health clinics

Recreation, physical education, and special education departments at local colleges and universities

State departments of welfare, or children and family services

State offices of education

State departments of correction

Local and regional service clubs

American Association for Health, Physical Education, and Recreation (AAHPER)
1210 16th St. N.W.
Washington, D.C. 20036

AAHPER serves as a clearinghouse for information on camps and camping. On request, the organization sends information to parents and professionals on programs for special populations. It distributes printed materials relevant to camping for the handicapped.

American Camping Association (ACA)
Bradford Woods
Martinsville, Ind. 46151

ACA publishes the *National Directory of Accredited Camps* for boys and girls. The *Directory*

costs approximately $3.00 and includes a state-by-state list of private, independent organizations and church camps. The *Directory* indexes specialized camps and describes the populations served. Publications on camping for special populations are available from the handicapped division of ACA.

Association for Children with Learning Disabilities (ACLD)
5225 Grace St., Lower Level
Pittsburg, Pa. 15236

ACLD publishes an annual camp directory and a variety of other materials relevant to camping for special children. Information can be obtained from ACLD's state and local affiliates.

225

Boys Scouts of America (BSA)
North Brunswick, N.J. 08902

The Boy Scouts encourage their councils to conduct camporees and camping programs for special children. Literature describing camporee activities and desirable physical facilities for camps admitting these children is available. Interested individuals are encouraged to contact regional BSA councils for assistance.

Girl Scouts of the USA (GSA)
830 Third Ave.
New York, N.Y. 10022

Some relevant literature is available from the national office of the GSA. Regional and state councils should be contacted for assistance.

The Joseph P. Kennedy, Jr., Foundation
Room 510, 719 Thirteenth Street, N.W.
Washington, D.C. 20005

The Foundation provides some information on physical education activities for the mentally retarded. In coordination with state and regional groups, it sponsors the Special Olympics.

Muscular Dystrophy Association of America, Inc. (MDAA)
810 Seventh Ave.
New York, N.Y. 10019

In 1973 MDAA sponsored 40 camps in 27 states, serving over 2,000 MD patients. The association publishes a pamphlet describing the camping program.

MDAA is not a clearinghouse for information on camps and camping for special children, but it will provide information when possible. Interested persons are encouraged to contact state and local affiliates.

National Association for Mental Health, Inc. (NAMH)
1800 North Kent St.
Arlington, Va. 22209

Requests to the NAMH for information on camps and camping for special children are referred to state and local affiliates.

National Association for Retarded Children (NARC)
2709 Avenue E. East
Arlington, Tex. 76011

Inquiries should be directed to state and local affiliates.

National Camping Association (NCA)
353 West 56th St.
New York, N.Y. 10019

The NCA has some information available on camps and camping for special populations.

National Catholic Camping Association (NCCA)

NCCA is no longer in existence as a distinct organizational entity. Inquires should be made directly to diocesan and archdiocesan offices of the Catholic Church throughout the nation and to the National Catholic Education Association, 1785 Massachusetts Ave., Northwest, Washington, D.C. 20036.

National Easter Seal Society for Crippled Children and Adults
2023 West Ogden Ave.
Chicago, Ill. 60612

Easter Seal publishes an annual directory of camps for special populations. On request, state and local affiliates provide information on camping. Some affiliates operate camps.

National Education Consultants, Inc. (NEC)
711 St. Paul St.
Baltimore, Md. 21202

NEC publishes the *Registry of Private Schools for Children with Special Educational Needs.* The *Registry* lists private schools and agencies serving special populations. Entries include references on camping and summer programs when this service is available. The *Registry* is updated frequently.

National Park Service (NPS)
U.S. Department of the Interior
Washington, D.C. 20402

National Park Guide for the Handicapped, a publication of the NPS, describes what the handicapped person may expect in the way of facilities in the national parks. The publication also describes the limitations of the available facilities. Information is cataloged state by state. Provisions for the deaf, the blind, wheelchair visitors, and visitors with heart and other physical health problems are described. This publication can be obtained from The Superintendent of Documents, U.S. Government Printing Office, Washington, D.C. 20402.

National Recreation and Park Association (NRPA)
1601 North Kent St.
Arlington, Va. 22209

NRPA distributes a catalog, *Publications on Parks, Recreation and Leisure,* that is a selected bibliography to assist individuals in recreation and allied fields in solving problems, planning, and administering park and recreation programs. Publications are available on recreation for special populations. Several membership classifications exist within the association. National Therapeutic Recreation Society (NTRS) is an affiliate of NRPA.

National Society for Autistic Children (NSAC)
Information and Referral Service
306 31st St.
Huntington, W. Va. 25702

NSAC provides an information and referral service for parents and professionals concerning camps and recreational facilities for special populations. The organization distributes printed materials pertaining to camps, camping, recreation, and physical education for special children.

National Special Education Information Center (Closer Look)
Box 1492
Washington, D.C. 20013

Closer Look disseminates information on special education services for children. The center does not disseminate materials concerning camps and camping for special children. Inquiries are referred to appropriate organizations and agencies.

Porter Sargent Publishers
11 Beacon St.
Boston, Mass. 02108

Porter Sargent publishes *The Directory for Exceptional Children* and *Summer Camps, Summer Schools.* The *Directory* lists several hundred public and private facilities and agencies serving children with handicapping conditions. Camps and summer programs are noted in the individual entries. Listings of national and state associations, societies, and foundations that offer assistance to exceptional children are included in this publication, which is revised frequently.

Summer Camps, Summer Schools is a directory of over 1,100 summer camping, recreational, travel, pioneering, and academic programs. Programs for special populations are noted in this publication.

President's Council on Youth Opportunity
801 19th St., Northwest
Washington, D.C. 20006

The Council's booklet, *Camping Opportunities for Disadvantaged Youth,* is available from the Superintendent of Documents, U.S. Government Printing Office, Washington, D.C. 20402. This booklet is a guide for communities planning, organizing, and coordinating camping opportunities for disadvantaged youth. By following this general plan for action, local officials may tap community resources and provide a variety of camping programs for young people.

Other assistance is available from the Council directly.

Superintendent of Documents
U.S. Government Printing Office
Washington, D.C. 20402

The U.S. Government Printing Office distributes a variety of printed material relative to camping, recreation, and physical education for special populations. Catalogs and bibliographies may be obtained from this agency.

Sample administrative forms and letters

GENERAL PERMISSION FORM

_____
(date)

TO: Coordinator, Camp R & R
        Southern Illinois University
        Edwardsville, Ill. 62025

FROM: _____
            (Parent or guardian—full name)

RE: General permission form

I agree to permit my child or ward, _____, to participate in all Camp R & R
                                              (child's name)
regular and extended activities, including field experiences, special events, and swimming.

Camp R & R has my permission to photograph and videotape my child or ward during his/her
period of enrollment. I understand these photographs and videotapes are used for professional purposes only.

Signature of parent or guardian _____

Signature of witness _____

LETTER OF ACCEPTANCE (TO PARENTS)

Camp R & R
Southern Illinois University
Edwardsville, Ill. 62025
April 10, 1976

Dear Mr. and Mrs. _____ :

We are very pleased to inform you that _____ has been accepted for attendance at Southern Illinois University's Summer Remediation and Recreation Program (Camp R & R). We are looking forward to providing this service to you, your child, and your community.

There has been some confusion concerning fees to be paid for this summer's program. There is a $5.00 application fee, which is not refundable, and a $5.00 per week camp fee. The total fee for attending Camp R & R for 6 weeks is $35.00. This fee is to be paid by the camper's parents or the local school district.

Camp begins at 9:00 AM, June 30, 1976, and closes at noon, August 8, 1976. Camp is open daily, Monday through Friday, from 9 AM to 2 PM. Camp is closed July 4. Your child is expected to attend daily.

Camp R & R is located on the SIU campus in Edwardsville. A map is included on the last page of the attached brochure.

_____ should bring a sack lunch to camp each day. Please *do not put* desserts or snacks in the sack. These are provided by the camp at no charge to you.

_____ may bring home small toys and trinkets. These are prizes or awards that he has earned. Please admire them and praise him for his hard work.

_____ is to wear sneakers or tennis shoes, daily.

All campers must wear a shirt, daily. The sun is *very* hot in southern Illinois, and we wish to avoid serious sunburns. Female campers must wear shorts or slacks, not dresses or skirts.

Please arrange _____'s transportation well in advance of the first day of camp. He will not want to miss the exciting first-day activities.

The counselors, instructors, and I are looking forward to a pleasant and productive summer in the company of _____ . Please feel free to call us any time if you have questions or wish to visit the camp. You are always most welcome.

Sincerely,

Coordinator, Camp R & R

TMS/mmb

Enclosures:
  Brochure
  Permission forms

LETTER OF ACCEPTANCE (TO AGENCY PERSONNEL)

MEMORANDUM   April 10, 1976

TO: Directors of special education
                        and
           referring agency personnel

FROM: Coordinator, Camp R & R
           Southern Illinois University
           Edwardsville, Ill. 62025

RE: Children accepted to camp

Attached is a roster of the children from _____ selected to attend Camp R & R during the summer of 1976. The campers and their parents or guardians have been notified of the child's acceptance. Their names and addresses are listed on the attached roster for your convenience.

In the parents' letter we have enclosed a brochure that should answer most of their questions about camp. However, we have referred them to your office for problems concerning fees and transportation. As you know, we cannot provide transportation to and from camp.

Please circulate the attached roster to all appropriate administrators, supervisors, and teachers in your agency.

The children are to attend camp from June 30 to August 8, 1976, with the exception of Saturdays, Sundays, and July 4. Please schedule transportation to ensure that the campers arrive promptly at 9 AM and depart at 2 PM.

Unfortunately, we could not accept all the children applying for admission to camp this year. We have invited 56 children to attend this session. The staff made every effort to serve the most needy children from each community in the metropolitan area.

We are not rejecting the unaccepted applicants at this time. If space and personnel become available to us, some of the unaccepted children will be invited to attend camp.

We thank you most sincerely for your cooperation and assistance. If we can be of additional help to you, please call the office.

Enclosures:
  Roster
  Brochures

PARENT PERMISSION-AGREEMENT FORM

_____
(date)

TO: Coordinator, Camp R & R
        Southern Illinois University
        Edwardsville, Ill. 62025

FROM: _____
           (parent or guardian—full name)

RE: Parent permission-agreement form

I, _____, understand that the SIU Camp R & R is engaged in training and
      (name)
research activities as well as in service to children.

Therefore, I agree to permit the camp staff to observe and record in writing and/or on videotape the parent interviews and conferences in which I participate.

I agree to participate in at least three conferences relative to my child during the camp session.

I agree that the records kept of these conferences and interviews are the property of Camp R & R. I understand that these records are used for professional purposes only.

Signature of parent or guardian _____

Signature of witness _____

WILDERNESS CAMP PERMISSION FORM

_____
(date)

TO: Coordinator, Wilderness Camp Project
        Southern Illinois University
        Edwardsville, Ill. 62025

FROM: _____
          parent or guardian (full name)

RE: Wilderness Camp Permission Form

I agree to permit my child or ward, _____, to participate in all the Wilderness
                                         (child's name)
Camp Project's regular and extended activities including planning sessions, field experiences
(camping and backpacking), and related special events.

The camp has my permission to photograph and videotape my child or ward during his/her
period of enrollment. I understand that photographs and videotapes are used for professional
purposes only.

Signature of parent or guardian _____

Signature of witness _____

In addition, permission is granted to use photographs, videotapes, and descriptive materials
in popular magazines and local and/or regional news media.

Signature of parent or guardian _____

Signature of witness _____

ALTERNATE WILDERNESS CAMP PERMISSION FORM

Legal release form—Wilderness Camp Project
Southern Illinois University at Edwardsville

In consideration of educational and therapeutic benefits accruing to me and/or the child named below by way of Southern Illinois University at Edwardsville allowing me/my child (or ward), _____, to participate in the Wilderness Camp Project, I hereby authorize
(child's name)
Southern Illinois University, Edwardsville, to produce and disseminate any and all pictorial and descriptive material in which I and/or my child (or ward) _____ have par-
(child's name)
ticipated in any manner in the Wilderness Camp Project.

It is my wish, freely given, and I understand that such authorization shall release the Board of Trustees of Southern Illinois University and their agents from liability, course of action, or claims of whatever nature that may arise from such production and dissemination.

Signature of parent or guardian _____

Signature of witness _____

Date signed _____

DRUG (MEDICATION) ADMINISTRATION PERMISSION FORM

Camp R & R
Southern Illinois University at Edwardsville

_____
(date)

I, _____, request that the coordinator or his representative at Camp R & R ad-
(name)
minister to my child, _____, the following medication:
(child's name)

Name of drug	Dose (1 tablet, 1 teaspoon)	Hour
_____	_____	_____
_____	_____	_____
_____	_____	_____

This medication should be administered (before, after) meals.

I certify this is a prescription that I would normally give the child at home.

Prescribing physician's name _____

Physician's telephone number _____

Signature of physician _____

Signature of parent or guardian _____

EMERGENCY INFORMATION CARD

Name _____   Address _____

Phone _____   _____

Parents/spouse:

Name _____   Address _____

Home phone _____   _____

Business phone _____

Emergency contact person:

Name _____   Address _____

Phone _____   _____

Physician:

Name _____

Office phone _____

Emergency phone _____

Hospital of choice:

Name _____   Address _____

Phone _____   _____

Front

Handicapping conditions _____

_____

Unusual physical conditions and/or reactions _____

_____

_____

_____

_____

Back

END-OF-CAMP LETTER

Camp R & R
Southern Illinois University
Edwardsville, Ill. 62025
August 9, 1976

Dear Mr. and Mrs. _____ :

At noon on August 8, 1975, Camp R & R at Southern Illinois University ended its sixth year of service to children from the St. Louis metropolitan area.

It was an exciting and profitable 6-week session for all concerned. All of our children made gains socially and academically.

We were most blessed this year with a staff that included Ms. _____, Ms. _____, Mr. _____, and 15 graduate student counselors. They did a great job.

Our boys and girls came from many communities in Madison and St. Clair Counties. The children ranged in age from 5 to 12 years. They experienced many new and exciting activities while working very hard on their reading, writing, and arithmetic. We are proud of their efforts.

The enclosed reports are for your information. They are of great value if shared with your child's teacher and other professionals responsible for his education and rehabilitation.

Please remember that our testing is done by students. It is not of the caliber that you would derive from a psychologist or other certified diagnostician.

In closing, we most sincerely thank you for your support and help this summer.

We look forward to serving you again in the near future.

Sincerely,

Coordinator, Camp R & R

TMS/kja

Enclosure (1)

INDEX